SANDPLAY
THERAPY

SANDPLAY THERAPY

A Step-by-Step Manual for Psychotherapists of Diverse Orientations

BARBARA LABOVITZ BOIK

AND

E. ANNA GOODWIN

W. W. Norton & Company

NEW YORK | LONDON

BS

For information about permission to reproduce selections
from this book, write to
Permissions, W. W. Norton & Company, Inc., 500 Fifth Avenue,
New York, NY 10110

Composition by Bytheway Publishing Services
Manufacturing by Haddon Craftsmen
Book design by Susan Hood

Library of Congress Cataloging-in-Publication Data

Boik, Barbara Labovitz, 1944–
    Sandplay therapy : a step-by-step manual for psychotherapists of
    diverse orientations / Barbara Labovitz Boik, E. Anna Goodwin.
        p.   cm.
    Includes bibliographical references and index.
    ISBN 0-393-70319-3
    1. Sandplay—Therapeutic use Handbooks, manuals, etc.
    2. Psychotherapy Handbooks, manuals, etc.   3. Play therapy
    Handbooks, manuals, etc.   I. Goodwin, E. Anna.   II. Title.
    RC489.S25B65   2000
    616.89'165—dc21   99-32765   CIP

W. W. Norton & Company, Inc., 500 Fifth Avenue, New York, N.Y. 10110
www.wwnorton.com

W. W. Norton & Company, Ltd., 10 Coptic Street, London WC1A 1PU

3   4   5   6   7   8   9   0

1/7/05

This book is dedicated to our greatest teachers,
our parents, Paul and Diana Labovitz and
Cornelius and Anna Unger,
and E. Anna's children, Tonya and Jason Goodwin.

CONTENTS

*of "communication sand tray" work for couples who are distant
or have difficulty communicating, to break unproductive
patterns and promote communication. A detailed description of
the stages of "individuation sand tray" work for couples who are
enmeshed and/or not individuated, to facilitate integration.
Case examples are included. Summaries.*

ILLUSTRATIONS

Photographer: John Hooton

ACKNOWLEDGMENTS

Many people have been supportive and influential in our professional lives, and we are grateful for all of their contributions. There are, however, some who have had a direct bearing on the crystallization of this book. Without the encouragement of our sandplay therapy workshop participants, we very well may not have taken on this project. We thank them for being catalysts for this undertaking. We also thank our clients for sharing the innermost parts of themselves in their sandplay creations. We have learned much about sandplay, as well as about ourselves, in this process. Our clients' creations not only have served to teach us but have also provided material for us to share with those we wish to teach.

We are particularly beholden to our teachers. First, we thank Gisela De Domenico for sharing her expertise in her trainings in Oakland, CA. Her paradigm of conducting sandplay served as a foundation for our format. Second, we thank Donna Linn, who, in her workshop in Seattle, WA, taught techniques that we found invaluable with our clients. Other sandplay workshops we have attended, as well as scholarly works on the subject, have been important resources for us.

Throughout the writing of this book we received substantial support and help from Alanna Kathleen Brown, professor of English at Montana State University. The innumerable hours she spent helping to edit the drafts of the manuscript contributed immensely to the final product. We thank Susan Munro and Deborah Malmud, our editors at W. W. Norton, for their faith in us, their encouragement, and input that helped lead to the polished, completed book. We also thank our colleagues and friends, Julie Linden, psychologist, Ellen Lynn, licensed clinical professional counselor, and Malcolm Ringwalt, psychotherapist, for the time and effort they took to read the manuscript and to give us helpful feedback. In addition, we appreciate the hours John Hooton, associate professor of photography at Montana State University, spent taking, developing, and printing the photographs included in this book.

We are grateful for the patience and encouragement of our husbands, Robert J. Boik and Ronald H. Goodwin. Their loving support helped us through this ambitious adventure. We also thank Jason Goodwin for his willing assistance during our periodic hi-tech computer fatalities.

Last but not least we feel that we would be remiss if we did not express gratitude to each other. We have met each challenge along the way with kindness, respect, and love.

PREFACE

In a small tray of wet or dry sand the client arranges sand with or without miniature objects and creates a scene. The client, using the senses of touch, sight, sound, and smell, brings into physical form her/his innermost conscious and unconscious thoughts and feelings. Sandplay, through the use of active imagination and creative symbolic play, is a practical, experiential tool that can create a bridge from the unconscious to the conscious, from the mental and the spiritual to the physical, and from the nonverbal to the verbal. Often a client does not have words or intellectual understanding of the source or solution of her/his difficulties, pain, or conflict. When this dilemma occurs, sandplay provides an opportunity for the client to represent in images what is happening in the person's inner or outer world. That is, the images become a language through which the client can communicate unconscious material to the therapist and to her/himself, resulting in greater understanding and behavior change. Like art therapy, the visual form supplants verbal interchange and bypasses the defenses of the client. The additional advantage of sandplay is that it allows the client to create aspects of the entire issue with symbolic objects that can be touched and easily changed. This process of *play* helps the client move from feeling like a victim of experiences to being a creator of experiences. When the therapist trusts the unconscious mind of the client to reveal its own unique and perfect path to self-discovery, deep transformational work can occur for both the client and the therapist

Sandplay is now surfacing as a powerful tool for therapists of various therapeutic orientations. The World Technique, the predecessor to Jungian sandplay, was developed by Margaret Lowenfeld, a British pediatrician, in the late 1920s. Sandplay has found its place throughout Europe and the United States. Historically used primarily as a medium for children, sandplay is rapidly becoming a tool also utilized with adults, couples, families, and groups for healing, personal growth, communication enhancement, and problem-solving. Sandplay is utilized in outpatient and inpatient mental health facilities, hospitals, private practices, agencies, schools, and businesses. Although sandplay is typically practiced by mental health professionals, it can be very effectively employed for the same purposes by nurses, primary, middle and secondary school teachers, graduate school professors, supervisors and students, and organizational behavior facilitators trained in this approach.

As co-authors, we would each like to tell you how we came to sandplay.

Barbara: Before I tell you about my professional journey, I'd like to relate the story about the first sand world I created. A colleague had recently learned sandplay and asked if I wanted to construct a sand world in a tray. I had already been using sandplay with children, and I found the prospect of creating my own tray intriguing. But to my surprise, I was initially hesitant. In thinking about this afterwards, I realized that my experience with sandplay had come from the therapist part of me, not from the playful child. I had been a conscious observer and holder of the client's experience and, although my unconscious was actively involved as the therapist, I was not familiar with sandplay from the client's side of the tray. I sifted the sand through my hands, forming shapes and moving the sand in a variety of ways. I reexperienced the many hours I had spent building sand castles at the beach as a child. But choosing objects did not come naturally. Eventually, I became more centered and began feeling more relaxed, allowing myself to move from cognitive awareness to more unconscious functioning. I began choosing objects and creating a world unplanned by my conscious mind. The results were astounding to me. I created a scene of a frolicsome mermaid located in the center of the tray looking out at the world around her (see illustration #1). In talking with my colleague afterwards, I was profoundly aware that the child within me was awakened. I realized that, although I certainly enjoyed my life and was often playful, there was

Illustration #1. Barbara's Initial Sand World

a reserve that I had developed that inhibited the child in me. It was then that I understood on a deeper level the profound implications of the sandplay process, as well as its usefulness for myself personally and for my adult clients.

My professional career began as an elementary school teacher in the 1960s. I found that when I created opportunities for children to express themselves and to work and play in their own unique ways, the greatest learning and growth occurred. The constraints of the classroom with its limited focus on academic mastery, combined with the size of my classes (30+ at the time), interfered with my desire to work holistically with each child and nurture emotional as well as intellectual development. That desire led me to graduate school in counseling. My first counseling experience was in an urban school setting, where I used play as a primary modality to draw out the children and help them develop and move toward healing. After I completed my second master's degree in psychology, I began work-ing increasingly with adults and couples in a university counseling center and in private practice. I utilized a diverse range of techniques, including Gestalt therapy, hypnotherapy, narrative therapy, and ra-tional emotive therapy, still reserving play therapy for children. I found that I was often better able to acquire information, gain un-derstanding, and facilitate change, growth, problem-solving, and healing when I interacted with clients of all ages employing the more *indirect* modalities. I was able to access hidden material not readily available at the conscious level. These indirect, creative, imaginative methods were often less threatening and allowed the client to more naturally express her/himself. However, I continued to use appropriate direct and verbal approaches, depending upon specific client needs and situations.

In the 1980s, I became more familiar with sandplay as a therapeutic approach via colleagues, books, and sandplay workshops. After I created my initial sand world and continued to do my personal sandplay, I introduced the sand tray to adults in my practice. The results with these adults reflected the benefits that this modality provided. I increasingly experienced and trusted the power of the inner wisdom of my clients. When I think back to where this faith in others originated, I recall the unconditional acceptance that I received from my grandfather. It is this gift of acceptance that I want to share with my clients, honoring their uniqueness and trusting their process and inner wisdom. In the early 1990s, Anna, at that time an associate in the same group practice, participated in intensive workshops on the use of sandplay, which she shared with me.

Anna: There are many experiences in my life that have led me to adopt sandplay as an important modality for growth to be used with both clients and myself. I will mention only a few. My earlier nursing practice with children, involving both psychiatric care and medical surgical nursing, stressed the importance of the physical being and taught me how it interacts with the emotional, cognitive, and spiritual aspects of each person. At that time, and later as I watched my own children grow, I became increasingly aware of the value of play in the individuation process. I noticed that the senses of touch, sound, sight, smell, and taste greatly enhanced and facilitated this movement. I also realized that I could provide guidance, but that ultimately each child needed to determine and take charge of her/his life to become a healthy adult.

In the late 1970s I returned to graduate school to study child and adolescent counseling. Play and family systems therapy were the basic interventions taught, with an emphasis on treating the whole person and system. Although I was introduced to sandplay early in my career as a psychotherapist, I recognized it as an intervention for children only. From the first time I witnessed sandplay used with children, I realized that this was no ordinary technique. The children were drawn to the sand and figures like metal to magnets. They seemed lost in time and space, with no apparent memory of the present as

they played. Never having used sandplay personally, I did not understand the power of this approach for adults. In my private practice I
specialized in the area of physical and sexual abuse, working with
children, adults and families. I became increasingly cognizant of the
importance of respecting and trusting each client's inner wisdom,
which could direct her/his unique healing process. I also realized
that the child did not disappear as the adult emerged. Even as an
adult, play remained essential to release creativity and feelings.

I found that using less directive, nonjudgmental techniques gave
clients permission to be themselves and to fully explore their own
processes. Gestalt, hypnosis, storytelling, and other play techniques
were successful on the intellectual and emotional levels. However,
there still seemed to be something missing. It became evident that
adult clients as well as children had difficulty breaking through physical blocks related to body memories. After reading several books on
sandplay, employing a colleague's sandplay room with selected adults
and children, doing my own sand trays and studying extensively with
Dr. Gisela De Domenico in Oakland, California, I realized that sandplay could indeed create that necessary physical link. Physically recreating, experiencing, seeing, touching and shifting the symbols that
reflected the client's issues and traumas facilitated dramatic movement.

Barbara and Anna: In the late 1980s and early 1990s, we began to
co-facilitate workshops for therapists and educators on innovative approaches to working with children including sandplay, as well as a
variety of play and storytelling techniques. After a few years, it became clear to us that greater benefits would derive from an in-depth,
focused workshop on sandplay therapy. Initially we concentrated on
sandplay with individuals, both children and adults. By the mid
1990s we expanded the trainings to include how to use sandplay
with families and couples, finding it an invaluable tool to enhance
communication around problem areas within relationships. We continue to use sandplay extensively for ourselves and our clients, teach
workshops, present seminars, and consult with university faculty,
training them in the use of sandplay and in the creation of a sandplay
room. We also present demonstrations and professional development
workshops for therapists in Montana and at conferences throughout
the United States.

The conception of this book originated from suggestions of therapists who attended our sandplay therapy workshops. There is a pau-

city of books published on sandplay therapy, although the number is slowly increasing. The books and articles that are available successfully describe the history, theory, and value of sandplay and present in-depth case studies. However, we know of no book that delineates the specific step-by-step *mechanics* of how to use sandplay. We decided that to fill this void we would write a practical guide to doing sandplay.

In this book we do not adhere to any one theory or approach. We have, however, adapted Gisela De Domenico's phases of a Sandtray Worldplay session and find them very useful. Although our theoretical tenets may differ somewhat, we have found her philosophy of working with clients very similar to ours and her paradigm of conducting sandplay very effective. The methods she developed directly served as a foundation for our format. Much of the seminal sandplay work as developed by Dora Kalff and perpetuated by Jungian analysts has come from a Jungian perspective. We comply with the distinction that Harriet S. Friedman emphasized in her presentation at the Association for Play Therapy International Conference (San Francisco, 1995), referring to Kalffian Jungian Sandplay with a capital "S" and sandplay which has diverged from a strict Jungian approach with a lower case "s." For those of you who prefer a strictly Jungian approach or would like to review extensive case materials, there are several books annotated in the suggested readings list at the end of this book. We do not present complete cases and analyses of clients' work. However, we do illustrate aspects of the sandplay process by sharing experiences of clients' journeys in their sand trays. We have altered the names and particulars about the clients to conceal their identities. The examples reflect our successes and mistakes. In the interest of clarity, we have chosen to remain simple and directive in our writing. We have struggled with the use of a masculine or feminine pronoun when referring to clients and therapists. Taking into account both readability and fairness to both sexes, we arrived at: *s/he, her/himself,* and *her/his,* etc. We use *we* when describing work that either of us has done as therapists individually instead of identifying which one of us worked with the illustrated client. When we give instruction to the reader, we directly address the reader as *you;* in other instances, we write in the third person. A glossary is appended at the end of the book in order to elucidate how we use particular terms.

We do not propose that this book replace training. We believe that firsthand experience is the most efficacious method to learn and internalize knowledge and skills. For that reason our workshops are primarily experiential. Although experience is the best teacher, a guidebook can be very helpful in introducing, reviewing, and strengthening a skill. *Sandplay Therapy: A Step-by-Step Manual for Psychotherapists of Diverse Orientations* is such a guidebook.

SANDPLAY
THERAPY

OVERVIEW OF SANDPLAY

What Is Sandplay?

Before we begin, we would like to relate the story of a sandplay experience we had with one of our clients. Alice, a 40-year-old divorced woman, had come to see us when she began to remember severe childhood sexual and physical abuse by her grandfather. Using hypnosis, Gestalt, and cognitive therapy, she worked through many issues. However, she remained resistant to the idea of play as a form of therapy. Play had not been a part of her life, and the idea was threatening.

Near the end of her therapy process, she stated that there was one traumatic incident with her grandfather that continued to follow her into her daily life. As a young child, Alice was very willful. Her grandfather, in his rage over her lack of adherence to his demands, shoved Alice into a small cage filled with little birds and locked the door. Alice lay silently shaking at the bottom of the cage as the terrified birds fluttered, scratched, and pecked at her. That was where her memory ended. Throughout her life she had been unable to be near birds without a feeling of dread. She would become pale and begin to shake even at the sight of feathers. In the session she relived the memory, but the power of the incident had only been slightly diminished. We suggested that sandplay might be able to help her with this trauma in ways that other therapies had not, because it would allow her to actually physically see and touch the objects that she feared. Because she trusted us at this point and was anxious to rid herself of this phobia, she decided to try sandplay.

As she entered the sandplay room and began looking at all the objects, she suddenly froze. She became very pale and began to shake, unable to speak. However, she pointed at two bird wings lying on the shelf. Finally she turned her head away from the wings and burst into tears. When she calmed down she shook her head, repeatedly saying, "I just can't touch them. I can't even look at them!" After a minute of silence we finally asked, "Would you like to continue if we place the wings and feathers where you want them?" "Yes, I think so," she said. "I really want to finish with this. I don't want my grandfather continuing to ruin my life." We gently took the wings and feathers she identified and placed them into the specified positions in the tray. As she continued working in the tray on her own, memories of the incident crystallized. She realized that the association between the birds and her grandfather was what caused this phobia. The birds had meant her no harm (see illustration #2).

Toward the end of the session, Alice tenderly picked up one of the wings and held it to her heart. Tears spilled onto her cheeks and onto the wing as she stroked and whispered to it. She stood there for some time, crying and talking. When she was done she smiled, laughed, and then said, "I'm done." In our discussion with Alice at the end of the session, she indicated that it was important for her to mourn for her past so that she could leave it behind. We asked how she might be

Illustration #2. Alice's Sand World

able to do this. She immediately stated that the next dead bird she came upon she needed to cradle and bury, because the dead bird symbolized the death of her ability to fly and be free in childhood.

Alice called the next afternoon. Her voice sounded strong as she related what had happened to her when she left the office. A friend who knew none of her abuse history stopped her in the parking lot and said, "I have something for you. I found this and I just know it belongs to you." She handed Alice a beautiful, soft sandhill crane feather, which Alice accepted. The next morning, when Alice left her house to go to work, she found a small dead sparrow on her porch. Her first instinct was to run, but instead she dug a small hole at the foot of her weeping birch and gently took the little sparrow and buried it. She stood there weeping over the lost years and the delicate, graceful sparrow that she perceived had sacrificed his life to set her free at last. And on the grave marker she wrote, "Fly high, little one, fly high." "You know," she said before she hung up, "I couldn't have done it without the sand tray." As C.G. Jung wrote in his essay, "The Transcendent Function," "Often it is necessary to clarify a vague content by giving it visible form. . . . Often the hands know how to solve a riddle with which the intellect has wrestled in vain" (1960, p. 86). Like Alice, many of our clients have experienced this to be true.

So what, in fact, is sandplay? In sandplay therapy the therapist provides a sand tray, water, and a multitude of objects and materials with which to imaginatively create scenes in the circumscribed space of the sand tray. Sandplay can be used effectively with children, adults, couples, families, and groups. As Ruth Ammann analogized, the sand tray is like "a soul garden," a kind of container for the display of the client's psychic life. The sand tray is an "in-between-space," where the client's inner and outer life can develop and reveal itself. The tray is that free and empty space where the client has the opportunity to create her/his own world and transform her/his existing world with fresh insight. The therapist provides a safe and accepting environment in which the client can allow her/his inner voice to speak. To continue Ammann's metaphor, this "in-between-space," in which the conscious and unconscious material can unfold, come together, and be made concrete, is also the space between the client and the therapist. This is the space where the unconscious and conscious of the therapist and the client meet and interact (Ammann, 1994).

Sandplay provides the client access to her/his innermost feeling core or psyche. In sandplay therapy the client represents in images what is happening in her/his inner and outer world. By making concrete what the inner voice is expressing, the client brings into external reality her/his own relationship with her/himself and allows unconscious material to be revealed. This concrete, observable manifestation of subliminal material brings into greater consciousness that which has heretofore been repressed or unknown.

In the course of people's lives they create personas to interface with the external world. They often repress feelings and thoughts and lose touch with their Selves, the center of their psyches. The constant activity and demands of individuals' everyday lives, the dissociation from traumatic and painful experiences, the messages people receive to shut off their feelings, to be rational or think linearly, to conform and to subdue their imaginations, all serve to block them from their Selves. The more people are blocked, the more disparate the persona is from the Self. "The deeper the emotions and feelings are covered up, the more distanced from consciousness memories and a part of our personalities have become, the less likely it is that we can find the words to express them" (Ammann, 1993, p. 2). As they become more aware of their unconscious processes by allowing the unknown to be seen through the creation of the sand world, individuals can gain energies and insights which were denied to them. In describing Jungian theory, David Hart, in an interview with Adelaide Bry, stated that "the cooperation of conscious and unconscious life leads to a greater unity and greater strength within the individual" (in Centerpoint I, 1995, p. 19). Sandplay can provide the framework for this cooperation.

Sandplay takes many forms. The connection with the sand in and of itself helps to ground, center, and/or regress the client to a place that needs healing. One of the reasons that this occurs is because as children most people played in the sand and in the dirt. Sandplay often takes a person back to some childhood memory. Some clients use no objects at all; they touch, move, and make formations in the sand. Some use few objects; some use many. Some use the sand dry; some wet the sand with water. Some build their scene quickly; some work slowly. Some create a static world; some create an ongoing, moving story. Some report the experience as very centering and tranquil. Some enjoy the playfulness of sandplay. Some experience very deep emotions, reexperiencing past pain. There is no right way or right outcome. It is important to trust that each client will do what s/he needs to do at that moment in time. It is also important for the therapist to be as aware as possible of her/his biases, values, and unresolved issues.

This awareness allows the therapist to be open to receiving what the client is experiencing, with minimal judgment.

"Sandplay therapy is a prime facilitator for the individuation process" (Weinrib, 1983, p. 88). We concur with the Jungian precept that the psyche naturally moves toward healing and wholeness. This aspiration for wholeness toward which the client may have been striving unconsciously becomes increasingly realized as the unconscious becomes conscious. The client reconciles her/himself to, and becomes more aware of, different aspects of her/his personality and the blocks and wounds that have interfered with healing and wholeness. Sandplay is like a dream experience, in that it brings to consciousness what the client doesn't see in reality. This helps compensate for her/his lack of awareness.

We see sandplay as an adjunct to therapy. Therefore therapists will continue to use the techniques that have served them well in their professional careers. It is important for therapists to honor their own style and theoretical orientations. Sandplay complements many different therapeutic approaches. Gestalt techniques, visualization and imagery, psychodrama, body work and movement, cognitive restructuring, art therapy, and hypnosis are some of the therapeutic strategies that interface with and augment the sandplay process.

History and Current Trends of Sandplay

Prior to the formal therapeutic use of sand and symbols, indigenous tribes drew protective circles in the earth and created sand paintings. According to Weinrib, sandplay therapy parallels the historical cultural "sand paintings of the Navajo religion wherein ritual sand pictures are used extensively in ceremonies of healing, as well as for divination, exorcism and other purposes" (1983, p. 3). Clare Baker, in her article "Navaho Sand Painting and Sandplay" (1993) elaborated on the parallels between sand paintings and sandplay. Both Navaho sand paintings and sandplay are healing modalities that activate psychic energy and initiate passage from one state of mind to another. In addition, they both enhance communication between the participants.

The use of the sand tray extends back to the late 1920s, with many events contributing to the growth and development of its application in therapy. Play and creativity as a part of the therapeutic process were already being used extensively, especially for children. Melanie Klein, Anna Freud, Erik Erikson, Charlotte Buhler, Helga Bolgar, and Lisolette Fischer, to name a few, were proponents of using toys and miniatures for therapeutic, diagnostic, and research purposes (Mitchell & Friedman, 1994). Their practices reinforced Jung's advocacy of the use of imagination and creativity in the growing and individuating process. Before sandplay was developed as a Jungian modality and named in the 1950s by Dora Kalff, a Swiss Jungian analyst, the creation of scenes using miniatures in the sand had already found its place in therapeutic circles. In 1929, Margaret Lowenfeld, a British pediatrician, originated the "World Technique," also known as "Worldplay," which was the precursor to sandplay.

In the 1920s Lowenfeld moved from orthodox pediatrics to child psychiatry. Her goal was to find a medium that would be attractive to children and provide a means through which the observer and child could communicate. She recognized the potential of using small toys to enable children to make known their deepest, preverbal thoughts and feelings. Her personal history, including an unhappy childhood, many illnesses, her parents' divorce and mother's eventual demise, coupled with her work as a medical officer during the Russo-Polish war, served as a backdrop for Lowenfeld's thinking. Her past experiences facilitated her understanding of the inner life of children and the recognition that nonverbal tools were expeditious in paving the way for interpersonal communication (Mitchell & Friedman, 1994). Fortuitously, as a youth, Lowenfeld had read *Floor Games*, written in 1911 by H.G. Wells. Wells, author of *War of the Worlds* and *The Time Machine*, among other achievements, had a profound belief that play provided an environment for expansive and innovative ideas in adulthood. In *Floor Games* he described the activities in which he participated with his two sons. Equipped with pieces of wood, paper, plasticine, and miniatures of people and animals, they played games and built cities and islands. Wells made an important contribution by recognizing suitable materials and types of play that encouraged inventiveness and honored the activity of creative imagination. With the inspiration from Wells, the backdrop of Lowenfeld's own experiences, and her goal of finding a way to provide an opportunity for communication with children and an understanding of them, the World Technique was launched.

Prior to opening the Institute of Child Psychology in England in the late 1920s, Lowenfeld had a collection of many small toys and miniatures, paper shapes, colored sticks, etc., and kept them in a box, which the children named the "Wonder Box." In the move to the

Institute the objects were stored in a cabinet with small drawers, which the children then named the "World." Lowenfeld set up two zinc boxes, one filled with sand and the other with water. The children began to use the objects together with the boxes. The World Technique involved the client spontaneously arranging the sand and or miniatures in wet or dry sand to create a picture or world. Lowenfeld believed that children thought in experientially vivid images instead of words or archetypes. She found that in the sand tray children communicated conscious and unconscious thoughts. She was not a psychoanalyst and did not analyze her clients' work. She believed that the value in the World Technique was realized through experiencing it. According to Lowenfeld, the aim was to "have the created world confront its maker, rather than having the therapist confront the maker of the world" (in Gisela De Domenico, 1988, p. 13). She believed that the World Technique could be applied by therapists from a wide variety of therapeutic orientations.

In the 1950s, Dora Kalff studied with Lowenfeld. Being a Jungian analyst, Kalff adapted the World Technique to Jungian theory and named it "Sandplay." Her views reflected her study of Eastern philosophies, her own highly developed intuitive capabilities, her long history of using sand trays, the influence of Neumann's developmental theory, and her studies with Jung and Lowenfeld (Mitchell & Friedman, 1994). Kalff's sandplay was based on Jung's belief that the psyche can be activated to move toward wholeness and healing. Kalff saw sandplay as a tool that allowed children to express both the archetypal and intrapersonal worlds, and connected the child to outer everyday reality. She postulated that symbolic play created a communication between the conscious and the unconscious mind. "The blending of all of these dimensions within a safe and protected space created by the therapist encouraged images of reconciliation and wholeness and re-established the connection between the ego and Self" (Mitchell & Friedman, 1994, p. 50). After observing the children function in a more balanced and congruent manner with this reactivated joining of the ego and Self, Kalff began using sandplay with adults as well.

Dora Kalff lectured and trained other Jungian therapists/analysts internationally and was a catalyst for its widespread use. In the psychoanalytic mode of sandplay, unlike the World Technique, it is the therapist who confronts the client (De Domenico, 1988). In her process, Kalff used two trays of prescribed dimensions (see "Sand Trays" in chapter 2), one wet and one dry, with blue bottoms and sides to represent water and sky. She emphasized that silence should be maintained by the therapist to allow the building of the scene to take place without interference. She encouraged that interpretation be withheld until after several trays have been created. Photographs are taken of each scene and can be reviewed at a later time, joining the cognitive awareness to the deeply felt experience.

In the early 1980s, Gisela De Domenico conducted phenomenological research with normal preschool children, using a variety of shapes and sizes of sand trays. She also did clinical and transformational work with children, adolescents, adults, couples, families, and groups. Her theory and practice of sandplay, which she calls Sandtray-Worldplay, evolved from this research. Her theory is based on her findings while conducting play sessions and from the observations she made about how the psyche reveals itself during play with sand, water, and images in small containers of a variety of colored sands. Her focus is on fully experiencing the process, the products of the play, and the healing "meaning-making" that occurs during the different phases of the sandplay process.

Like her predecessors, De Domenico emphasizes the healing power of the psyche. Rather than emphasizing the depths of the "unconscious psyche," she works directly with the depths of human consciousness by facilitating clients' process of experiencing the world and themselves and by eliminating both silent and verbalized therapist interpretation. She emphasizes trusting the psyche and its play products to faithfully indicate the client's movement toward healing and growth. She sees the function of the sandplay therapist as a mediator between the client's "growing edge" and the "communal-social" expectations placed on each person.

De Domenico approaches the psyche quite differently from Lowenfeld and Kalff. She experiences humans as multidimensional beings who are conscious in many different dimensions and use different bodies of consciousness [not unconsciousness] to experience, respond to, create, and modify the different aspects of reality. She sees the images and the sand formations as real (not symbolic), once they are placed in the tray. Unlike Lowenfeld and Kalff, De Domenico believes that the realms and bodies of human consciousness function in each individual regardless of the client's diagnosis. She believes that sandplay always activates them. De Domenico believes that, when therapists are present to clients' "various bodies of experience," they need not interpret the sandplay worlds of their clients, and thus can forego the role of the expert and become coexplorers of the world. Like Lowenfeld, she starts with the personal experience of the client, and, like Kalff, she honors the archetypal planes of experiences of the client, but does not interpret them. She also includes the familial, social, ancestral, transpersonal, and universal realms of experience in her work with sandplay. De Domenico teaches her students the client's story, rather than the therapist's story, about the play.

In the course of her work, she has created techniques that allow clients to deeply experience their sandplay worlds, be aware of their center, and to take responsibility for themselves. Unlike other sandplay therapists, De Domenico has developed protocols not only for individual, but also for joint sandplay sessions. She asks clients to apply the sandplay experiences to their daily lives. She believes that therapists should also use sandplay for self discovery as often as possible.

Sandplay continues to gain in popularity among therapists as well as educators and business consultants. Although Kalffian sandplay with its Jungian symbolic approach is widely practiced, and De Domenico's Sandtray-Worldplay is at present reaching many therapists, in recent years therapists of many orientations are exploring its application for their clients. Sandplay, as we define it, allows for many different ways to play in the sand in a therapeutic milieu. It incorporates not only aspects of the paradigms previously mentioned, but also the multitude of possibilities that evolve out of the creativity of the therapists and the clients who use the sand tray. In our experience, sandplay in itself, regardless of associated theory, has been extremely beneficial for the healing and growth of most of our clients and ourselves. We have found that De Domenico's methods are very effective and most closely resemble our own philosophy and approach to therapy. In order not to reinvent an already excellent model of therapy, we have adapted her format and some of her techniques in our work.

Sandplay is being used as an adjunct to therapy, incorporating both verbal and nonverbal approaches. The trend seems to be away from rigid rules and interpretations. Settings in which sandplay is practiced include outpatient and inpatient mental health facilities, hospitals, private practice, agencies, schools, retreats for personal growth, and businesses.

Therapeutic Benefits of Sandplay

What is the power of sandplay? Why is it that in the 1990s this technique is being utilized by an ever increasing number of individuals who work therapeutically with both adults and children? How is sandplay distinct from other forms of play therapy? In this section we report several authors' answers to these questions, as well as our own perspectives. Lowenfeld, Kalff, Weinrib, De Domenico, Bradway, and many other therapists who have used sandplay, have readily experienced the following benefits.

First, healing professionals have known for some time that fantasy play in children facilitates the individuation process and fosters mastery of the adult world. According to Piaget (1951), play is the leading source of development in preschool children. Jung stated, "[fantasy] is the mother of all possibilities where, like all psychological opposites, the inner and outer worlds are joined together in a living union" (1971, p. 52). In recent years the rediscovery of the power of the child within each person, young and old, male and female, has encouraged mental health workers to use play therapy and other experiential therapies for all clients. Humans have a need and desire for play to free creativity, inner feelings, perceptions, and memories and to bring them into outer reality.

Sand and water are particularly powerful tools to use in fantasy play. For children, sandplay is a natural form of expression and they are readily drawn to it. Most adults have already had some childhood experience with sand, either at the beach or in a sandbox. Therefore, sandplay serves as a link to, or reminder of, past experiences and creates a doorway to the realm of childhood. For the child within, sand and water are magnets that automatically invite spontaneous play. Most of the children who enter our therapy rooms are immediately drawn to the sand trays and the multitude of objects available for them to use. Adults, as well, are usually curious about the sandplay area, although some are more hesitant than children to play. Because most adults and children have experienced no need for artistic skills and no particular cultural restrictions in their childhood sand play, they feel free to create without self-criticism or constraint. There is no wrong or right way to play in the sand. Worlds can be created without adult modeling or interference and are thus authentic to the inner world of the creator.

Second, and what most distinguishes sandplay from other forms of therapy, is that it allows the client to create a world that provides concrete testimony to inner thoughts and feelings. This world can be viewed, touched, experienced, changed, discussed, and photographed. Some clients need to externalize and objectify certain experiences or traumas in their lives before the traumas can be resolved. As Alice, the client in our story, said, "I couldn't have done it without the sand tray." Although several other forms of therapy are effective, most do not allow the client to create and recreate experiences using actual physical forms. According to Jung (1971), an emotional experience that cannot be understood or resolved by cognitive means can often be dealt with by giving it visible shape. In the creation of the world using sand, water, objects, and the hands, something magical appears to occur and the solution that only the client's unconscious knows is transmitted to the hands of the builder. An integrated entity is manifested in the tray. The client may have an "aha" experience. In children, for whom play and life tend to be almost synonymous, the objectification of the unconscious material in sandplay leads to integration into the present reality. For adults, insight can be rapid and complete and is often felt physically as well as emotionally, mentally, and spiritually. When clients cannot resolve an issue by the use of other types of therapies, or when clients are perplexed about what they are feeling or why they are behaving a certain way, sand worlds that can be touched, seen, heard, and smelled can provide the answer.

In addition to being physical, sand and water are natural archetypal symbols connecting and grounding humankind to the planet earth. Like the psyche, they flow and move, changing constantly. Sand and water link mind and spirit with body and physical form, providing an opportunity for the spirit and body to influence each other consciously and unconsciously. While creating the world, the builder continuously converts mind into matter.

Third, the symbols of the objects and materials used in sandplay can serve as a common language. Children often do not have the capacity to articulate or name what is happening to them. Adults, such as Alice, also often have no words for their feelings. Sandplay can provide an avenue for clients to express their innermost thoughts and feelings. Because sand and water tap prenatal, perinatal, and preverbal consciousness, language skills are not necessary for understanding the expressions of the psyche. For this reason sandplay can be used across languages, cultures, races, ages, and developmental levels. The use of earth and symbols are familiar to many cultures around the world (e.g., indigenous American people with their sand paintings, Oriental countries with their courtyard "meditation" gardens). In addition, an excess of words can hinder therapeutic progress. For those clients who speak incessantly and use language to intellectualize and avoid issues, sandplay discourages the rational mind and allows the unconscious to tell its story while grounding the body in the here and now. Sandplay, therefore, allows for nonverbal articulation. Deep inner experiences can be expressed and communicated to the client and the therapist symbolically. The sharing of these experiences can create a close bond between therapist and client, which is frequently difficult to establish verbally.

Fourth, when clients are resistant to therapists' inquiries into difficult issues, sandplay can be a less threatening approach than talk therapies. Sandplay allows defenses to soften and resistance to diminish. Clients' concerns can then surface on their own, without words, in the sand tray. This brings to mind a resistant teenager with whom we worked. When we encouraged her to address her family issues, she appeared pressured and withdrew. She was, however, able to create worlds in the sand, without speaking, revealing the true story of her abuse by her mother and father.

Fifth, sandplay can be an adjunct to therapists' present techniques. Although it is practiced mostly as a Jungian technique, sandplay can be used as a tool in conjunction with many other approaches. For example, if a therapist's methodology is mainly cognitive in nature, it is unlikely that analysis will be used in sandplay. It is more likely that the therapist will work with the client in the tray to help restructure her/his thinking. It is unnecessary for therapists to learn a completely new theoretical approach, especially when their present methods are working satisfactorily. We incorporate the techniques with which we are most familiar, such as Gestalt techniques, imaging, psychodrama and cognitive restructuring, and we provide no or little interpretation.

Although many therapists are satisfied with their usual approach to therapy, there are times, as we have found, when those techniques fail, and stagnation and frustration occur for both client and therapist. When techniques are not adequate to portray the whole or the complexity of the person's intrapsychic experience, the sand world, with its multilevel, three-dimensional symbols, can overcome this limit. "[T]he nonverbal sandtray world enables the sandplayer to portray events on many levels at the same time—in the way they are presented in dreams" (Thompson, 1990, p. 18). The client creates a bridge from the unconscious to the conscious, from the inner to the outer world, the mental and the spiritual to the physical, and the nonverbal to the verbal. The process also goes in the reverse, for once the unconscious is objectified in image it serves as a catalyst for inner change. A direct link between the conscious and the unconscious has been forged.

Sixth, the use of sand and water automatically transports clients back to those areas of human experience that need to be healed and integrated. During sandplay an experience or trauma is defined, confined, and eventually mastered in a free, protected environment. This process occurs in the presence of someone who can honor and respect, without judgment, the person and the creation. As the client builds, s/he is constantly changing the world, destroying the old and creating the new. By creating and destroying, creating and destroying, clients can claim and view their own worlds as they build them. In time they move from feeling like victims of experiences to being masters of old experiences and creators of new ones.

Seventh, because sandplay activates the innate healing powers of the individual's unconscious and provides the opportunity to move from victim to creator, it empowers each person to determine her/his own course of therapy. Clients are in control of what they will or will not reveal to themselves or will learn in this process. Only material with which clients are ready to deal will become conscious. The images they create outwardly reflect the inner world of the unconscious and will enlarge their comprehension of themselves. Because clients are actively and consciously involved in the healing process, they can overcome feelings of helplessness and inferiority. As therapists honor the clients' creations and personal interpretations of their worlds and do not give their own explanations, the clients' unique experiences and insights are validated. Each client appreciates her/himself as a knowledgeable and respected human being in charge of her/his life.

Last, because the sand tray is a powerful tool to deal with many life events including traumas, relationship matters, personal growth, integration and transformation of the Self, therapists as well as clients can benefit from sandplay. Therapists can address issues of countertransference and personal growth in the tray (see chapter 10). Also because, like Lowenfeld, we use the sand tray (and not the therapist) to confront the client and hold the client's projections, there is an additional benefit for the sandplay therapist. We agree with Linda Cunningham's explanation of why sandplay therapy is less depleting for the therapist than verbal therapy. Because many of the client's projections are placed into the sand tray instead of onto the therapist, the energy required to deal with transference issues is minimized. As Cunningham wrote,

> It is my hypothesis that the doing of sandplay therapy is less exhausting for the therapist because the sandtray itself becomes the

container for [what Jung called] the *participation mystique/* [and what Klein called] projective identifications. The client symbolically places unconscious, disowned parts of self and the connected affect in the tray, and the tray silently returns these affects and parts of the self in a more tolerable and usable form. The therapist's subjective experience of the transference is then not as wrenching because the transference has already manifested and transformed in the container of the sandtray. (1997, p. 122)

Role of the Sandplay Therapist

While sandplay can be a rich addition to techniques already quite effective for the therapist, doing sandplay requires a different kind of focused concentration. Gisela De Domenico enumerated a number of requirements for performing this experiential type of therapy. She stated that it "requires belief in the reality of symbolic, pictographic intrapsychic images. It requires the ability to spontaneously enter fully into experience. It requires the ability to tolerate new experiences. It requires the ability to let go and step back from the experience by first utilizing the observer function . . . and, then, upon termination of experiential involvement, switching to the reflective function that allows for conscious remembering and integration of experience" (1986a, p. 4).

The therapist in a sandplay therapy session serves the client in a pivotal way by becoming a *psychological container* who holds what is happening in the tray and in the therapy room, making it safe for the client to allow her/his inner voice to speak. This is especially important for children, because they have not yet developed a strong ego and need the support of a nonjudgmental adult. The therapist also *models* for the client the act of really listening and being present. In modeling this attentiveness, the therapist demonstrates the capacity to observe, without judgment, the creative and meaning-making process. In addition, the therapist serves as a *bond or link* for the client to her/his sandplay. The therapist helps the client see how the world or scene s/he is creating reflects some of the psychic content that was held in the unconscious. Because the sandplay process often evokes deep emotion and insight and brings to an observable and conscious level that which has been hidden, the therapist must serve as a *helper/supporter* to the client as the client experiences and deals with the emotions and memories that surface.

Sandplay is a journey of exploration for the client. The therapist is a *co-explorer* on this journey. Together they move through the psychic topography. The client takes the lead in meaning-making; the therapist provides questions and suggestions, following the client's lead. It is important to be patient and to let the client's narrative unfold. The therapist must be cautious to be only as active a co-explorer as will stimulate the client's exploration. Ammann eloquently provided an image describing this balance: "the flames on which the vessel containing the psychic process of the analysand is cooking must be carefully tended by the analyst. The fire mustn't go out. But neither should the flames flair too vigorously lest the contents of the pot boil over or be ruined in some other way" (1993, p. 5).

The therapist enhances the process of constellating the unconscious in serving as *witness* and *mirror*. It is validating and reinforcing for the client to have someone whom s/he trusts and respects witness something that may be alien to the conscious. It is not uncommon for clients to be unsure of themselves or of their new insights. When the therapist verbally reflects back what s/he is observing of the client's experience, it often helps the client to see it for her/himself, as if looking in a mirror from a different perspective. We have found that when we simply reflect back what we are seeing, clients will often be triggered to go a step further in applying the sand world to their own lives.

So, how can a therapist be all this for her/his clients? There are a number of qualities and skills a therapist must possess to effectively do this deep work with a client. Certainly, as in any therapeutic orientation, it is important to have a basic understanding and foundation in human development, psychological processes, and therapeutic interventions. In sandplay therapy, it is also helpful to have some understanding of the psyche, the language of the collective unconscious and the knowledge of archetypes. Additionally, it is advantageous but not necessary to have some knowledge of the body and somatic illnesses.

It is also important that the therapist be committed to exploring her/his own "soul-garden", thus moving toward wholeness and individuation. By doing her/his own sandplay, the therapist experiences the process of sandplay from the client side of the tray. This enhances her/his ability to understand what clients experience. By undergoing sandplay therapy, therapists not only fine-tune and strengthen their powers of observation and abilities to use all of their senses, but they also develop their abilities to nurture creativity and imagination. Furthermore, therapists bring into awareness their hidden unconscious material, thus allowing their shadows to be less projected onto clients, and this permits a more or less unfiltered exchange. The therapist must be aware that learning never stops and that the interaction between the therapist and client is a learning process for both (Ammann, 1994).

Just as sandplay therapy is not congruent with the needs or proclivities of all clients, it is not an intervention of choice for all therapists. In reviewing the necessary skills and tasks of a sandplay therapist delineated in this section, it is important for therapists to assess if this mode of treatment is compatible for them.

What is Sandplay?

- Imaginative activity in the sand
- Natural mirror for the individuation process
- Access to innermost feeling core
- Observable manifestation of subliminal material
- Symbolic language for communication
- Safe and accepting environment
- Within a circumscribed space
- With or without water
- With or without objects
- Static or moving world
- Adjunct to therapy
- Used with children, adults, couples, families, groups

Benefits of Sandplay

- Facilitates the individuation process
- Frees creativity, inner feelings, perceptions and memories, bringing them into outer reality and providing concrete testimony
- Utilizes most of the senses, providing an expanded experience
- Regresses the client to past experiences, allowing healing and integration
- Creates bridges from the unconscious to the conscious, the inner to the outer world, mental and spiritual to physical, nonverbal to verbal, thus revealing hidden material
- Invites spontaneous play; no right or wrong way
- Allows defenses to diminish because it is nonthreatening
- Functions as a natural language for children and a common language for use with diverse cultures and developmental stages
- Empowers the client by allowing movement from the position of victim to creator and by impacting her/his own course of therapy
- Serves as an adjunct to therapy, making sandplay available for use by therapists of various orientations
- Provides therapist the opportunity to do personal work

. . . .

Role of the Sandplay Therapist

- *Psychological Container:* Holding for the client what is happening in the sand tray and in the therapy room
- *Model:* Modeling attentive listening, nonjudgmental behavior, and being totally present
- *Bond/Link:* Linking the client with her/his sandplay: the unconscious content with the conscious and the sandplay with the external world
- *Helper/Support:* Supporting the emotions that are evoked and helping the client to experience those feelings
- *Co-explorer:* Exploring with the client her/his creation and what it means to her/him
- *Witness/Mirror:* Witnessing and reflecting back the client's process, validating and strengthening the experience

. . . .

Important Qualities for the Therapist

- Theoretical knowledge
- Clinical experience
- Understanding of the psyche
- Commitment to self-understanding and personal growth
- Experience with her/his own sandplay
- Ability to tolerate new experiences
- Belief in symbolic internal images
- Knowledge of the body and somatic illnesses

·· 2 ··

SETTING UP A
SANDPLAY SPACE

Once you decide sandplay is something you would like to pursue, it is time to set up your workspace and collect your materials. Although you may think that your workspace is inadequate or that your budget is insufficient, this is probably not true. We will show you how you can begin with minimal space and expense. The basic materials that you must have are sand, one or two sand trays, some miniature objects, art and construction materials, a pitcher for water, a camera, a small table, and some shelves or storage containers. We describe in detail various possibilities for the sand tray room to give you a variety of options and ideas.

In the process of integrating sandplay into your practice it is important to spend some time reading books and articles on the topic. To help you get started, a suggested reading list is included at the back of this book. If at all possible we also advocate that you take one or more workshops facilitated by a qualified practitioner of sandplay. Preferably workshops should be experiential, allowing you to experience being both the client and the therapist. You will find that learning will be at a deeper level if you actually participate in sandplay. This will help you determine whether sandplay is a tool that is appropriate for you to use as an adjunct to your present techniques.

Sand Trays

There are a variety of types, shapes, and sizes of trays or boxes that can be used successfully as holders for the sand. If possible, have at least two containers at your disposal. One will hold sand that clients can wet, and one will hold sand that will remain dry. This allows the client a choice. A third empty tray is sometimes useful, especially for children. We discuss this later in chapter 4. Lowenfeld provided rectangular trays made of zinc that measured 20″ × 30″ and were 3″ deep. Kalff's trays were usually made of wood and lined with sheet metal or rigid plastic. To simulate sky and water she painted the insides of the trays blue. Her boxes measured 57 cm (19.5″) × 72 cm (28.5″) and were 7 cm (3″) deep.

Kalff's reasons for using this specific size container were multiple. She felt clients should be able to see the entire world at one glance without shifting their eyes. This allowed clients to fully comprehend and appreciate their creations. Each area of the tray was also to be easily accessible and within arms' reach. The size was kept purposely small to limit the space in which clients could create their worlds in safety. Kalff stated that the tray actually "limits the player's imagination and thus acts as a regulating, protecting factor," discouraging the builder's imagination from going beyond control (1980, p. 31). Joel Ryce-Menuhin stated that "the delimited space of the sandbox enables the player's fantasy both to be bounded and held within limits, and to go free" (1992, p. 6). De Domenico's research study with a variety of sizes of trays also concluded that the small trays that Lowenfeld and Kalff advocated helped clients focus and crystallize their worlds. Children played for longer periods of time and expressed their intrapsychic world views more clearly in a reflective symbolic mode of experiencing than they did in larger containers. When using sandboxes or trays large enough to climb into, children exhibited diminished attention span, increased physical movement, and increased incidence of alternative play activities. De Domenico stated that, in effect, the tray held and limited both the player and the creation. She believed that "the psyche will manifest itself most fully in a limited safe space" (1988, p. 19).

Although many of our wooden sand trays are approximately 20″ × 30″ × 3″, like De Domenico (1988), we have found that different sizes and shapes of containers are useful, depending on the client's process. In addition to rectangular trays, we provide one that is square and one that is round (see illustration #3). Usually we suggest to clients that they choose the tray in which they wish to work for that particular session. We believe that the unconscious will direct the selection. Occasionally, however, we direct a client to the particular tray that we feel

Illustration #3. Round and Square Trays and Stacking Tables

will best facilitate a specific process. The rectangular and square shapes depict opposites and conflicts more clearly than round trays and usually allow for a slow, natural process of integration to occur. The round trays tend to facilitate pictures of centering. Conflicts and dualities often find places of connection in a circle. Scenes tend to be more idealistic and soothing (De Domenico, 1988). The round tray might therefore be selected by you, the therapist, to facilitate the reduction of anxiety and agitation of the client. If a client frequently selects a round container, keeping the scenes anxiety free, you may wish to suggest the use of a rectangular or square one to facilitate the client's dealing with her/his issues. Direct the client at your discretion.

Wooden trays are both aesthetic and useful. We have lined ours with blue Formica. The Formica provides the color blue to simulate water and sky and also creates a waterproof surface. Wooden trays may be built by a contractor or friend, or by yourself if you are adept at woodworking. Sand trays of different materials can also be purchased from sources such as those listed in Appendix 3: Suggested Readings and Resources. Generally these trays range from $150.00 to $300.00.

Although the usual rectangular tray is adequate for couples therapy, we have had a somewhat larger one (approximately 20″ × 42″ × 4″) built for work with couples and families (see illustration #4). Our other sand tray that is worth mentioning is a traveling combination of tray and storage compartments (see illustration #5). This container is particularly useful for therapists, such as mental health workers, public health nurses, social workers, and school counselors, who travel in their

Illustration #4. Couple/Family Sand Tray and Sand Tray Tables

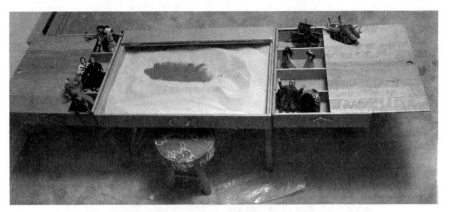

Illustration #5. Traveling Sand Tray

work. It is also beneficial in small or shared offices, where space is at a minimum. Our tray is approximately 19″ × 28″ × 3″ and has small covered compartments on each side (19″ × 14″ × 3″ with adjustable separators) for different categories of miniature objects. This composite folds up entirely, including the retractable legs, which stand 12″ high. It can be carried by a built-in handle. The sand can be removed for travel if the filled tray is too heavy.

Although many therapists prefer wooden trays, we have found that sturdy plastic trays can be just as useful. Plastic trays are inexpensive and can be flooded with water without damage. Wal-Mart, K-Mart, and other discount stores sell inexpensive translucent blue or clear Rubbermaid storage containers (see illustration #6). Usually the containers have a blue or white cover. Covers are important if you need to stack trays. Trays come in a variety of sizes and costs. The size of the plastic tray we frequently use is 20″ × 30″ × 6″. This container costs approximately $15.00. A smaller tray that we use as well is 15″ × 21″ × 6″. The cost is approximately $5.00. If possible, buy a tray that is blue to simulate sky and water. Trays that are 3″– 4″ deep are often preferred by world builders as they are somewhat easier to work in than deeper ones. Clients are also able to more easily see the scenes that they are creating from different angles in a shallower tray. However, we have not found inexpensive Rubbermaid containers that are only 3″ deep. Photographic equipment stores carry 20″ × 24″ × 3″ developing trays that cost approximately $27.00. Usually these can be found only in white but occasionally they are also sold in blue. These trays, however, do not have a cover. If you are unable to find a satisfac-

Illustration #6. Rubbermaid Tray and Storage Unit and Shelves

tory tray at the types of stores we have mentioned, you might explore toy stores, hardware stores, and plastic supplier catalogues.

To simulate water you may wish to paint the outside bottom of your translucent plastic tray blue or place the container on a piece of blue cloth, contact paper or shelf paper. If the cover of the container is blue, you have the option of placing the tray on top of it. With an opaque tray, you may want to paint the inside blue or line it with blue contact paper. We have yet to find a paint that does not chip off with a lot of use. If you have clients who frequently flood the sand with water, you may wish to cut a small round hole, sized to fit a rubber stopper, in the side of the tray near the bottom. Cover the hole with a fine mesh screen slightly protruding into the tray and place the rubber stopper into the hole from the outside of the tray. The hole will facilitate draining the water when you are ready. To remove excess water between uses, simply raise the end that does not have the hole, remove the stopper, and use your hand or some other barrier to restrain the sand from the opening.

Our round tray is cut from the lower portion of a plastic drum. These drums can be found as containers for fertilizer and other agricultural substances and must be cleaned carefully and thoroughly before using. If they are not blue, you can paint them to simulate sky and water. Also, look at discount or hardware stores for large, round, clear or blue containers or garbage cans 20″–30″ in diameter that you can cut down to a height of 3″–4″.

As you begin to explore your and the clients' personal needs and desires more fully, you will be able to select the container(s) best suited for your practice. Initially, you may choose just one tray. Once you are more experienced in using sandplay you will have a better idea of how you wish to expand your collection.

Tables

We have found that most young children and some older children and adults prefer to work with the tray on the floor. However, most adolescents and adults like to sit or stand. It is therefore important to provide at least one table for the tray being used. The surface should be large enough to hold a pitcher of water, a roll of paper towels, a box of tissues, and objects that the client has selected to place into the tray. The table should be approximately waist high so that clients can choose to sit or stand while they create. Ideally, it should have wheels, so that it can easily be moved to a desirable location.

You might wish to place the table or tray on a plastic tarp to protect the carpet or floor. If needed, a quick sweeping or hand vacuuming of the tarp or the floor between sessions keeps the workspace clean and neat. Roll up the tarp to the legs of the table when the sand tray is not in use. This decreases the likelihood of the client tripping over the tarp. If you have extra trays, they can be stacked under the table to conserve space.

If you wish to have both your wet and your dry tray available but have a minimum of space, you can store them on "stacking tables" (see illustration #3). For easy access and storing, the tables should be on wheels. The smaller, shorter table can then be slipped under the other when not in use. Heights should be different enough to allow the lower tray to remain on the table while tables are stored. You can have someone build these tables of varying heights and sizes or you can modify existing tables or buy a smaller one that fits under your larger one. If necessary, cut the smaller table's legs to the desired height and place casters or wheels on the ends of the legs. Wheels or castors can be found at most hardware stores. This table can then be moved under the larger one. If your expense account is limited, you may be able to find tables that are suitable and inexpensive at garage sales or thrift shops. We also have two wooden sand tray tables of different heights and sizes (so that the smaller, shorter table can be easily rolled under the taller table). These tables are merely sand trays with legs on wheels. They have lids and are built specifically to our design (see illustration #4). When not in use as a sand tray, the covered tray can serve as an all-purpose table. The disadvantage of these tables is that they lack space to place objects and materials while the client is working. You can remedy this by placing a surface next to the sand tray table to provide adequate space for materials.

Display

There are several ways of displaying the miniature objects you will be collecting. Objects should be exhibited or stored together neatly in categories to facilitate fast and easy access for clients. The choice of display is up to you. We describe several possibilities; you may find others that are suitable to your needs.

Lowenfeld (1935) believed that the toys themselves should not offer suggestions to the client, and that the client should not be over-whelmed by a multiplicity of choices. In her work with children, she found that the most satisfactory form of storage was a cabinet of drawers that pulled out to their fullest extent but could not be taken out completely. Lowenfeld preferred that one drawer close entirely to allow another one to open, thus decreasing the possibility of overstimulation. On the other hand, Kalff, like most Jungian analysts, uses an open shelf display. Miniature objects are displayed in full view on shelves that line the play area.

In our practices we use primarily the open shelf display (illustration #7). We have found that this attracts many clients to the objects and therefore to sandplay. The objects seem to activate the curiosity and creativity innately present in everyone. We have not found that the open display overly arouses most of our clients. Instead, it tends to open the client up to many possibilities. Where overstimulation or distraction is an issue, facing the client away from the shelves while s/he is working in the tray or not participating in sandplay usually eliminates the problem.

In situations where you work frequently with very young or attention deficit hyperactive clients who may be in more danger of distraction than your other clients, you may find the Lowenfeld manner of object storage most appropriate. There are, however, other ways to reduce exposure if you prefer shelves. You can install doors, curtains, or roll-up shades to cover your objects. Shades and doors can be as long and as wide as you wish. This allows you to display no objects, a certain category of objects, or all objects, as is appropriate for the session (see illustration #7).

We have found that using open shelves with some containers works best for us. The containers allow us to use less space and somewhat reduce visual stimulation. Multiple objects such as soldiers, flowers, small rocks, and gems can be stored readily in baskets, bowls, storage bins, or small boxes. Containers remain uncovered so that objects are visible. Note, however, that we have found that stored articles, even when they are not covered, are not as frequently used as openly displayed objects.

Closed shelves and storage bins that can be placed in a closet are often the most suitable when you have an office space that is used by several therapists (see illustration #6). For a therapist who works in more than one site, plastic storage containers similar to the small plastic covered Rubbermaid sand trays discussed previously can be divided into small sections to hold categories of objects. Tool boxes or tool storage containers may also serve this purpose. If you are a therapist who has very little time between clients and needs to have your objects

Illustration #7. Open Shelf Display; Shades Covering Shelves

cleared before the next session, storage bins or a combination of containers and shelves may work best. This reduces cleanup time considerably.

Our shelves are 4″–12″ deep and 6′–8′ wide. Ideally, they should be no deeper than 6″–8″. The limited depth allows clients to pick up and replace miniatures with less disturbance to surrounding objects. It also allows clients to see objects without obstruction. Our shelves are wood and particle board and have been built by a contractor. You may have yours built or build them yourself. Display units made of bricks and boards are easily and rapidly set up and are utilitarian. You can also purchase shallow bookcases of wood, particle board, plastic, or metal very reasonably at garage sales, thrift shops, or discount stores. Most of our displays are approximately 6′ high. Although we place the objects that are most popular with children on the lower shelves at their eye level, we provide a sturdy folding stepping stool for children and clients who are unable to reach and view objects on the higher shelves. Bracketed shelves that can be raised or lowered are most serviceable, as the distance between the shelves can be changed according to the size of the objects.

To limit confusion and facilitate easy location, objects of the same category should be exhibited together. We have made two exceptions to this rule. First, we, like De Domenico, display tall objects from various categories, which require a greater distance between shelves, on the bottom. By doing this, we are able to place our other shelves closer together and thus provide more space on which to display a greater number of objects (see illustration #8). Second, we have a miscellaneous category of objects—those that defy classification either because there are very few objects that are related   (e.g., time items, communication items, planetary items) or we are perplexed as to where to place them.

Workspace

Some sandplay therapists prefer to have a separate room for the sand tray and the miniatures because it makes the process separate and special. This is especially true of therapists who have a separate play therapy room. We have found, however, that placing the tray in a prominent position in the office elicits many questions and responses. This facilitates introduction and integration of sandplay into our regular sessions with both children and adults. Whether you choose one or two rooms is your prerogative.

Realistically, most therapists' choices are limited by space and budget. If you are one of the few therapists who chooses to create a separate play room, line your walls with shelves. Place your sand tray in the middle of the room where clients are not directly facing the objects. If, however, you have only one small room, line one wall or corner with shelves and store the sand trays on stacking tables in the corner near the shelves. On the top table place a large pitcher of water to wet the sand. Some clients may also wish to use the water to wash their hands periodically while doing sandplay. Also provide paper towels so

Illustration #8. Tall Objects Placed Together with Moveable Shelves

that your clients can dry or clean their hands when desired. Don't forget a box of tissues! Of course, no therapy room is without tissues, but make sure the box is easily accessible to your client. A folding stepstool near the shelves facilitates client viewing and selection of objects on the higher shelves. Have two chairs available close to the tables in case you and your client wish to sit during the session.

The camera you and your client will be using to take pictures of the client's scene can be placed on the table with the other materials between sessions. We have found, however, that cameras are better kept on our desks away from the sand and water. This prevents any accidental damage.

Arrange your regular consulting space somewhat separate from the sand tray and miniature display, if possible. Often one area or corner of the room can be designated as the play area and another area as the consulting space. To avoid distraction, situate the seating in the consulting space in such a way that the client faces away from the exhibit of objects.

When your client chooses to use the sand tray in a session, pull the tray that s/he selects away from the display as far as you can. It is important to allow enough space for the client to walk freely around the tray. S/he may choose to sit or stand at the tray or sit on the floor next to it. Like De Domenico, we have found that the standing position is described by many builders as the one that most places them in charge of the world they are creating and allows for freedom of movement. Standing tends to facilitate a more active mode of play than does sitting. Play with the tray on the floor is apt to encourage regressive behavior in clients. If the client chooses the floor, remember to join her/him so that the two of you are on an equal level.

These directions are only recommendations based on our experiences and our readings. Use the design that best meets the needs of you and your clients. It is your space and you are the one who will be using it for many hours a week. We have always believed, however, that it is important to keep your workspace neat and orderly. It is easier to feel inner order when outer order is maintained.

Camera

Have a camera available at all sandplay sessions. In most cases photographs are taken only of the finished world. If the clients wish, they may take a picture of their final world to take home. We have found that clients frequently choose to do this, in which case a Polaroid camera is advisable. It is especially important to have a Polaroid camera available when your clients want or need an immediate physical reminder of their work. Although pictures taken during the building of the world can be very revealing of the client's process, this is not often done. Repetitive photographing may be intrusive to the client. If you choose to photograph the process and/or the completed scene, ask for the client's consent.

Usually you will take another picture for your records during the session after your client takes hers/his. Sometimes you will take it after s/he leaves. A 35mm camera is best used for this purpose because the picture is less expensive than a Polaroid picture and is clearer, showing more detail and depth. Slides are useful if you will be reviewing them with the client. For more information on picture documentation, see chapter 3.

Sand and Water

Sand and water are highly symbolic and connect people to the planet Earth. Water flows, cleanses, dissolves, and regenerates, and is frequently representative of the unconscious and the emotions. It can be a metaphor for the feminine principle, fertility, and the fountain of life. Water is the source of all potentialities in existence. Sand frequently symbolizes the earth, the concrete and the physical. Children and adults alike often unconsciously work or play in the earth to ground themselves in physical reality. The earth can also be seen as the feminine, the bearer of life that provides nourishment, fertility, and love. According to De Domenico, "Sand is the foundation for the world being created. Sand supports, hides, covers or destroys the images in the tray" (1988, p. 23). Both sand and water tend to regress people to early childhood experiences. These elements can also facilitate individuation through the birthing and rebirthing process of the Self. Depending on whether the sand is wet or dry, it remains constant, holding the shape of things, or flows and changes endlessly as the creator commands. For clients who require a more concrete connection to earth than the sand provides, some therapists choose to supply soil.

Keeping these metaphors in mind, select your sand carefully. For those of you with only one or two trays, you will have fewer options. However, we are describing the full range of grits we use. Each different grit and texture evokes unique feelings. Our sand varies from 20 to 90 mesh. The higher the number, the finer the sand. The finer grits are usually soothing and tend to evoke a deeper altered state than the courser grits. For some clients the very fine grit is disturbing. Coarse sands tend to be more grounding. If possible, supply at least two grits from which clients can choose. Clients may use a finer grit one session and a coarser one the next session, depending on their emotional state at the time. Some clients may prefer sandbox sand, which is composed of several grits, because it is familiar. The advantage of this texture is that it often rapidly regresses clients to childhood. The disadvantage is that some of the sand is very fine and therefore very dusty. The dust might present problems for people with allergies.

Because it has been brought to our attention that there could be some deleterious effects of using sand with silicon as a component, we want to briefly address this issue. We were told by an industrial hygienist at Occupational Safety and Health Agency (OSHA) that silicosis, a scarring of the lungs caused by silicon, may result when the dust particles are imbedded in the lining of the lungs. This can occur if one breathes in the powder raised during sandblasting, when working on or frequently driving through construction sites. We were assured that the use of the sand in the sand tray does not present a hazard.

De Domenico taught us the importance of color when selecting sand. If you supply more than one tray, consider using more than one color. The natural colors range from light to dark beige, white, black, red garnet, green, and coral. Different colors evoke different feelings. The client will select the color according to her/his need. As an example, one of our clients selected the dark red sand when doing a spontaneous tray. She was unaware of the issue she would be working on when she felt drawn to the tray. She proceeded to create a tray that focused on the trauma of finding her mother in a pool of drying blood. In retrospect, she realized why she had chosen the red sand.

Usually local brick and cement companies will sell sand of varying grits. However, the sand is often sold in white or light beige only and comes in 100 lb. bags for about $5.00 a bag. Colored sands can be found at different beaches or sand dunes around the country. You can find a beautiful soft coral sand in Utah and a fine silky black sand in Hawaii (a possible tax write-off!). Some people say they have used dyed terrarium sand or have dyed the sand themselves. We, however, have no knowledge of whether the colors remain permanent, especially when the sand is wet. You could experiment with this if you wish. You can also buy natural sand of varying colors at specialty sand and gravel stores in large metropolitan areas. We are aware of suppliers in the San Francisco and Los Angeles areas. The cost is approximately $15.00–$25.00 for a 100 lb. bag. Shipping may be expensive.

Fill your trays with sand 1.5″–2″ deep. One bag of sand will be enough to fill two 20″ × 30″ trays to this depth. There will be enough sand remaining to replenish trays when sand is lost by natural attrition or when clients request more sand. Keep a bag with the same grit and color sand available for occasions when clients request more sand or wish to remove sand from the tray. If you would like two different grits or colors of sand for your trays, you might wish to share bags of sand with another therapist. In addition, provide a large pitcher of clean water accessible next to the tray so that clients can wet or flood the tray, sprinkle or pour water, or place water into containers. You might also supply a sprayer or water gun. If possible, have easy access to extra water in case more is needed.

When using sandplay with very young children or developmentally disabled clients who like to eat the sand, cornmeal, rice, or semolina can be substituted. The advantage is that your concern will be lessened and your clients will be able to play as they wish. The disadvantage is that the connection to the earth will be diminished.

After you have chosen the grits, composition, and color of sand you wish to use and have set up your table with sand trays and a pitcher of water, you are ready to facilitate sandplay with your clients. Most therapists supply miniature objects. A selection of items is important but not essential. Some clients choose to play only with sand or with sand and water. Always remember to trust your client's unconscious mind to choose the grit and color of sand s/he needs to play in to resolve her/his issues in the best possible way. Occasionally, when clients are stuck in their process, we direct them to a particular color or grit of sand to help them deal with specific issues.

Miniature Objects

When you begin to select objects for sandplay, remember that the objects you are collecting will be the symbolic language of the conscious and the unconscious mind of the builder. The more diverse the objects and the larger number of objects that you make available (at least to a point), the richer and more creative the vocabulary of the client can be. Each piece used is like a new word learned and expands the client's symbolic vocabulary. Include as many objects as possible that trigger the senses of sight, sound, smell, taste, and touch. A large selection of miniatures encourages the client to explore the diverse possibilities available in life. In collecting objects "your aim is to bring forth all which is a vital aspect of the collective, individual, racial, cultural, historical, spiritual, physiological and emotional heritage of humanity and the planet" (De Domenico, 1988, p. 45).

On the other hand, some therapists prefer to present a simple array of objects. They perceive this simplicity as less confusing and stimulating to their clients who may already be overwhelmed. In addition, when clients create their own symbolic objects, the work seems to come more from the unconscious mind (Ammann, 1993). Usually the therapist provides multipurpose materials such as fabric, pipe cleaners, string, clay, plasticine, construction paper, and magic markers so that clients can create their own objects to make the exact statements they wish. Regardless of how many miniatures are available, it is helpful to provide materials for clients to make their own objects, because clients may not find the exact ones they need to express their inner experience.

Start your collection by selecting at least a few objects from each category listed in this chapter. "Remember you are not creating an art gallery. Nor are you creating a world of deprivation. Therefore you need to include that which repels you, that which magnetically draws you, that which bores you, that which is tasteless, that which is horrifying, that which is good, that which is evil, that which is harmonious, that which is absurd, etc." (De Domenico, 1988, p. 45). Make sure you select as many objects that are aversive as are attractive to you. This provides the psyche the opportunity to express and integrate polarities and inner conflicts.

Collect objects of different sizes, colors, textures, and materials. Objects should range from large to tiny, without color to bright colors, transparent to opaque, rough to smooth, and be made of a variety of materials, such as pewter, glass, clay, wood, and plastic. Collect very defined objects as well as amorphous ones. Each size, color, texture, and material will elicit a unique meaning from the builder, depending on what the unconscious wishes to express at that moment. Usually, size denotes the level of dominance. Defined figures are thought to be closer to consciousness than are sand and unformed or amorphous materials. Collect natural objects in as many categories as you can. Actual feathers, seashells, pine cones, twigs, rocks, etc., can facilitate the client's process when s/he feels uncomfortable with manmade miniatures or needs to connect to nature. Natural objects can provide an environment where the client can feel strength and peace.

When you explore the world with clients, they will usually be able to convey the significance of each object. If they are unable to discover the meaning for themselves, you may allow them to remain in their confusion, create an amplification tray (see "Amplification" in chapter 6), or ask them if they would like to consult a symbol dictionary for possible clarity. Let them know that the dictionary explanation may or not apply to their trays. Symbol dictionaries can be ordered or purchased from most bookstores. If you are interested in exploring the meaning of the object but the client is not, you might check the dictionary after the client leaves to help shed light on the sand world. This is done to help you make sense of your client's world. Just remember that the meaning in the dictionary may or may not be applicable to the client's tray. Symbols may be archetypal but most of all their meanings are unique to the builder.

Objects can be collected from a variety of sources. Natural objects can be found on hikes and trips. There will be some specialty items such as gods and goddesses that you will probably wish to buy at the appropriate boutique. Most objects can be inexpensive. Dollar stores and cake decorating stores provide unique low-cost items. Also check thrift shops and garage sales regularly. If you have a mate or know friends who like to scavenge or peruse garage sales, give them a list of the items you need and they will probably enjoy finding them for you. You might also wish to rummage through your own trinkets or your children's outdated objects and toys for suitable miniatures. If you are a school counselor, you might let the parent association and teachers know the types of objects that you can use. This way any toys or objects that families are ready to discard can be contributed to your sandplay collection. As gifts, request special objects that you would not ordinarily buy. Friends and relatives are often looking for a list of things you want for birthdays and special occasions.

Acrylic paints can be used to paint objects that are colorless or are not the color you want. Because it may be difficult to find figures of different races and ages, you may wish to change skin and hair color on some of your figures. Sometimes it is difficult to find metal objects. Repainting objects bronze, gold, or silver can simulate metal. We have found that creating our own miniatures out of Sculpey, clay, wood or papier-mâché is inexpensive and allows us to provide symbols not usually available (see illustration #9).

Illustration #9. Self-made Objects and Sky Hooks

Working in three dimensions seems to provide even more possibilities for the builder. For this purpose we have developed *sky hooks*. Sky hooks are made of a piece of bent metal (we use hangers) glued between two large heavy washers. The hanger extends upwards with a hook at the top (see illustration #9). The washers sink into the sand and disappear, leaving only the extended wire. This allows clients to suspend objects found in the sky such as the sun, clouds, airplanes, and birds.

Sometimes we encourage clients to bring in their own meaningful objects to use. Often personal, cultural, or religious artifacts, objects from childhood, and articles special in a relationship, such as photographs, are brought in to resolve client issues. For example, we had a client from China who brought in a box filled with Chinese ornaments, gods and goddesses, and family treasures whenever she planned to create a world. Another client, grieving his father's death, brought in photographs and special belongings of his father.

De Domenico suggests in her workshops that, as therapists acquire new miniatures for their displays, they should build a world of their own using these objects in their sand tray. She believes that this helps therapists incorporate the symbols into their collection. You might wish to try this approach. However, be aware that your clients may or may not use the objects as you do.

When you begin to collect your objects for sandplay, you will probably find that your view of the world changes. Almost everything you see will be a potential sandplay item to collect or to make. Whenever you take a hike, go on a vacation, or simply walk into a room or a store, objects beckon. We offer a word of warning: It is easy to become obsessed with collecting. Maybe a new 12-step program is in order! On the positive side, we have found that we have become much more aware of our surroundings. We often view our environment as a sand world with all the symbolic magical meanings the objects in that world convey. Happy hunting!

Categories

As you collect an array of objects from the categories described in this section, display them in an orderly fashion. Contributors to the sandplay therapy field have classified miniatures in a variety of ways. De Domenico's impressive collection certainly influenced us as we enlarged our sandplay space. You may display the objects in categories as we list them here, or you may choose to exhibit your objects as listed in other books, such as *Sand Tray World Play* (De Domenico, 1988). Or you may create classifications that seem to be most applicable to your individual situation. The following is a general summary of the categories we have found to be most useful to us. We have provided an extensive list of possibilities. Your space, budget, and clients' needs will dictate the number and kind of objects you select. Remember to choose at least a few objects from each category.

PEOPLE

People are frequently used as symbols of actual individuals in the client's life or are used as prototypes of distinct personalities that have an impact on the client (e.g., aggressive or loving dispositions). People also symbolize aspects of the client's personality.

For all of the following categories of people, supply miniatures of both sexes from various races, cultures, and ages. Include a variety of colors and sizes. The smallest figures should be able to fit into toy toilets, beds, and drawers. Also include group composites, such as parent and child, couples (same and opposite sex), families, embracing lovers, or wedding couples. Materials can be glass, clay, porcelain, metal, wood, or plastic. They should be painted and unpainted, transparent, translucent, and opaque. Provide faceless, amorphous and androgynous figures. Clients can attribute a wide variety of meanings to these objects. Interestingly, our faceless little wooden blue and red figures are used frequently by clients to represent a myriad of people in their lives. Depressed clients often begin by using colorless or gray pewter people in their tray and then gradually move to a language of color. Provide people in different developmental stages of life such as infancy, childhood, aging, and pregnancy. Include symbols of sexuality, death, accidents, and illness. Make sure figures represent a range of human emotions. Include people who are crying, frowning, angry, smiling, and laughing. We have found that most figures have very little expression.

Any objects, such as apparel, tools, and belongings used by the group of people you are displaying, may be placed as a subcategory adjacent to the figures to whom the personal effects pertain. For example, the clothes and hats of ordinary people would be displayed as a collection next to the group of ordinary people.

Ordinary People. Supply a sufficient number of ordinary people to represent the individuals in your clients' lives or to represent a community or a family. Include duplicates to represent twins, triplets, groupings, etc. Different ages, sexes, races, and cultures are essential to portray a full range of experiences. Some figures should be standing, some walking, some running, and some seated. It is valuable to have some people with rigid, and some with bending, arms, legs, and heads. Make sure to include nude as well as dressed people. If possible, include clothes designed specifically for the naked figures in addition to the separate category of clothes, hats, shoes, jewelry, and makeup that ordinary people wear.

People in a Variety of Recreational Activities. Include men, women, and children in both summer and winter sports and hobbies. Reading, dancing, playing music, skating, skiing, sledding, golfing, fishing, bicycling, bowling, running, hiking, riding horseback, and playing baseball, football, tennis and basketball are examples of such activities. Make sure that the activities most frequently performed in your area are represented in your collection. Include items used in recreational activities, such as footballs, skates, tennis rackets, and clothes such as football helmets and tennis shoes. These items can be placed separately, but as a subgroup of the recreational activity category. Include objects that make sounds, such as bells and whistles. Include symbols of the arts, such as musical instruments, record players, sheet music, paints and brushes.

People in a Variety of Occupations. Include men and women from both rural and urban settings. Include figures such as farmers, laborers, police officers, firefighters, clergy, ambulance workers, business people, doctors, nurses, teachers, scientists, astronauts, entertainers, clowns, and any other occupational characters you can find. Don't forget to include children at their school desks. School is a child's work. Also include tools and products, as well as clothes of the trade, in a subsection.

Unique People of the Past and the Present. Incorporate men, women, and children in period dress, such as queens, kings, princes, princesses, emperors, pirates, pioneers, primitive tribes, and stone age people. Also include icons from the past and the present, such as Marilyn Monroe, Elvis Presley, and Princess Diana. In a separate subsection include items worn or associated with these people, such as crowns, thrones, and treasures.

Fantasy, Folklore, Mythological, and Magical People. Include creatures half-human/ half-animal, monstrous humanoid creatures, space aliens, science fiction figures, characters from cartoons, fairy tales, current movies, and books. Such characters as Superman, Batman, Power Rangers, Darth Vader, and Yoda can be symbolic of the inner battle of good and evil, for young and old alike. Be familiar with the characters who are currently popular among children and adolescents. Include giants, dwarfs and gnomes, wizards, witches, fairies, Disney characters, Santa Claus, and Dracula. Replicas of famous human statues, such as the Statue of Liberty, the Pieta, or the Thinker, can also be incorporated here. In a separate subsection, group items specific to this category, such as magic wands, light sabers, wishing wells, and glittering stars.

Fighting, Warring, and Enslaved People. Include both men and women of the past and the present in this category, if you can find them. Make sure to include the various branches of the military, such as the army, navy, and air force. Include soldiers from two different armies (e.g., American and German), so that people can play out fully their inner conflicts. These conflicts often portray what clients consider to be good and evil. Soldiers should be mounted on horses, in tanks, and on foot, running and shooting if possible. Include wounded soldiers on stretchers with bearers, and people who are in bondage or are imprisoned. If figures are difficult to find (e.g., people in bondage), you can create them out of clay or Sculpey.

Include knights in armor, cavalry men, and several cowboys and Indians with weapons. Include primitive people holding clubs and spears as well as warriors of different cultures such as samurai warriors. In a separate subsection include paraphernalia of war, such as guns, spears, and swords, and objects of enslavement, such as handcuffs and chains.

Death Figures. Include death symbols such as the grim reaper, the devil, zombies, skeletons, skulls, shrouded figures, gravestones, and coffins. Note that different cultures have different symbols of death.

Religious and Spiritual People and Objects. It is important to include people and objects from a variety of different religious and spiritual beliefs. Incorporate figures from the Christian, Buddhist, Hindu, Jewish, Islamic, and indigenous religions. Include items such as the nativity scene, the Virgin Mary, Jesus, angels, the saints, a priest, a clergyman, a rabbi, a nun, a child taking first communion, Shiva, Buddha, Native American totemic figures, and ancient gods and goddesses. Also include religious objects such as a cross, rosary beads, an African mask, a Jewish star and dreidel, a Native American kachina doll, the ankh, and other images specific to different religions. Remember to provide the people and objects that would be most relevant for your client population. If you cannot procure the needed objects, ask your clients to bring specific religious objects they might wish to use for sand tray sessions.

Other Races and Cultures. We prefer to include other races and cultures in all the different categories already listed, as we see people as people regardless of race or culture. You will find, however, that some other authors tend to list this category separately. The choice is yours. We do, however, stress the importance of including miniatures of other races and cultures than the dominant ones in your community. Make sure to also include artifacts and apparel of different cultures.

Body Parts. Include body parts such as hands, eyes, feet, legs, heads, breasts, and penises. Keep broken and damaged figures such as broken dolls and miniatures of people and display them in this category. These objects are probably as valuable as whole ones, because they may be seen as powerful symbols representing the feelings of the client. Remember, many clients feel broken and damaged inside when they come for therapy.

ANIMALS

Animals can symbolize intuitive life and the instinct as distinct from the intellect, will and reason, and are often used anthropomorphically. Animals in the client's sand world can depict the different aspects of humankind's nature. For example, the lion can depict the strong and aggressive side, and the lamb can depict the vulnerable side of the client. However, it is important to remember that people outside the Judeo-Christian tradition may experience an interconnectedness with animals that derives from a different spiritual awareness.

Collect animal objects in various sizes, colors, sexes, ages, species, and groupings, such as families, pairs, and communities. Include mothers with suckling babies. Include animals that are constituted from a variety of materials and textures, such as soft and furry or hard and smooth. Include miniatures that are transparent, colorless, and colored, and ones that are defined and amorphous. Some animals should be grazing and some should be running. Predatory animals should be shown in aggressive stances as well as in peaceful ones. Include animals that live in different areas of the world. Within each of the animal categories, create subsections according to where the animals live, such as land, water, and air.

Wild Animals and Creatures. Group various types of land animals together. Include predatory animals such as tigers, lions, bears, wolves, hyenas, snakes, and lizards. Include herbivorous animals such as deer, antelope, camels, elephants, monkeys and apes, kangaroos, rhinoceroses, hippopotamuses, giraffes, zebras, buffalo, moose, and rodents such as squirrels, rats, mice, and rabbits. Also include land dwelling spiders, worms, scorpions, and insects.

Group water animals together. Include whales, sharks, alligators, dolphins, seals, turtles, octopuses, squid, shrimps, crabs, lobsters, and fish. It is particularly useful to have creatures such as sharks, alligators, and whales with open mouths and hollow insides. Clients, especially children, often like to place objects inside animals.

Group air animals together. Include birds of prey such as eagles, hawks, and owls. Also include any other kinds of birds you can find, such as penguins, robins, swans, and hummingbirds. Include bats and flying insects, such as flies, bees, mosquitoes, and butterflies.

Domestic Animals and Creatures. This category consists of animals living in a home, on a farm, or on a ranch. Include pets such as dogs, cats, guinea pigs, hamsters, rabbits, hermit crabs, goldfish, and tropical fish. Include parrots, songbirds, and other birds in cages. Also include pigeons and peacocks. Also collect a sufficient quantity of animals to create a farm community. Supply farm animals such as cows, sheep, goats, pigs, chickens, donkeys, horses, turkeys, and geese.

Extinct, Mythological, and Fantasy Animals and Creatures. Include prehistoric animals such as saber toothed tigers, woolly mammoths, and dinosaurs. Include mythological animals such as Pegasus and Minotaur, unicorns, dragons, gargoyles, and monsters with several heads. Include fantasy animals such as characters from movies and cartoons, monsters, and space creatures. If you can find animals from common tales and legends of different cultures, include these as well.

Animal Habitats. Include cages, nests, zoos, and caves. Also include nets to capture animals.

Animal Parts and Broken Animals. Include natural animal parts such as bones, claws, fur, feathers, teeth, and eggshells and casings. Also include seashells, starfish, coral, sand dollars, and fossils. Include miniatures that are broken and animal parts of miniatures such as heads, legs, or tails.

PLANT LIFE

Plants also sometimes are used anthropomorphically. For many people plants symbolize the cycle of life, the life force, death, and resurrection. The seasons remind us of the changing qualities of the physical world. Plants are grounding and are seen as closely connected with the Great Mother, goddess of the earth, and fertility.

When you collect plants, include groups of various plant forms from a variety of places, such as the sea, the mountains, the tropics, and the desert. Include plants of different sizes, colors, textures, and materials. Objects should reflect all aspects of the life cycle from seed to bloom to barren or dead. Include natural as well as artificial plant forms.

Natural Plants. Include a selection of twigs, driftwood with interesting shapes, branches that are smooth, and branches that have thorns. Include dried flowers, leaves and weeds, moss, lichens on rocks and twigs, seed pods, grains and seeds, pine cones and chestnuts. Include some small living plants that take their food and moisture from the air. If you have access to fresh plants, you may wish to provide some for your clients. We have found that clients greatly enjoy using freshly cut flowers and branches. The color and the fragrance of flowers and evergreen branches often trigger clients' memories of special places and events. Often we cut small, fresh branches of cedar and spruce that clients may break into whatever size they wish.

Artificial Plants. Include shrubs, bushes, hedges, houseplants, cacti, deciduous, evergreen, and palm trees in various stages of their life cycles. Include plants as they appear in spring, summer, autumn, and winter. Include seedlings, flowering plants, fruiting trees, dying plants, and dead plants. Include vegetables and fruits. (You may choose to include these in this category and/or the food category.) Include silk and plastic flowers of different colors and sizes as well as silver, bronze, and gold flowers, trees, shrubs, and leaves to be used in creating magical worlds. Also include Christmas trees.

MINERALS

Minerals such as rocks, metals, and gems may symbolize stability, permanence, solidity, and coldness. Rocks are seen as representing strength and refuge. To some clients cut and shaped jewel-like stones signify the soul shaped from the rough irregular stone into a beautiful treasure, the gem or the jewel.

Include in your display a variety of rocks, metals, and gems of various sizes, colors, shapes, textures, and materials, so that clients may replicate various landscapes and topographies. Include ordinary as well as exotic rocks. Include rocks that contain holes or fossils. Also include geodes, cut and polished slabs of rock, crystals (single and clusters), semi-precious stones such as amethyst and tiger eye that are tumbled, cut, or in their natural form, and rocks with fool's gold or other metals. Include metals, glass beads, marbles, artificial gems, and jewelry.

ENVIRONMENTS

The environments of people often have great significance. For instance, the home may be seen as a symbol of shelter and protection or of violation and abandonment. On an expanded scale, the home can be the center of the Self and the cosmos.

When you are collecting for this category, remember to include objects of different sizes made of a variety of materials. Include miniatures of various cultures, lifestyles, and religions from the past, present, and future. See if you can find a variety of homes, such as houses, teepees, igloos, castles, fortresses, caves, and space stations. Include barns, stores, churches, temples, schools, jails, hospitals, playgrounds, lighthouses, and pyramids. Include damaged and burnt-out homes and buildings. Many clients have lived through disasters or feel destroyed inside and need a method to express that in the tray.

Include home furnishings of all kinds, such as tables, chairs, beds, cribs, toilets, tubs, and appliances. Also include tools and implements, such as shovels, rakes, lawnmowers, pliers, saws, and screwdrivers. If tools have already been included in the "people with occupations" section, it is unnecessary to duplicate them here. Include fences, gates, bridges, columns, arches, traffic lights, signs, and other items often found in the environment.

TRANSPORTATION

Transportation may be a metaphor for the psychophysiological experience of the client. Vehicles may symbolize movement and change. They may represent control, release, escape, and power in the client's life. Remember to collect modes of transportation of various sizes, colors, and materials. Include wrecked as well as intact vehicles.

Land Vehicles. Collect ordinary vehicles, such as cars, trucks, buses, taxis, farm implements, carts, bicycles, motorcycles, sleighs, and wagons. Include the cars and engines of trains, special period vehicles such as streetcars, stagecoaches, covered wagons, and chariots. Group emergency vehicles such as fire engines, police cars, and ambulances together. Include vehicles of aggression, such as tanks and other armored military vehicles.

Water Vehicles. In this category include water vehicles, such as civilian and military ships, sailing vessels, boats, canoes, rafts, submarines, aircraft carriers, and battleships.

Air Vehicles. Incorporate into your collection civilian and military propeller and jet airplanes, seaplanes, helicopters, airliners, air balloons, zeppelins, space shuttles, and space ships. Also include warring vehicles such as bombers, fighters, and troop carriers.

MISCELLANEOUS OBJECTS

This category includes those items not easily classified or too few to warrant a category of their own.

Planetary and Earth Symbols. Planetary objects sometimes represent the interaction of all the fundamental forces of the universe and nature. Include objects such as the sun, moon, earth and other planets, stars, clouds, snowflakes, and rainbows. The sky hooks that we discussed earlier in this chapter can be used to suspend planetary and earth symbols. Place sky hooks in a place where they can be easily reached.

Reflective Surfaces. Reflective objects such as mirrors can symbolize truth, self-realization, wisdom, the soul, divine intelligence, and truth. Include various shaped mirrors, sheet metals, glass balls, and spheres. These can often be found as Christmas tree decorations.

Illuminating Objects. Light often symbolizes the illumination of the mind (gnosis), the manifestation of the divine, and is seen as having the power to dispel evil and the forces of darkness. Light imparts truth, glory, splendor, and joy. Include candle holders and candles of different shapes, colors, and sizes. Also include small oil lamps, flashlights, and any other battery operated lights. Be sure to have matches available to light the candles.

Aromatic Objects. The sense of smell, as well as sight, sound, and touch, is important in portraying a full range of experiences in a client's life. Include items such as potpourri, incense, smudge sticks, old perfume bottles, small bottles of essential oils, sprigs of herbs, sage, mint, and lavender.

Addiction and Medical Objects. Many clients struggle with their own or family members' addictions and medical problems. Addiction and medical objects are often pivotal elements in a client's tray. Include small empty bottles of alcoholic beverages such as you can obtain on an airplane, empty prescription pill containers, cigarette packages with cigarettes, syringes, medic alert bracelets, etc. If clients have specific medical problems, they may wish to bring in the particular items that pertain to their condition.

Communication Articles. We are living in an age where objects of communication have become central to our way of life. Include tiny books, pens and pencils, telephones, televisions, cameras, computers, radios, and tape recorders.

Containers. Containers provide a special place for secrets and treasures. They serve as limiting spaces to restrain and confine as well as a receptacle to hold the various things that life presents. Include containers of various sizes, shapes, colors, and materials. Some containers should be waterproof so they can hold liquids as well as sand. Include vases, bottles, glass bowls, boxes, and baskets.

Food. Food tends to symbolize nurturing and nourishment. Food is essential to sustaining life. It also can be an obsession. Include foods that are healthy, such as fruits, vegetables, cheeses, milk, meats and cereals, as well as foods that people tend to crave, such as sweet and salty foods, fast foods, pizza, candy, and pastries. You may wish to include wrapped hard candy and other foods that do not spoil. You might give clients permission to open and eat the candy. Taste is another sense that enlarges the sand tray experience.

Multipurpose Materials. Sometimes clients cannot find objects that represent fully what they wish to portray. When materials are made available, many clients will create their own objects. As discussed earlier, objects that are made by the client often reveal the unconscious to a greater extent than do manufactured objects. Include materials such as construction paper of various colors, plasticine, clay, string, fabrics, carpet pieces, glitter, confetti, pipe cleaners, pencils, scissors, and glue. As clients create their own objects, you will become familiar with their requests, and you will learn what additional materials you need to supply.

Other Supplies. Have a kitchen strainer or sieve available to strain the sand when needed. Small pieces of natural objects such as branches and bark often remain in the sand after clearing the tray and need to be removed prior to the next client's use of the sand tray. Strainers are sometimes used by clients to sift the sand lightly onto their created worlds. Also, have small serving trays available; these can be used to hold objects while clients collect materials through the "Constructing the World" phase (see chapter 3). Include a symbol dictionary among your books to be used if clients want clarification of the meaning of an object.

Our list is extensive and is used merely to suggest possible items you might wish to incorporate in each category in your display. Sandplay can be effective with only a few objects from each category. The symbolic language of the objects is a gift from you to your clients. Each article that you collect expands your clients' opportunities for expression. As you collect items, experience them. Create sand trays of your own using the new objects. "A sandplay miniature collection is not simply a massing of important symbols. It is a reflection of the relationship of the individual therapist to those symbols. A person who sees your collection will be looking at you and your soul" (Hegeman, 1992, p. 101). Remember, "A collection grows and changes as you do. Through your self exploration you will discover your collection. What has gone into the building of the collection is as important as what is in the collection" (Hegeman, 1992, p. 106).

. . . .

The Sandplay Room

- *Sand Trays:*
    Number: One, two, or more; one dry and one wet
    Size: Approx. 20″ × 30″ × 3″; larger for families and couples
    Shape: Rectangular, square, round or other
    Type: Wood, metal, or plastic; with blue bottom and sides

- *Tables:*
    Number: One or more
    Size: Large enough to hold tray, water, tissues, and objects
    Height: Various heights; if only one, at waist level

- *Display:*
    Open shelves, storage containers, drawer, and/or cabinets

- *Workspace:*
    Separate sandplay area or room
    Neat and orderly

- *Sand and Water:*
    Grit of Sand: 20 to 90 mesh
    Color of Sand: White or natural silica, black, red, etc.
    Water: Pitcher of clean water to wet sand and wash hands

- *Other Materials:*

Miniatures/objects	Construction materials
Paper towels, tissues	Pitcher/container for water
Tarp to protect floor	Camera: Polaroid, 35mm

. . . .

Objects for the Sand Tray

- *Arrange:*
  Carefully and in categories

- *Collect:*
  A few objects from each category
  As many aversive as attractive objects
  A wide array of sizes, colors, textures, and materials
  Duplicates
  Amorphous and defined miniatures
  Natural and artificial items

- *Create:*
  Figures you can't find, or suggest clients create figures

- *Encourage:*
  Clients to bring in pertinent personal objects

- *Multipurpose Material:*
  Construction materials: String, plasticine, clay, Play-doh, paper, coloring materials, fabric, confetti, scissors, glue; sky hooks, water containers, sifters, small serving trays; symbol dictionaries

- *Sources for Objects:*
  Catalogs; garage sales; discount, cake decorating, second-hand, specialty, and toy stores; old toys and figurines of yours and friends

. . . .

Categories of Objects

- *People:*
  Ordinary; in recreational activities; in a variety of occupations; from the past and present; fantasy, mythological, and magical; fighting, warring, and enslaved; death figures; religious and spiritual people and objects; diverse races and cultures; body parts

- *Animals:*
  Wild animals of the land, sea, and air; domestic; extinct, mythological and fantasy; animal habitats; bones, shells, and feathers

- *Plant life:*
  Natural and artificial; complete plant life cycle

- *Minerals:*
  Rocks; natural and artificial gems; marbles and beads

- *Environments:*
  Habitats of various cultures and areas; fences and bridges

- *Transportation:*
  Land, water, and air; emergency and military vehicles

- *Miscellaneous Objects:*
  Planetary and earth symbols; objects that reflect and illuminate; addiction and medical symbols; aromatic objects; communication objects; containers; food; construction materials

·· 3 ··

SPONTANEOUS SAND TRAYS
WITH INDIVIDUAL ADULTS

Sandplay therapy is as unique for each client as the clients are themselves. For some clients, the initial tray reflects how they would like their life to look. For others, it reveals a current pressing issue. For others, it is a deeply centering and relaxing experience. Just as clients differ, so do therapists. There is no one way to conduct a session, no one course of therapy. Each clinician must honor her/his own theoretical orientation. However, there appears to be a pattern in how clients progress along their therapy journey, as well as a sequence within the sandplay therapy session. In our work we have discovered that the session unfolds in a very productive way when clients move from silent, unconscious play to more verbal, conscious play. Initially, the therapist encourages clients to allow their *inner voices* to guide the process; then the therapist takes a more interactive role.

Louis Stewart (1982) elaborated on P. Aite's concept that early in the sandplay process it seems that the ego is relatively inactive and consciousness appears fragmented. He wrote, "While it is evident that there is a collaboration between the unconscious fantasy image and the ego-consciousness, it is clear that the lead in the process is taken by the unconscious images" (p. 206). Ruth Ammann added to this concept when she wrote, "During the initial formative phase the analysand [client] is led away from critical, rational consciousness. . . . What is activated, rather, is the power of the imagination and the sensation function, that is the senses and especially the sense of touch. The power of the imagination and its connection to reality unite while activating the emotions and feelings and form the image of the sand picture" (Ammann, 1993, p. 7). Gradually, the ego collaborates with the fantasies being played out. This process is similar to what Jung describes as active imagination. As this collaboration occurs, all aspects of the therapy begin to coalesce and clients are able to exhibit new attitudes and behaviors. This change often occurs more than once in the course of therapy and is frequently seen after a pivotal sand tray world has been created. Sandplay enables clients to utilize their unconscious material and integrate it on a conscious level. It is our job as therapists to facilitate this process.

Through our training and experience we have found that the therapist can best promote this collaboration by providing some guidance. It is important to *follow the client's lead*, because the client's creation and the meaning that the client attributes to the creation is of utmost significance. It is essential to honor the images presented by the client and understand them as symbols of the unconscious. From Jung's perspective, image and meaning are synonymous. Therefore, as the image takes shape the meaning is conveyed; no interpretation is required. It is for this reason that during the sandplay process the therapist must *follow the client's lead* and not make interpretations, even when the therapist takes an interactive role.

Just as there appears to be a general process through the course of sandplay therapy, there is also a pattern that we see within one session. Although this is true for static worlds where clients create a scene to completion, this schema does not apply with moving worlds, where clients change the scene as the action takes place. What we describe in this chapter is a sequence that we have found useful when clients build static worlds. In order to facilitate progress in the most productive manner, we have directly adapted the five phases of a sandplay session, and the observations and the directions for the therapist that we learned from Gisela De Domenico. (De Domenico has, however, changed her phases since the earlier training.) We found her delineation of the session, her conceptualization of static and moving trays, and her distinction between spontaneous and directed trays to be invaluable and, although our stages have diverged somewhat from hers, we wish to acknowledge her groundbreaking work.

As De Domenico pointed out, in the sandplay therapy session the client does not always progress through all the stages. At times, only the first stage is completed. What we describe are guidelines for proceeding through a session. The process is continuous and flows as is appropriate. The stages are not separate or delineated. How therapists work with their clients in a session depends on the therapist's own therapeutic orientation and the needs of the client at the time. Although a 50-minute session can suffice, we recommend scheduling an hour and a half for sandplay. The extended session generally allows clients to progress through all the stages, permitting sufficient time for silent creating, therapeutic work in a more overt, conscious manner, and processing.

The stages as Gisela De Domenico originated them were: (1) building phase, (2) first experiencing phase, (3) second experiencing phase, (4) photographing phase, and (5) dismantling phase. As we used with our clients the format that De Domenico taught in the early 1990s, our delineation of stages evolved as follows:

Stage 1: Creating the world
Stage 2: Experiencing and rearranging
Stage 3: Therapy
Stage 4: Documentation
Stage 5: Transition
Stage 6: Dismantling the world

In the "creating the world" stage, which corresponds to De Domenico's "building phase," clients are introduced to the sandplay process and begin creating their worlds. De Domenico described in her "building phase" that this is a time for clients to create their worlds however they wish, allowing themselves to be propelled by their own "inner promptings." "The doing of sandplay itself can invite the psyche, jump-start the unconscious, and nudge the ego into a cooperative position, and can evoke or set in motion the flow—and labor—of inner work" (Signell & Bradway, 1995, p. 20). The "experiencing and rearranging" stage provides the opportunity for expanding the client's inner work and for helping her/him go deeper. This stage was drawn from De Domenico's "first experiencing phase," in which clients were directed to silently experience and breathe in their worlds and rearrange them if needed. Clients have the opportunity to free associate to her/his world, sharing with the therapist any thoughts or feelings that are evoked. The therapist supports the clients by "reflective mirroring." During these first two stages of sandplay therapy, clients generally create from the unconscious and experience their process on a deep level, not unlike the altered state of consciousness during hypnosis. This segment of therapy is often conducted in silence subsequent to the initial introduction and explanation.

Although the therapist has been very present and available to the client, the therapist becomes more interactive in the third stage, the "therapy" stage. This corresponds to De Domenico's "second experiencing phase," when the therapist joins the client on her/his side of the sand tray. As Lowenfeld stated, the client is the expert of her/his world. De Domenico suggested that the client serve as the guide and take the therapist "on a tour" of the world. She emphasized that the therapist allow her/himself "to experience and observe the world through the builder's psyche" (1989, p. 21). The therapist asks questions to promote deepening of the experience but does not interject her/his impressions of the world. It is at this time that further exploration through the use of various therapeutic interventions occurs. Problem-solving, working through and healing of the presented issues, and a collaboration of the unconscious and conscious are evident. In the fourth or "documentation" stage (De Domenico's "photographing phase," when the therapist asks the client "how he/she wishes the World to be photographed and recorded" [1989, p. 21]), clients are given the opportunity to photograph the worlds they have created. In the fifth or "transition" stage, the therapist helps clients make a connection between their created worlds and their lives. Together they explore what bearing the created world may have on the clients' issues and how clients can apply what they have learned. De Domenico included this in her "second experiencing phase." In the sixth or "dismantling the world" stage, the therapist disassembles the world following the client's departure from the therapy room, reflecting on what has just transpired. De Domenico described the possible need for dismantling the tray prior to the client's departure from the therapy room. She suggested that the therapist allow the client to "'break the energy pattern' of the created, intact World" by having the client remove the first object (1989, p. 21).

As we describe each stage, we present in detail what may develop throughout the sandplay process. Each therapist will use her/his own language and style. The examples we offer are suggestions of how therapists may proceed.

Prior to the client's first sandplay session, there is initial groundwork to be laid. Often when a client first enters therapy, you'll discuss with her/him some of the approaches you may be using in the course of therapy. If you prominently display the sand trays and objects, you have an immediate opening for introducing sandplay as one of the modalities you use. Observe the client's response to seeing these objects and playthings. You might say: "These things are for adults as well as children" or "These objects and toys are not just for children. Many adults, couples, and families have really found using the sand trays and these objects very beneficial" or "Sandplay provides a language when we can't find the words or don't really understand what we are feeling. It allows our inner voices to speak. You may find that you'll want to play in the sand at some point." Give a cursory explanation of how sandplay works, including a few of the benefits or applications and how some clients have used sandplay, normalizing the process.

As you briefly show clients the sandplay materials, pay attention to their reactions. This will give you an initial insight into their openness to the sandplay process. Notice if they touch the sand or move toward it, look closely at particular objects, seem completely uninterested, or move quickly away from the play area.

When to Suggest Sandplay

Once therapy is in progress and trust has been established, sandplay may be utilized. Because it takes some time to build trust, sandplay will probably not be used in the first couple of sessions, although there are some exceptions. Sometimes a client may be referred to you specifically for a sandplay session. It is our belief that the client's unconscious will guide her/him to unveil whatever s/he needs to address at the time. As long as the therapist is present to hold what the client is experiencing and has provided a safe space, the client will do what is needed.

Some people believe that the therapist should wait for the adult client to initiate sandplay. Geraldine Spare warned, "All the psychic energy and impetus for using the sand tray . . . it is claimed, must come from the client. The therapist is enjoined from suggesting sandplay. If the therapist suggests that the client work in the sandtray, the patient, sensing power in the therapist, may feel himself in a one-down position, experiencing anger or resistance but wishing to please the authority. He will then be out of touch with his own inner world" (1990, p. 196). However, she proceeded to state that a criterion that perhaps supersedes this rule is the therapist's centeredness and ability to assess the client's needs accurately at certain critical moments and to unite with this outer assessment some personal inner clarity about what, if anything, to do. She defined centeredness as the therapist's willingness to initiate action on behalf of the client without "tearing the fabric" of the client's individual journey (1990, p. 196).

In our experience, we find that most adults do not initiate sandplay themselves. We usually make the suggestion for sandplay, emanating from an intuitive recognition and in-tunedness with the client that this would be a very fruitful experience for her/him at that moment. Because we have already established trust and the client knows that s/he has the choice of whether s/he will create a world in the sand, the element of power is minimized.

Most frequently, the therapist suggests sandplay during the early part of a session when something is addressed by the client that signals its beneficial use. There may be times when a particular issue or circumstance may be ongoing and the therapist may suggest to the client that sandplay would be apropos for the next session. A longer session may then be scheduled if available. Sometimes we have found that even if half the session has transpired, 20 or 25 minutes may be sufficient for the client to create a tray, thereby allowing the unconscious to reveal an answer heretofore hidden. There are innumerable circumstances that may lead the therapist to suggest creating a sand world. Some of the most common instances are when a client: (1) is stuck in her/his process, (2) is unable to find words to express feelings or thoughts, (3) is blocked in her/his feelings, (4) has a poignant dream s/he doesn't understand, (5) is confused, (6) is struggling with a decision s/he needs to make, (7) has a perplexing problem to solve, and (8) has a trauma to work through that s/he seems ready to face.

Once the preliminary groundwork has been laid and it has been determined that the client is prepared to play/work in the sand tray, you are ready to begin the sandplay process. We have divided the first stage, creating the world, into two phases: introducing sandplay to the client and constructing the world.

Stage 1. Creating the World

INTRODUCING SANDPLAY TO THE CLIENT

When you suggest that the client create a sand tray world, it is often helpful to reiterate the benefits that apply specifically to her/him. You may want to establish a positive expectation in the client. For example, you might say: "There's someone I was recently working with who was struggling with a similar dilemma. When he created a sand world he was able to allow the solution to emerge" or "This may be an ideal time to use the sand tray and just see what comes up for you" or "You seem to be feeling really stuck on this one. We often have answers within us, which are hidden from our awareness. Sometimes sandplay can be really helpful in revealing a solution. Would you like to try that today?"

Once the client has agreed to create a sand tray, introduce her/him to the trays, the objects, and the process in more detail. Have the client feel the different grits of sand (if you have a variety). At this time model using the sand tray by placing your hands in the tray and shifting the sand. By observing your comfort with the sand, the client may feel less inhibited to follow suit. Point out the blue bottom of the tray by moving the sand and clearing a spot. As you do this, explain how the blue color can simulate water and sky. Show the client the variety of objects and other materials and inform her/him that s/he may use no objects, a few objects, or as many as s/he chooses. Let her/him know that items are placed in categories, which will assist her/him to locate objects easily. Show the client the pitcher of water and the paper towels, and remind her/him that s/he may choose to use the sand dry or wet. Explain to the client that s/he may create anything s/he wishes and may change that creation at any time. For example, you might say, "You may build any world, make any picture or scene, or create any story in the sand that you wish. You don't have to think about it or understand it. Just do whatever comes. Take whatever objects seem to call to you. Sometimes taking things quickly without much thought reaps some insights you would never expect. You may choose objects that you consider attractive or positive. And you may choose objects that seem aversive or negative. No matter what you do, there is no right or wrong way of doing sandplay."

Let the client know that s/he may sit, stand, or place the tray on the floor. Tell the client that s/he may be silent, talk, and/or ask for help. You may want to encourage silence, as this allows the client to work more deeply. For example, you might say, "You may play in the sand and choose objects from the shelves as you wish. Some people find that they get right into the play and are so focused on what they are doing that they don't talk at all. But some people do talk during their play. If you can't find something you are looking for, you may ask me. I can show you where you might find it or you may wish to use some of these materials (pointing out the construction and art supplies) to create it. I will be silent while you are doing this unless you need something from me." Some clients prefer to speak or interact with you. If this is the case, your responses should be reflective only. Avoid providing interpretations, insights, ideas, or questions that could in any way lead or influence the client.

Ask the client where s/he would like you to sit. If you sit across the tray from the client, the communication can go from the client through the tray to you and back through the tray to the client. Sitting across from the client also provides you with the back view of her/his world (De Domenico, 1988). This facilitates the flow of energy between the two of you, thus enhancing the intimacy and power of the exchange. Space in the office does not always permit this seating arrangement. An alternative to this is sitting at the side of the tray, about three to five feet away from the client. This location is comfortable for most clients. Often the client will say that it doesn't matter where you position yourself. However, there may be occasions when clients have some embarrassment or reticence about creating a world or have a need for greater space and privacy. They might request that you place yourself some distance away. Clients may even request that you leave the room. Some therapists believe that this request should be honored. Some believe that remaining in the room in a position where you cannot see the actual production but can still hold the energy for the client, if the client agrees, provides greater safety and succor for the client. Whichever you choose, do not intrude in the client's space. Before the client begins, ask her/him for permission to record, if you plan to take notes. Also ask her/him to please inform you when the sand world is complete.

There may be times when you have forgotten to say something to the client. You can always add it at a time when it does not seem too disruptive. For example, if you have forgotten to ask the client to let you know when s/he has finished and you think of it while s/he is choosing objects or building her/his world, you can interject the statement. If the client seems to have already shifted to a deeper state of focus, you may decide not to give this direction. Clients will naturally let you know when they have completed their scene.

CONSTRUCTING THE WORLD

Now that you have introduced the client to the process, it is time for her/him to choose a tray and objects. Remain quiet as the client decides how s/he wishes to proceed. "At the beginning of an hour they [clients] sometimes sit there full of indecision, perplexed and wavering, or absorbed in themselves, saying that they have no idea what to do with the sand. Then we [therapists] just wait quietly. When using the sandplay method, one does not need to do anything; rather we try, if possible, to turn off and exclude this will and desire to act" (Ammann, 1993, p. 33). If you recognize that the client is uncomfortable you may choose to remain silent or you might say: "Just take your time. Do whatever feels comfortable. There's no hurry. Whatever you do is fine" or "This is something new for you. Sometimes people have no idea what to do. But then after they take a moment or two, they begin doing something and get right into it." If the immobility persists, you may want to explore what the client is experiencing.

Once a shift in consciousness occurs and clients become engrossed and focused or feel more relaxed, most clients begin to choose objects. If they do so, maintain a position from which you are able to view the selection. You may remain stationary if you are able to observe the client from that location. If the shelves are spaced around the room in a manner that impedes your ability to view the client's movements, ask permission to walk with her/him. For example, you might say, "Would it be all right with you if I walk around with you as you choose your objects? If you would like me to hold something for you or would like me to help you find something, just let me know. Here are small serving trays to hold your objects if you would like to use one."

Record mentally the sequence in which the objects are chosen and the manner in which they are selected and handled. Notice which objects the client seems particularly attracted to, repelled by, or interested in. Sometimes the client will pick up an object and examine it and then replace it on the shelf. The objects that s/he examines and decides not to use may have as much relevance as those that s/he chooses to use. Some clients choose one object at a time, place it in the sand tray and then return to the shelf and choose another. Some select several objects at once, place them either in the tray or to the side of the tray and then create their worlds. Some clients opt for many objects; some opt for few. At a later time in the therapy you may want to comment on your observations.

It is imperative to remember that it is your role as therapist to witness, honor, and respectfully hold the experience for the client. It is your responsibility to create a safe, protected space and to maintain this sense of safety. Remember that creating a world in the sand can be a very exposing and deep experience for the client. As Karen Signell and Kay Bradway stated, "The trays are the client's process. It is the very making of the tray that is the healing and individuation process. We who witness the making of the tray are privileged to see the process as it is made visible in the tray. . . . Each step initiates the next step" (1995, p. 20). Remain silent, unless the client invites you to speak. As the client builds her/his world, stay very present, paying close attention to nonverbal cues (e.g., facial expressions, energy in the body, sighs). Objectively observe the process. If you wish, record, with permission, what your client does. (Recording is discussed in chapter 7.) Remember to keep your hands outside of the sand tray. Do not get actively involved in the play in any way, unless the client makes a specific request for interaction or help. You convey to the client your confidence in the self-healing process of the psyche by virtue of her/his own creativity and expression, not by what you say or do (Weinrib, 1983).

There are several other features and behaviors you should notice as clients are creating their worlds, because these observations will be important when you move into the therapy stage. Then you will have the opportunity to verbally explore the significance or essence of these actions, verbalizations, or nonverbal cues. For now, merely pay attention to clients' modes of approaching sandplay, choosing objects, and building the world. Some work very quickly; some work methodically and thoughtfully. Some take time to move the sand around, form a terrain, or just feel the sand for a few moments. This often can be grounding or centering. In some cases, clients may feel more comfortable playing in the sand than playing with toys. These clients may choose to do no more than manipulate the sand, which has value in itself. A 32-year-old client with a strong sense that he had buried a large part of himself spent his sandplay session using no objects. He moved and shifted the sand until he eventually cleared an area. He stated that he had unburied the spiritual part of himself. This was a climacteric for him on his journey to exploring the *black space of the unknown* within himself that frightened him.

Pay attention to the attributes of the objects selected. Note the color, texture, size, shape, and material used. Observe the sequence and manner with which objects are placed and handled. Sometimes clients place objects very emphatically in the tray; sometimes they place them hesitantly. Clients may move or remove objects that already have a place in the world. For example, objects may be in a pair or group and then be separated and placed in different sections of the tray. When an object is moved or removed, notice the demeanor of the client. Notice groupings of twos, threes, etc., of families and opposites. Observe the direction objects are facing. Recognize whether they are facing away from or toward other objects, away from or toward the client or the therapist. Note where in the tray objects are placed: Are they above or below the surface? Are they buried or hidden? Are they clustered in one area? Is a portion of the tray barren? Notice separations and partitions between objects and areas of the tray. Recognize if sand or miniatures are positioned in geometric patterns. Your total presence to the sand world gives you integral information to later explore with the client.

Ammann described succinctly what often happens for the therapist as the world is taking shape. "During the creative formative phase what becomes active for me are the more instinctual, physical reactions. These depend on subtle sensory perceptions, body feelings, and intuition and on empathic emotional relationship with the analysand. This does not happen unconsciously but rather from a conscious turning toward this more receptive attitude which can grip the whole person" (1993, p. 6). Remember, everything clients do has meaning. The information you gather as you observe the client will serve as the groundwork for the therapy stage.

To recall how clients' worlds come into being, it may be helpful to take notes as clients create their worlds. Some therapists find that note-taking facilitates easy recollection and disciplines their minds to focus on the sequence of and changes in the construction of the world. It also provides a record of the feeling states and nonverbal cues that occur throughout the building process. De Domenico was an advocate of note-taking and provided some guidelines in her training (see 1989, pp. 26–31). Some therapists find the recording cumbersome and distracting. Whatever the therapist's preference, we suggest that s/he practice note-taking several times initially to train her/his mind to hold all the information that helps her/him address what happened in the creation of the world along the way. Some therapists have video equipment set up in their offices, which provides a serviceable and effortless way to record. This is useful for review of the session but is not readily utilized during the therapy stage of that session.

As therapists, we often have ideas about what the client's actions or choices of objects mean. However, it is important to suspend any interpretation or assumption. This is not always easy. It may be automatic for you to form hypotheses. If this is the case, allow yourself to form hypotheses, then set them aside until, during the therapy stage, you determine if the client's explanations confirm your ideas. Misinterpretations can stem from three sources. First, they may be projections of what the objects mean for you. The meaning that you give to a client's object may reveal as much about you as it does about the client— or more. This can occur whether the client is new to you or is someone you know well. Second, this can happen when there is an ascribed archetypal, cultural, or psychological meaning to particular objects. You must be careful not to attribute the generally accepted meaning to the client's object. This is more likely to occur when you do not have a long history with the client and/or you are well versed in Jungian archetypes. Third, misinterpretation may happen when you know the client well. You may assume that you know the meaning of the object because of your past experience with the client or because you have knowledge of her/his history. By making unspoken interpretations you may jump to conclusions and follow a line of logic that has nothing to do with the client's issues. You must also be careful not to convey messages nonverbally to the client. If you are attending to your own thoughts and have stopped *hearing* the client, you are not entirely present and holding the experience for her/him.

These situations often present themselves in our sandplay therapy workshops. Participants taking the role of therapists have frequently commented on how the meaning they attributed to an object placed in the tray by their client partners was completely different from what the *clients* later revealed. In one workshop a client participant placed a large Native American man in the tray. The therapist partner later disclosed that she had an ominous feeling that this figure was dangerous, and this was revealed to the client by the therapist's facial expression. The therapist, not remaining completely present to the client, proceeded to act on her hunch during the therapy stage and encouraged the client to deal with her fears. The client felt misunderstood and invalidated. She finally asserted herself and clearly indicated to her therapist partner that the Native American symbolized a protector and overseer. Contrary to evoking fear, the figure gave the client a feeling of safety and comfort.

When clients indicate to you that they have finished, it is time to move into the experiencing and rearranging stage. The duration of the creating the world stage, including the introduction, choosing of the objects, and building of the world, varies greatly from client to client.

Some clients construct their worlds very quickly, at times within five or ten minutes. This may be their general style of functioning, or it may indicate avoidance behavior, discomfort with the process, or operating on a more conscious, analytic level. If the creating the world stage has been brief, you can encourage some deepening of the experience in the experiencing and rearranging stage. Generally clients take from 15 to 30 minutes or even longer. Some clients take the entire session on this task. Allow clients the time they need. Inasmuch as sessions are time-limited, gently let clients know when the session is close to ending and suggest that they leave the world as desired for that day. You might say, "It seems that you are not quite finished creating your world but it is almost time for us to end. You might want to leave your world as you would like it for today. Remember, this is how it is for now. You may want to recreate it next time or you may want to do something different." Allow time for the client to take a photograph of her/his completed world (documentation stage) and allow time for a brief transition before ending the session.

Stage 2. Experiencing and Rearranging

EXPERIENCING

This phase provides an opportunity for the client to further deepen the experience of her/his creation. This is a time for quiet reflection. Sit silently as the client more fully assimilates the world. Encourage the client to immerse her/himself in the world. You might say, "This sand world is your world. Just take some time to be in it. Let it touch you inside. Experience it not just with your eyes but with all your senses. Explore it and get to know it. You may remain silent or you may share anything that comes to you."

The client is likely to shift again to a deeper level. Both the silent building and subsequent experiencing are exceptionally meaningful and valuable for her/him. "It is not a silence of embarrassment but a conscious silence. Both the therapist and the client direct their attention to the client's inner world leading to greater understanding" (Ammann, 1993, p. 6). Remember to treat every world with respect and honor, suspending any judgment. You may not understand the world. It may seem mundane or simple to you. Dismiss these evaluations. Your task is to respectfully and unconditionally accept the client and her/his creation.

If clients choose to speak at this time, use only reflective responses.

If clients exhibit obvious emotional nonverbal cues, you may respond in a reflective way to their body language. For example, if the client sighs with a sad expression as s/he is experiencing the world, you might say, "That seems to touch you deeply," without any interpretation or suggestion of the emotion you think the client is feeling. Do not ask questions or make suggestions of any kind. The dialogue at this point is solely between the client and her/his world. Your responses or comments are meant only to let her/him know that you hear and are attending to her/his statements. Make verbal comments only if you sense that the client needs the reassurance of your presence. Be aware that your words could be intrusive.

As De Domenico taught, we encourage the client to walk around the tray and observe the world from different angles. By doing this the client not only views the scene from different perspectives but is also able to notice aspects of objects that s/he could not see from the front of the tray. You might say, "Often things look different from different perspectives. You might want to walk around the tray and look at it from the sides, from the back, from above the tray, from the tray level." These instructions should be given either at the very beginning of the experiencing phase when you initially suggest being with the world or after the client seems to have fully taken in the world from the front of the tray.

As clients are experiencing their worlds, observe nonverbal responses. For example, watch for changes in feeling states as clients look at particular objects. Notice where clients' eyes seem to pause and which objects appear to trigger some emotions. Observe where they scan quickly over or intentionally avoid objects. Recognize if and where clients sigh, smile, or breathe heavily. Certainly it is not possible to attend to and remember everything. We mention all of the above circumstances to remind you that clients are giving you information continually and that this information can be of therapeutic significance. The more present you are, the more these nonverbal cues will register and remain in your awareness.

The experiencing phase usually takes approximately five minutes. Some clients spend a minute or less and say that they are finished. If this occurs, encourage them to reenter the world and take a little more time. Sometimes there is resistance to going deeper or discomfort in being inactive in the world once the creative activity has ended. You might encourage the client by saying, "If it's all right with you, why don't you take a few more minutes. Just imagine that you are in that world. Imagine walking around in it and seeing what it is like in different parts of your world."

REARRANGING

As clients fully experience their sand worlds, they may react to certain aspects of it. These reactions often elicit movement within clients, provoking the need to move things within the world. At this time clients frequently choose to alter the placement of objects and/or remove or add objects. Let clients know that they may leave the world as it is or make any changes they wish to make. It is important to include the message that they may leave the world as it is, so that clients, especially those who are perfectionists or who are hypersensitive to criticism, do not feel that some judgment is being made and that there is something *wrong* with the world as it is or that something *should* be changed. You might say, "Now that you are fully experiencing the world, you may find that it is just how you want it to be. Or you may find that something needs to change in the world. You may move any of the objects or add or remove whatever seems fitting for the world right now." If clients have made changes, encourage them to reexperience the world as it is after the changes were made. Pay attention to any shifts within the client that have occurred with the transformation of the world.

Stage 3. Therapy

The silent building and experiencing of the world in and of themselves have therapeutic, healing value. Clients have had an opportunity to release into the tray their innermost thoughts and feelings in an observable way. "In creatively building a sand construction, an image is set out in a step-by-step fashion, without concern as to the 'maturity level' of its final appearance. This enables the dropping of many defences autonomously without concern as to *how* defences might be overcome" (Ryce-Menuhin, 1992, p. 13). Thus far you have held and witnessed the client's process with quiet patience and acceptance. It is now time for you to evaluate whether or not to bring words into the session. "The fragility within the power of the sandplayer's expression should never be underestimated by a therapist. The psyche—naked—may need to be observed at first, never interpreted irrevocably" (Ryce-Menuhin, 1992, p. 15). If you determine that the client may be in a very vulnerable space and that speaking about the client's creation would be ill-advised, you may gently allow the client to be with the world. End the sandplay by letting the client know that if s/he chooses to tell you something about the world s/he may do so, or, if s/he chooses not to, s/he will have other opportunities. If you determine that further verbal exploration would be beneficial, you may take a more interactive role. This is the time that clients, if they choose, share their worlds verbally with you. Although clients may, with speaking, move out of their *altered state* to some extent, the work that you will be doing together will deepen and broaden the experience for them, facilitating the collaboration of the conscious and unconscious.

During the therapy stage clients are your guides through their sand worlds, supplying the meaning of the objects and the essence of the creation. You are the clients' guide in expediting further exploration and bridging their unconscious inner knowledge with their outer lives. This is the essence of therapeutic work that clients will be doing on a more conscious, intentional plane. We have divided this stage into two phases: touring the world and therapeutic interventions.

TOURING THE WORLD

Initially ask clients if you may join them on their side of the tray in order to see the world from their perspective. You might say, "You are the creator of this world. I really don't know much about it. I wonder if you would be my guide through the world and teach me about it. Perhaps you could take me on a tour, recount how this world came into being, and acquaint me with the people and objects in this world." When you join the client at the front of the tray, note the objects that you could not see from your perspective during the constructing phase. Also note the objects that were visible to you but not to the client (e.g., the client has placed an object behind a large rock). Encourage the client to retrace the making of the scene. Clients may actually guide you through the world in the sequence that they placed the objects in the tray. They may describe all the objects in the tray and comply closely with your instructions. When that happens, listen silently and attentively so that you can see the world as the client does.

If the client gives a cursory overview, De Domenico suggested encouraging her/him to retrace the making of the world and describe exactly what s/he sees. You might say, "I really don't know who or what all these people or things are. Could we take a look at all of the objects and perhaps you could describe just what you see? I really want to experience the world as you do." Another approach is to ask the

client to tell you a story about the world. This is often effective with
creative clients who may feel less threatened if they can distance from
their own issues. You might even have the client imagine that you are
from another country or planet and know nothing about their world.
Another possible strategy in dealing with a perfunctory description and
possible reluctance to go into more detail is to ask specific questions.
You might ask: "Could you tell me something about this object (pointing to an object)?" or "Could you tell me more about this object
(pointing to an object)?" or "What experiences or feelings does this
object evoke?" or "What age or sex is this object?" These questions
may vary and may be applied to each item individually.

Attend to the client's demeanor. If it is clear to you that the client
is resistant and wishes to remain silent and not describe the world,
honor that need. You might say, "Is there anything else you want to
tell me about this world? Or would you rather just be with it for a
moment and not talk about it?" This brings to mind one client with
whom we worked. She was a 50-year-old woman who had already
done a few sand trays in the course of her therapy. We had planned
several times for her to use the sand tray in subsequent sessions. Each
time, she managed to avoid creating a world in the sand. After this
occurred several times, she reported that she had recognized that she
kept avoiding the sand tray. She realized that the impediment was not
the creating of the world; her resistance was talking about it afterwards.
She felt that for her the verbalization detracted from the experience
and, furthermore, evoked in her the possibility of judgment and interpretation.

Some clients identify the characters in the tray as themselves and
people in their lives. They may relate the world to specific experiences.
Whatever way clients present the world, it is important for you to see
it through their eyes (and psyches). Remain open to all that the client
describes, and function as if you know nothing about the world except
what meaning the client places on it. If you deem it therapeutically
valuable to make comments on the objects as the client is taking you
on the tour, you will reflect only what the client has related. If you
determine that it would be judicious to receive the total tour before
doing further exploration, comments or questions may be delayed until you move into the therapeutic intervention phase.

Remember that this world has been created from a deep place
within the client. Do not touch any objects or intrude in any way,
physically or psychically. As the client describes the world, give your

undivided attention and learn the experiential language of the images. It is important to use the client's language when referring to the objects. Remember not to give a sexual identity to a figure unless the client has already done so. If you feel it is essential to have that information, you may ask the client. On occasion, we have made the mistake of naming an object before the client has named it, conveying a different meaning to that object than the client intended. For example, we recall one client who did not name an object that we called a mouse. When we referred to the animal as a mouse a second time the client firmly expressed her disdain and corrected us. She made it very clear that it was a rat and not a mouse. It was significant to her that it was a rat. It is important to use not only the client's language but also the client's tone or personal interpretation. For example, a snake may mean one thing to a client and another to you. Your care in not attributing your feeling about a snake, even in a nonverbal way, is essential.

As clients describe their worlds, notice not just the words they speak but also their body language and facial expressions. Notice what clients may be experiencing in their bodies. If there seems to be a strong reaction as the client is describing the scene, you might ask: "What are you experiencing in your body?" or "Where do you feel that in your body?" Do not ask the question in a leading way, for example, "You seem sad, angry, upset. Where do you feel that anger in your body?" It is crucial that you accept how the client responds. Do not urge the client to give an interpretation or report a feeling if the client has none. If the client does give an explanation, do not push for another one, even if you believe there is something deeper that s/he isn't identifying. Wait until the therapeutic intervention phase and allow the tour to be completed without interruption. However, if a client exhibits strong emotion during this touring phase, address the situation.

As feelings emerge, encourage clients to stay with the emotion. Clients will sometimes have the impulse to move away from a difficult feeling. If you are uncomfortable with the expression of difficult or deep emotions, the potential exists for you to collude with clients and hinder their forward movement. On the other hand, by helping clients connect with what they are experiencing without analyzing, you create greater possibilities for healing and resolution.

If a client has buried an object or has failed to describe an object, ask about that omission before leaving the touring phase. For instance, if a client has completed taking you on the tour but failed to mention an object, you might say, "I noticed that (name the object) over there.

Could you tell me something about it?" Beware of the possibility of your unconsciously colluding with the client's unconscious desire not to address an issue. In sandplay therapy you are so connected with the client that the likelihood of collusion is greater than in most talk therapies. An example of this comes to mind. A 35-year-old man who was very unhappy in his marriage had created a world in which there was a bridge. Beneath the bridge he buried a bottle. As he did this, we noted that his expression implied that this bottle probably had considerable significance to him and that this would be something to address later. The client never mentioned the bottle during the touring phase and we forgot to question him about it. After the session ended and the client left, we immediately remembered the buried bottle. With the client gone, there was no longer a need for collusion. In the following session, we mentioned that we had failed to talk about the buried bottle under the bridge and suggested that the client create a scene with these two objects. What transpired was profound for the client. Following our suggestion he created a scene and realized that he had a great deal of fear of leaving his wife because of her threat to kill herself by taking pills if he did. On an unconscious level the bridge was his path out of the marriage and to a new life and the bottle represented a bottle of pills. The fear and guilt he would feel if he left his wife and she committed suicide prevented him from crossing the bridge. He was so frightened that his unconscious defended him against remembering the bottle. We had colluded with his fear and guilt.

Also pay attention to different groupings and encourage the client to note basic groupings of objects, i.e., things that seem to belong together in the world. You might say: "I notice that there are three animals over here, three seashells in that corner, and three trees over there" or "There seem to be a cluster of animals in this corner and they are separated from the rest the world." Mentioning groupings that you notice is often a catalyst that triggers important revelations about the client's life. For example, the client may recognize that s/he isolates from others. There are instances when the client notices groupings on her/his own and recognizes how the world reflects her/his life. It may be appropriate to defer comment on this until the therapeutic intervention portion of the session.

During the touring phase, you may do very little interacting. The client may conduct the tour on her/his own, giving you all the information you need to understand the essence of the world. It is only when strong feelings emerge or a superficial depiction is related that you may take a more active role. This is a time of gathering information using the client's spoken narrative. The touring the world phase usually takes from five to ten minutes, depending on the complexity of the scene and number of objects. If therapy activities transpire during the tour, this will flow into the therapeutic intervention phase and will take longer.

THERAPEUTIC INTERVENTIONS

Through the creating the world stage, "the therapist receives the client's creative process as a communicative dialogue and begins to learn the unique image language of the client" (De Domenico, 1986b, p. 5). Through the touring the world phase the therapist learns the client's verbal language. Now you and the client become co-explorers of the client's world. "With the client's active participation, the experienced therapist begins to translate the idiosyncratic image language into conventional language. This fosters the client's capacity to reveal him/herself through action and communication with those he/she contacts in daily life" (De Domenico, 1986b, p. 5).

Commence questioning about the world. Encourage the client to experience, experiment with, and explore the world or specific aspects of the world more extensively. Links with the client's life or memories may arise, but do not analyze the experience. As you make comments on or ask questions about the objects, reflect only what the client has related, focusing on the world, not on the client. For example, you might say, "That woman is turning away from that man," as opposed to, "You are turning away from your husband," even if the client has identified the woman as herself and the man as her husband. You might say, "What changed when this object (naming or pointing to the object) came into the world or changed position in the world?" as opposed to, "What was it like when you moved this object?" By keeping the focus on the tray, you provide neutrality that allows the client to sufficiently dissociate and, in effect, reduce the possible threat of whatever the client fears.

Taking cues from how the client has described the world, you will have an idea of what issues are portrayed in the scene. If nothing stood out during the constructing or touring phases, your knowledge of and insight into the client will guide you, and you may begin at a place in the tray that you deem appropriate. However, if the issues are apparent and you feel that the client is not able to handle the intensity of the major concern, begin with a less intimidating issue. If your assessment is that the client is able to deal with the most pressing one at this time, focus the client's attention on this theme. Begin with an area of the tray related to the problem, but not its most emotion-laden aspect. Take care initially not to catapult the client to a place that may be exceedingly threatening to her/him.

We have found that deferring focus on the most painful area provides an opportunity for the client to prepare for more intense work. A client who comes to mind is a 40-year-old woman who entered therapy with several current issues in her life: a relationship crisis, her stress at work, and her struggle to become pregnant. The tray that she created appeared to incorporate images symbolizing all of these themes. As she guided us through the world, her nonverbal cues signaled that there was deep pain around the unfulfilled desire to have a child. We focused initially on the area of the tray where a woman and a man were facing each other. We began there because the client indicated during the touring phase that the couple was in stress. We felt that this would be a good entry point. We pursued dialoguing in this less threatening area and gradually moved to an area where a baby was lying in the crib. The movement of some objects, dialoguing with the man and then the unborn baby, and bringing in a wise owl to answer questions relating to the baby issue, led to deeply expressed pain. Had we coerced attention initially to that corner of the tray, we surmise that the client would not have been ready to allow herself to experience the pain or examine different perspectives and possible solutions.

Because it is the content of the client's psyche and ego that have been objectified in symbols in the tray, it is the creation, not the therapist, that should confront the client. Like Lowenfeld, we believe that in sandplay therapy transference mostly occurs between the created world and the client, not between the therapist and the client. What this implies is that the client, in essence, is confronting her/himself in the tray. As Jung stated, "The years when I was pursuing my inner images were the most important of my life. . . . the later [years] are only supplements and clarifications of the material that burst forth from the unconscious, and at first swamped me. It was the *prima materia* for a lifetime's work" (Jung, 1963, p. 199).

The therapeutic intervention phase lends itself well to a variety of therapeutic modalities. You will employ the techniques and theoretical approaches with which you are familiar and at which you are adept, choosing strategies that seem therapeutically germane at the moment. Techniques we have found useful include, but are not limited to, Gestalt approaches, psychodrama, imagery, regressive methods, art therapy, cognitive restructuring, and body awareness. The possibilities are restricted only by your range of knowledge and skill and the willingness of the client. The choice of interventions depends on you. In this section we describe approaches that we have found effective.

A technique we frequently utilize simulates the Gestalt two-chair technique. In the tray this approach plays out by having characters or objects dialogue with each other. If there are unresolved issues between two people or other symbols in the world, it is helpful to have those characters communicate with each other. For example, you might say, "What would the bird like to say to the cat?" If the client indicates that s/he feels foolish having the miniatures talk to each other, it is sometimes helpful to have the client pretend, e.g., "If the bird could speak, what might it say to the cat?"

We saw a 23-year-old woman in therapy who had been in a relationship with a man for two years and was questioning the future of the relationship. She had created a tray with a lovely woman dressed in white sitting on a very peaceful island and surrounded by flowers and butterflies. A man on the mainland was looking over at her. As the therapy proceeded, the man joined her on the island and the tranquillity seemed to disappear. We asked the client what the woman wanted to say to the man. The client had the woman say, "Jim, you always insist on having your way and when I tell you what I am feeling you never hear me. I don't even know if I want to stay with you. When you came over to the island, everything changed. My sense of peace with myself just disappeared." We had our client give the man a voice. The man stated, "I didn't realize I was so inattentive and controlling." The man and the woman in the tray continued their dialogue, doing problem-solving and negotiating about what each of them needed to do to make the relationship work. Through the play of creative imagination and the opportunity for dissociation, the client was able to face squarely the problems in her relationship. Prior to the safety of the sand tray, she had not been able to divulge her fear of being alone. After the sandplay, she was able to recognize her fear and her need to be heard and acknowledged within the relationship. The next time we met, Jim joined her for a conjoint session and she was able to address these issues openly with him.

As the client's story unfolds and some discovery has occurred, it may seem evident that there is an object in a position in the tray that is disconcerting to her/him. Once you and the client have discussed what the discomfort is and ascertained that some modification of placement may be helpful, you might suggest that s/he relocate the object. You might say, "What would happen if the child moved away from the man? Would you like to try it?" It is imperative that the client have the choice to move the object or not and that the client do the actual moving of the object. If the client moves the miniature, explore how the world changes and how both characters' feelings alter.

A 41-year-old woman in therapy had been physically and emotionally abused by her father when she was a child. She had managed to distance herself sufficiently from him and to remove herself from the abuse, but now his health was failing and she wanted to make peace with him before he died. When she began spending more time with him, both of them reverted to old behaviors. In fact, she allowed some of the emotional abuse to resume in order to maintain peace and avoid confrontation. This was very uncomfortable for her. She told us that she wanted to find a way to resolve her fear of and anger at him.

In the tray she placed a small child next to a large man in a city scene. The buildings were sparse toward the center of the tray and a stand of trees separated the city and outskirts of the city from a bucolic setting on the left side of the tray. After the woman described the world and began to speak of the girl's fear, we asked her if the girl would like to move away from the man. She proceeded to have the girl move through the trees and described this as being a little scary for the girl. When the girl reached the meadow full of flowers, the client seemed to breathe easier. The woman said that the girl's apprehension diminished gradually as she moved further from the man. Once the girl was in the meadow, she felt the warmth of the sun. She found that she wanted to pick the flowers and take them to her father. We asked the client if she would like to do that. The woman placed the flowers in the girl's hands and moved her back through the trees. In the transition stage, the client realized that in her distance from her father she had retracted the love that he needed to assuage his anger and pain. In the tray, when the girl gave him the flowers she was offering the love he needed and his anger dissipated. The woman was able to apply this to her situation. She knew that she could not control her father's moods but that she had the capability to treat him with kindness. She could also leave and go to a peaceful and safe place when she was feeling abused by him, even if she was afraid that he wouldn't understand.

Frequently a character or object placed in a client's tray appears to require assistance. This often occurs with clients who have low self-esteem, are depressed or highly anxious, are in a crisis, or have been victimized in some way. These clients need, through the symbolic images in the tray, to find some help from within or outside themselves. With clients such as these, it is often productive to suggest that there may be someone or something that could help the character or object. You might say, "Is there anyone or anything in this world that could help (naming the object) not be so frightened?" or "Would you like to bring in someone who could help (name the object)?" or "What would help (name the object) feel less confused?"

A 37-year-old client who was at a crisis point in his professional life and struggling in his marriage was in therapy with us. He had completed sand trays in past sessions. In this session he was disturbed by his impatience and irritability. He created a tray in which there were several children playing together on one side of a fence. On the other side was the beast from "Beauty and the Beast." The client said that the world needed the fence to protect the children from the beast. After exploring this, we asked him what the beast needed. He sat in silence for a moment, then went to the shelf and chose several small, soft teddy bears, which he placed in the tray encircling the beast. The client's body relaxed and again he sat in silence. He then sighed, "Ahh, the beast needs the soft warm comfort to soothe his pain and his anger. When I am so irritable, I need my wife's softness and I need her to comfort me." This was a revelation to him.

There are times when the client describes a character or object in the world as exhibiting a strong feeling. It is apparent to you that the client is experiencing that feeling strongly, evidenced by a change in her/his breathing, sighing or becoming tearful, or touching a part of her/his body (e.g., her/his heart or stomach). Direct the client's attention momentarily out of the tray and into her/his body. This facilitates body awareness and integration of body, mind, and emotion. You might ask, "Where do you feel that in your body?" or "I notice that your hand is on your chest. What's going on?"

An example of this technique is demonstrated in the case of a 48-year-old woman who created a sand world with the Wizard of Oz characters. As Dorothy was approaching the Tin Man and dialoguing with him, it was evident to us that strong feelings were present. Initially the client brought a porcelain hand with a rose into the world to soothe the Tin Man's heart. We suggested that she take the hand and soothe her own heart. The client appeared to breathe in the soothing, feeling the comfort that came from the hand object. She then used her own hand to soothe her heart. After experiencing the comfort in her body, she returned to the sand tray. She noticed that the Tin Man figure actually had his hand on his heart. Her body experience enabled her to recognize that the Tin Man did indeed have a heart and could ease it whenever he needed relief from pain. She also realized that she had the power to soothe herself.

Another way to shift the client's focus from the tray to her/his body and to deepen the emotion is to use body movement or psychodrama. A poignant example is the case of a 68-year-old woman who had recently been informed that she had terminal cancer. Within the tray she had placed a large rock, and during the process of the therapy she repeatedly poured water over the rock, creating a waterfall. She was unclear as to the meaning of this action. We asked her if she was willing to try something to help clarify the significance of the waterfall. She agreed, and we asked her to pretend that she was the flowing water and to act as the waterfall. Initially she was reticent to do this so we joined her by dramatizing the act of being the water. She accompanied us in the psychodrama. In the process of being the water, she crumpled to the floor in tears. After her weeping subsided, we asked, "Would you like to talk about what just happened, or would you like to just be with it for a while?" She revealed her fear of helplessness and lack of control over her illness. It became clear that the falling water was a metaphor for her sense of powerlessness. In several subsequent sessions we explored how she could deal with the impact of her illness. Importantly, she later came to a personal realization that water was also a symbol of ongoing life for her.

There may be instances when the use of visualization or imagery is advantageous. You might suggest to the client that s/he imagine something that may be difficult to actualize in the tray. An illustration of this is a 35-year-old client who was struggling in his relationship with a partner he felt was controlling and intractable. In his sand tray he had placed a miniature composite figure of two men playing a board game. The client named the men; the controlled man's name was George and the controlling man's name was Marshall. As the client's story of the world unfolded, George wanted to conclude the game and move on to another activity. Marshall wanted to continue with the game. However, the couple literally could not be separated from each other or the game board because the configuration was one object. In the client's life he had difficulty stating his preferences when they differed from his partner's. We asked the client if he could imagine

George leaving the game board and doing what he wanted to do. The client visualized George going to the lake and taking a swim. He was able to imagine George feeling refreshed, relieved and free. George was no longer bound to Marshall. A few minutes later, the client found an object to symbolize George as a separate individual.

An imbalance of power also lends itself to the use of visualization, e.g., when a perpetrator and victim are symbolized in the tray. The therapist may make a suggestion to imagine the perpetrator shrinking and/or the victim becoming larger. The client can visualize the weaker character or object in a position of growing power. S/he can then play out this increased power in whatever form it takes, e.g., picking up the newly empowered object and having it stomp on the originally more powerful character. Active imagination is synonymous with sandplay and ultimately healing.

Cognitive restructuring can also be played out in the tray. In actuality, many of the interventions we have described are examples of reframing or restructuring the client's thoughts and behaviors. Cognitive restructuring techniques can be readily applied when a client is stuck and unable to see alternatives. You might help the client explore different options or ways of perceiving the situation. For example, a 32-year-old accountant we saw was depressed because he lost his job and could not find another one. Through several sessions it became clear that his negative thoughts were keeping him stuck. We did Rational Emotive Therapy (RET) with him, but he seemed unable to apply the principles of RET to change his self-talk and beliefs about himself and the world. We suggested sandplay as an approach that often helps people who feel stuck.

He created a world with little color. Among his objects were a large rock, a man, a fence, several animals, and some books. After the tour of the world and some brief discussion, we asked him what the man would say if he could speak. He had the man say, "I will never be able to get a job. My life is a disaster. No one will hire me because I'm Black." We responded, "Is there anyone or anything in this world that can help the man?" He replied with an emphatic "No!" We then asked, "Is there an object you could bring in to help him?" He looked around for a few minutes and brought in a sun. We asked him, "What would the sun say to the man?" The client was unable to come up with anything. At this point we asked the client if we could take the role of the sun. He acquiesced. We had the sun say, "What is it that you need from me?" The client said, looking at us, "I need help. My life is a disaster." We redirected the client into the tray by asking what the man would say. The client then had the man say, "I need your help. My life is a disaster. I'm never going to be able to support my family." The sun responded, "You really feel like your life is a mess. But let's take a closer look at what is really going on for you. Is all of your life a disaster?" The client had the man respond, "Well, not everything. I have a wife and children who love me. I have a comfortable home but I am going to lose it."

We asked him if he would like to bring the man's family and home into the tray. He put them next to the man. We noticed a change in the client's demeanor when the man had the physical closeness of his family. We, as the sun, then reiterated the man's recognition that everything was not a disaster and encouraged the man to examine his statement about losing his comfortable house. The man said, "Without a job I won't be able to pay my mortgage payments. And no one is going to hire me." The sun responded, "So you can see into the future?" "Well, no, but I was fired from my job and no one will ever want me." "So you were fired from one job. Have you ever been hired before?" "Of course." "So were you Black then?" The client smiled and said, "Of course." We, as the sun, validated the man, "I know that statistically young Black men have a higher unemployment rate. So I understand your concern. But are you good at what you do?" "Sure. I was at the top of my class and got good evaluations at the other two jobs I had." "Do you think you are worth hiring?" "Well, yes."

In helping the male figure in the tray recognize his irrational thoughts—e.g., his overgeneralizations, all-or-nothing thinking, presumption of negative conclusions, and disqualification of the positive—the sun facilitated a change in attitude in the male figure. As the man continued talking to the sun, the client suddenly laughed and said, "This man really does sound pretty irrational." By telling the story about the man in the tray, the client unconsciously distanced himself from his own situation. This, as well as the objectifying of the issue and actual acting out of the reality of the situation, enabled him to affirm himself in more positive and active ways.

There are innumerable procedures and styles that can effectively further self-exploration, deepen the experience, allow the psyche to reveal itself to the client, and facilitate healing. As long as the client is respected and accepted by the therapist and is given permission to make her/his own choices about any changes to be made in the world and to follow only those suggestions s/he chooses to act on, whatever approaches are utilized allow forward movement.

The therapeutic intervention phase usually takes at least 15 minutes, although this varies according to the client and the availability of time. When the session is close to completion, ask the client how s/he would like to leave the world for today. You might say, "It's almost time for us to end for today. You can leave the world as you would like it for this moment. You may leave it just as it is or you may make changes. This is how the world is for now."

Stage 4. Documentation

Once clients have proceeded through the processing and modifying of their worlds and have positioned all the objects as they wish to leave them, give them an opportunity to record the symbolic image by taking a photograph. Also take a photograph yourself, with their permission. It is advantageous for you to have two cameras: a Polaroid or any camera that has immediate development and a 35mm camera with slide or print film. The Polaroid serves as the camera for the client so that s/he will have an image of the scene to take home. The 35mm camera enables you to have a clearer image with greater depth. If you choose to take slides and have a slide projector, you will be able to project a larger scene for you and your client. However, we have found photographs adequate for review purposes.

Most sandplay therapists agree that documenting the world is valuable. How it should be done varies. Photography is probably the most frequently used method. Some, including Lowenfeld, prefer diagrams. Erik Erikson moved from photographs to schematic sketches. Concretizing the sand tray image serves therapeutic, diagnostic, and research purposes. Lowenfeld used diagrams of the sand worlds to study the thinking of her clients. She also pointed out that the diagram can be productively used in consultation sessions with one's supervisor or colleagues, because the drawing represents the raw material that has not been processed through the therapist's psyche like other material the therapist is sharing. Erikson was interested in studying his clients' constructions for comparison with other data. Kalff used photographs for reviewing the course of therapy. Some may use photographs to check clinical hunches about groups of people, based on differences between sexes, ages, cultures, etc. (Thompson, 1990). For example, a therapist may want to know the answer to the following question: How do females explore aggression differently than males in our society? The therapist can conduct an observational study looking at several response categories (e.g., modes of expression and objects used). S/he can then compare the created worlds of males and females. By measuring how often subjects perform predefined acts, the researcher can draw some conclusions as to differences between the ways aggression is expressed in her/his population.

If you choose to use photography as your form of documentation, remember that the photograph documents the final result of the process the client has just experienced. This photograph is a "record of the psychic material held for symbolic and dynamic interpretation" (Ryce-Menuhin, 1992, p. 106). It allows for analysis or review even after the creation in the tray has been dismantled. Often our involvement in the client's process impels us to focus so closely that we see the world only through the client's eyes. The client's perspective becomes our perspective. The photograph thus becomes a helpful device to attain divergent viewpoints. As Dundas wrote, "When the sand picture is completed, I photograph it. . . . Later the slides help me see shapes and forms that were not apparent when I first looked at the sand picture. Viewing slides alone, I gain a different perspective and fresh approach that add to my understanding" (1990, p. 3). Also, we can review the client's psychological journey alone or with her/him by reflecting on the series of photographs that have been taken throughout the therapy process. "The completed trays are a record for the therapist and the client. They make visible what is happening at the time, and what happened, and what is ripening—portends toward the future. In reviewing the series, you affirm the route taken" (Signell & Bradway, 1995, p. 19).

The photograph also serves as a kind of transitional object for the client. S/he usually takes the picture with her/him and therefore has a tangible representation to hold, in addition to having the image and experience in her/his mind's eye or unconscious. The photograph helps to keep the image alive, even after the scene is disassembled. Dundas stated that "When I do this [photograph the sand picture], a child realizes his creation will live in a photograph" (1990, p. 3). In addition, the photograph serves as a reminder for the client of what s/he has learned from creating, exploring, and experiencing the world. It displays the process in visual form, utilizing the sense of sight and reinforcing the experience.

Moreover, because clients are in continual movement, their worlds continue to change. The constructions with which they were once pleased sometimes need to be altered. The photograph of a past scene can be critical in helping the client see, remember, and then reconstruct a world. Seeing the change often leads to significant therapeutic movement. An ongoing photographic record of each step of the sandplay process, along with the therapist's inquiry into the inner and outer life of the client, can lead to profound insights.

Another, more expensive option is to videotape sessions. Although the video is not viewed during the therapy stage, it is a valuable tool for the therapist after the session is completed. This allows the therapist to view the entire process, including all the changes, expressed insights, and verbal and nonverbal behavior. With client consent the therapist can also use the video during supervision sessions and for teaching purposes. In addition, it may also be useful in the transition stage or during a subsequent session for the client to study. The video gives the client the opportunity to observe her/himself and see things from a fresh perspective.

We'd like to reiterate a point that Ammann emphasized. Although the photograph is a valuable tool, it is important to remember that it is a concrete image of the process, not just the final product of an experience. Ammann insisted that "it is incorrect to say that an analysand 'makes' the sand picture, rather he composes a picture or mediates an impulse which flows into him from the unconscious. He represents the movement of his soul in the sand at that particular time and place" (1993, p. 33).

CLIENT'S PHOTOGRAPH

At this point in the sandplay therapy session the client has completed her/his symbolic work. S/he is preparing to leave the office, taking with her/him what has been learned. Ask the client if s/he would like to photograph the scene. You might say, "When people have finished with their worlds for the day, they always have the opportunity to take a photograph of their world. Would you like to have a photograph of your world?" If they respond affirmatively, ask them if they would like to take the picture themselves or would like you to take it. Whether the client takes the photograph or you take it, give the client the choice of the angle from which the picture is taken. In some cases clients indicate that they can remember the world and do not need a photograph. Some state that they do not want a photograph. By saying this, they may be minimizing the significance of the tray and the experience. Some clients choose not to take a picture because they feel that it detracts from the experience and makes it less meaningful. Whatever their choice, honor it.

THERAPIST'S PHOTOGRAPH

After the client has taken her/his picture, ask for permission to take a photograph for yourself. You might say, "Would it be all right with you if I also take a photograph? That way I'll have a record of the world you created. It will not only help me remember all that you did, but at some later time we can look at it together." Ask the client from what position s/he wishes you to photograph the world. Usually clients allow you to take a picture for yourself and indicate that you may take it from the angle of your choice. We frequently take it from the same perspective that the client chose and/or from the front of the tray.

If the client has chosen not to take a picture, you may take a photograph for your file after s/he has left, with or without her/his permission. If you have not received permission to photograph, we suggest that you do not show the photograph to the client at any time. Revealing to the client a picture that s/he chose not to take might feel like a betrayal. If we have asked and the client has denied permission, we respect the client's wishes and do not take a photograph, even after the client has left.

We generally take our photograph from the front of the tray. If the tray is complex and seems to have hidden material or areas of great energy, we sometimes take additional photographs. Since there is generally not sufficient time to spend with the tray before it has to be dismantled for your next client, the photograph will enable you, as De Domenico taught, to recreate the scene to increase clarity and understanding of the client's world. More detailed information of the process can be recorded, as described in chapter 8.

Stage 5. Transition

Now that the symbolic, unconscious work is completed, ask the client to join you in your consultation area. As you would in any session, help the client transition into the real world prior to leaving the office. Continue to engender clients' integration of their experiences of the sandplay on a more conscious level. Help clients bridge the gap between the symbolic images in their created worlds and representational meaning of these images in their lives. Encourage clients to recognize the connection between what transpired in the tray and the realities of everyday occurrences. The photograph has captured the final product of the process of sandplay. Now further crystallize the process within clients by encouraging them to make sense of their worlds and the issues contained in the trays. Support the clients as they explore how they can apply what they learned during the sandplay experience to their current life situations. This is the opportunity for you to channel the newly awakened energies or newfound insights and material brought forth from the unconscious into constructive use.

MEANING-MAKING

What happens in the tray emanates from the client's unconscious and conscious experience. It is a reflection of what is occurring in the client's inner and outer world. Your role is to aid in the client's understanding and application of this material. If the client is confused about the significance of the use of repeated objects or themes, you may encourage the client to create in the next session an amplification tray where s/he can place her/his confusion (see chapter 6). Or you may suggest that the client look up the objects' meanings in symbol or mythology dictionaries. Let the client know that s/he should determine for her/himself whether these interpretations have relevance for her/his life. If appropriate, tell the client of archetypal or transpersonal experiences of mankind (e.g., Biblical stories, myths, fairytales). The meaning presented in the dictionary or in the stories may not resonate with the client; the client's perspective takes precedence.

CONNECTING THE SANDPLAY EXPERIENCE
TO THE CLIENT'S REAL WORLD

There are a number of ways to help the client utilize her/his understanding of the sandplay experience. Encourage the client to link the sandplay world to memories or current life issues. Your questions or comments will reflect what transpired in the session, depending on what emerged for the client. For example, if memories were triggered and the focus in the tray was past relationships or events, you might say, "You have just created and experienced a world. I wonder what things that happened in the tray brought up memories for you?" If the world focused on more current issues, you might say, "You have just created and experienced a world. How are the occurrences in the tray similar to what is going on in your life now?"

Encourage the client to be aware during her/his daily life of how her/his experiences are like what happened in this sandplay world. For example, if a client were to recognize that in the sand tray world she placed a woman (representing herself) next to dangerous objects, you might suggest that she notice in her everyday life how she does this.

You might say, "You may find that things that happened in the tray will surface as you go about your daily life. For example, the woman in the tray was standing next to the beast, which was a threat to her. You might pay attention to how often you find yourself in potentially dangerous or harmful situations."

As you would in any session, explore practical ways for the client to handle or tolerate threatening, dangerous, or uncomfortable situations or solve problems that arise. Give assignments if appropriate. For example, when the client in the illustration in the preceding paragraph recognized her pattern of putting herself in dangerous positions, you might inquire how she could change her behavior. If she were to respond that she could leave or call for assistance in such situations, her assignment would be to follow through on taking care of herself. If she were to realize that there are ways to stay out of these circumstances, the assignment might be to recognize potential danger ahead of time and make a conscious choice to avoid it.

Between sessions the client can become more conscious and function on a more rational level. Let the client know that dreams, memories, and/or feelings may or may not surface as a result of the sandplay experience. These often do arise as a result of sandplay, as well as other techniques that delve deeply into the unconscious. In instances where this does not naturally occur, the comment on follow-up dreams, etc., may have an effect similar to that of a post-hypnotic suggestion, engendering continued unconscious work after the client leaves the session.

Discuss ways to integrate these dreams or memories into the client's consciousness in the event that they occur, which is likely. You might say, "When you have done a sand tray, much of what comes out is unconscious. So you may not be immediately aware of what it means to you. But your inner voice has a wonderful way of telling you what is important for you to understand from the sandplay session. This can happen shortly after you have done the tray or it can happen several days later. Very often it comes out in dreams or triggers memories or feelings. These can be surprising or sometimes overwhelming to you." At this time it is appropriate to discuss what to do when the feelings, dreams, and memories occur. You might say, "I'm going to ask you to keep a journal of this material. You might find a thread that runs through this material and the sandplay and discover its meaning. You might find an answer to a question that has puzzled you for years. Let's explore what other things you can do to help you through the experience if things get tough." Create a plan that you know will be helpful or supportive to the client if intense emotions are triggered as a result of the session.

Stage 6. Dismantling the World

It is appropriate to give the client the choice of dismantling the scene before s/he leaves or leaving it intact. For some clients undoing what they have created reinforces their knowledge that they have the power to nullify what they have done (i.e., to remedy their mistakes). For some, dismantling the world serves to complete one act and open the way for new creations. If the client chooses to disassemble the world, have her/him do so prior to the transition stage. Most clients choose to leave the scene as they constructed it. Having the world remain intact allows the client to take that image along as s/he leaves the therapy room. A client we saw who chose not to take a photograph of her tray took a good look at the scene as she was leaving the session. She was on her way to a conference to present a paper. Upon her return she reported that on several occasions the image of the world came to mind, providing a sense of strength and empowerment.

If the client has not disassembled the scene, inform the client that you will do so after s/he leaves. When you dismantle the tray, take time to reflect on and record the experience. Occasionally, it may not be feasible to wait until the client leaves. For example, if you have a client scheduled immediately after the session and will not have time to disassemble the world between appointments, it may be necessary for you and the client to dismantle the scene prior to her/his leaving. In such a case, ask the client to remove one item from the tray before the two of you replace the objects on the shelves. Again, do this prior to the transition stage. The purpose of having the client remove the first piece is twofold. First, this has been a deep creative and expressive experience for the client; it is therefore important for the energy to be broken by the client. Second, the object the client removes first often holds much importance or power for her/him. This provides you with additional information to explore. After the client removes one item, ask if you may help her/him put away the rest of the objects. If it is clear to you that dismantling the scene in the client's presence would be discomfiting or destructive to her/his process, find another way of handling the situation. We find that having an extra sand tray is advantageous. We cover the tray intact and place it aside. The world is then hidden from the next client and a bare tray is available for use. The only disadvantage is that the objects the previous client used are not available if sandplay is again the modality of choice.

UNDERSTANDING THE WORLD

Dismantle the world thoughtfully. This is an opportune time to reexperience the client's process and learn more about the meaning of the world. We find that we gain additional insights at this time, as we focus on the tray and recognize particular placements or movement that we may have missed while attending to other aspects of the process. Often the world has gone through several metamorphoses. It is sometimes helpful in the dismantling process to remove some objects and reposition others as they were prior to the completion of the world. This often reveals significant changes that occurred for the client.

If the world does not make sense to you, rebuild it and rework it, duplicating the client's experience. Recreating the client's world when you are not rushed can be enlightening. You will have a photograph to aid you if you choose to review the tray at a later time. If you have an emotional reaction to any aspect of or object in the client's scene, build a world for yourself, beginning with that object. This is an excellent method for resolving countertransference issues (see chapter 10).

CLEARING THE WORLD

As you put the materials away, replace the objects in their correct categories to maintain the organization necessary for easy access and sense of order for other clients. After placing objects in their appropriate places on the shelves, complete your notes and reflect on the experience. We complete our note-taking subsequent to dismantling. We then have the additional insights gained from thoughtful handling of the objects. If you choose, you may make your notes prior to the dismantling.

As we stated, often these six stages are neither completed nor distinctly delineated. We encourage you to include time at the end of the session for a photograph and some debriefing before the client leaves the office, even if the client completed only the creating the world stage. If the client chooses not to reflect upon or discuss the process, at least s/he has the opportunity to address her/his reticence and gain greater awareness.

. . . .

Stages of a Sandplay Therapy Session for Individuals

STAGE 1: CREATING THE WORLD

- *Introducing Sandplay to the Client:* Create a safe, protected, and free space. Establish a positive expectation. Reintroduce the client to the trays, objects and the process. Place yourself in a position that is comfortable for the client. Let the client know there is no wrong way to do sandplay. Instruct her/him to let you know when s/he is finished.

- *Constructing the World:* The client creates a scene in the sand. Witness, honor, and respect the experience without interference or interpretation. The client builds the world with or without objects and with or without water. Remain silent and fully attentive.

STAGE 2: EXPERIENCING AND REARRANGING

- *Experiencing:* Encourage the client to fully experience the world. Sit quietly as the client reflects on the scene. This is a time of deepening the experience.

- *Rearranging:* Inform the client that s/he may leave the world as it is or make changes. Allow time for the client to experience the changed world.

STAGE 3: THERAPY

- *Touring the World:* Join the client on her/his side of the tray. Request a tour of the world. Attend to the language and nonverbal cues of the client. Stay outside of the tray. Encourage the client to stay with the emotions that arise.

- *Therapeutic Interventions:* Ask questions about the world, reflecting only what the client has related. Keep the focus on objects in the tray. Apply your choice of therapeutic interventions such as Gestalt techniques, psychodrama, imagery, regressive methods, cognitive restructuring, art therapy, and body work. More changes in the sand world often occur.

STAGE 4: DOCUMENTATION

- *Client's Photograph:* Provide an opportunity for the client to photograph her/his world from an angle of her/his choice, preferably with a Polaroid camera. The client may take the picture home.

- *Therapist's Photograph:* With the client's permission, take a photograph of the world for future reference.

STAGE 5: TRANSITION
- *Meaning-Making:* Help the client understand and apply the insights that have become conscious through sandplay.
- *Connecting the Sandplay to the Client's Real World:* Ask the client how the events in the tray reflect her/his life. Help the client make sense of the world. Encourage the client to notice how the issues in the tray appear in her/his daily life.

STAGE 6: DISMANTLING THE WORLD
- *Understanding the World:* Dismantle the world thoughtfully after the client has left the therapy room. Reflect on the client's process.
- *Clearing the World:* Notice changes that occurred. Replace objects in appropriate places on the shelves. Complete your notes.

• •

Things to Remember During Creating the World Stage

- Create a safe, protected and free space.
- Reintroduce the client to the trays, the objects, and the process.
- Place yourself in a position from which you can observe the client and that is comfortable for her/him.
- Direct the client to let you know when s/he is finished.
- Remain completely present.
- Remain silent unless the client invites you to speak or you feel it is important to respond to the client's body language.
- Notice nonverbal cues, e.g., facial expressions, sighs, energy in the body.
- Pay attention to the sequence and manner of the creation of the scene.
- Do not get actively involved unless the client requests it.
- Stay outside of the sand tray.
- Objectively observe (and record), without interpretation, what the client does.

• •

Things to Observe

- Use of sand, water, and objects; movement toward or away from
- Sequence and manner of choosing and placing objects; those chosen and those touched but rejected; those attracted to or repelled by
- Manner of creating the world: speed, intensity, quantity of objects
- Patterns in the tray: repetition of numbers, colors, groupings, opposites, geometric patterns
- Attributes of objects: texture, color, size, etc.
- Use of space: above, below; clusters and barren areas
- Direction objects are facing
- Nonverbal cues: facial expression, evidence of energy in the body, sighs, internal and external shifts
- Changes made in the tray: addition, removal, movement and separation of objects and sand
- Language the client uses in naming the objects
- Buried and hidden objects

SPONTANEOUS SAND TRAYS
WITH COUPLES

In the previous chapter we described in detail how to do sandplay with individuals, delineating the stages of a sandplay session. Here we address working with any dyadic relationship (e.g., romantic unions, family relationships, friendships, and work connections). Because most couples who come to therapy are in intimate relationships, we will focus on such relationships. As you know if you have worked therapeutically with couples, there are some fundamental theoretical premises and therapeutic considerations that apply whether your clients are individuals or couples (e.g., recognizing that past experience contributes to present attitudes and behaviors, the importance of being very present to clients, and trust in the clients' wisdom). However, there are understandings about how couples and therapists function and the dynamics in relationships that distinguish couple therapy from individual therapy. In this chapter we describe some basic characteristics of couples and their communication. We also discuss aspects of the dynamics within the dyad that dictate when sandplay is indicated, identify which methods to use, and delineate the stages of a couple's sandplay session.

We are making the assumption that if you are planning to do sandplay with couples, you have a basic theoretical knowledge of relationship development and communication theory, as well as therapeutic experience in working with couples. We therefore present only a few rudimentary and pertinent assertions pertaining to couples that we have garnered from other theoreticians and therapists and our own experiences over the years. When we mention particular theories, we by no means imply that these are the most auspicious perspectives on relationships. It is beyond the scope of this book to enumerate the multitude of fundamental principles about couples or detail any of them.

First, when two people come together, each brings with her/him the legacies from her/his family of origin. Murray Bowen postulated that the greatest influence on individuals' perceptions of themselves and others is "the quality of their emotional dependency in family relationships" (Hall, 1991, p. xii). The influences on one's beliefs, values, perspectives, interactions with others, etc., cannot be separated from one's current being in the world and intimate relationships. We look at each partner in the couple as part of his or her family of origin, as well as of the new system the partners have formed. It is essential to take into account what each brings to the relationship. The amount of differentiation or lack thereof (i.e., integration and individuation or fusion and enmeshment) affects how emotionally cut off and distant or how enmeshed and dependent a person is in her/his intimate relationships. This directly reveals itself in aspects such as closeness and distance and behaviors such as pursuing and withdrawing. Understanding and working therapeutically with family-of-origin issues helps individuals gain greater awareness of themselves and each other, leading to improved ability to act objectively. When partners share in the sand on a more symbolic level, especially when there is a focus on family of origin, they are more open to seeing what they have contributed to the issues that brought them into therapy. This also helps the therapist learn more about the couple and assess what they are bringing to the relationship and where the problem areas may lie.

A particular client comes to mind. While working individually with Franni, it became evident that the sense of powerlessness and inequality in her relationship was key to her depression. She and her partner Marian were both willing to participate in conjoint therapy. When the couple created their sand world, the dynamics of their relationship became more evident to them and to us. Marian was more assertive in guiding the creation of the world, while Franni seemed increasingly afraid to participate. When they described the world from their own perspectives, each gained new information and insight into the other's inner workings and the baggage each carried from her families of origin. Marian never knew of Franni's experiences of being criticized by her parents because of her obesity in adolescence, which contributed to her low self-esteem and her fear of being known. Learning this helped Marian be more patient with Franni's distance and hypersensitivity. It also helped Franni understand her reasons for assuming the inferior position in the relationship and freed her to assert herself more and to share her feelings.

Second, many theorists have studied and written about individual personality traits and psychological types, and how these affect a relationship (see Keirsey & Bates, 1984). When the partners can understand and accept each other's way of being in the world, they can cooperate with each other. But when the diversity in their styles and personality traits, beliefs, or values clash, conflict may result. One analyst who identified psychological types was Jung. His typology has been studied and applied to understanding couples. Helping partners recognize and understand their own and each other's personalities, ways of thinking, and ways of relating to the world can lead to the growth of the individual as well as the blossoming of the relationship. Each partner contributes different strengths, as well as shortcomings. "If [one] begin[s] to sense what [her/his] typology is, [s/he] might realize where [her/his] strengths lie and also where some of [her/his] missing ingredients may be found. Whatever type [one] may be, it would help her/him get along with [her/his] friend or spouse if [s/he] could recognize the differences in their typologies" (The Educational Center, 1995, p. 46).

A couple with whom we worked demonstrates the dilemma that occurs when the partners are caught in their own "strengths" and unable to see the contributions of their spouse. The man had a highly developed spiritual self, and sought spiritual guidance in many places. His wife put much of her energy into outdoor, physical activity, having a highly developed physical self. The man had very little interest in physical pursuits, nor did he see value in expending so much energy in that way, believing that the spiritual path was of higher value. The woman felt that her way of being was preferable and more grounded, and that the neglect of the physical realm was unhealthy and irresponsible. In this case, the couple not only did not share core values but invalidated each other's contributions to the relationship. Sandplay helps partners recognize and understand that divergent behaviors that are a part of the person can complement the relationship. We have found that in sandplay partners often come to appreciate their contrasting contributions and respect their differences.

Third, people often enter partnerships with different expectations of the relationship. These expectations are frequently not verbalized and the partners unknowingly work toward different ends. Many times when we work with couples, we see that each partner believes that s/he is contributing to the well-being of the relationship. But because their beliefs and hopes are unspoken, they may act counterproductively to the other's expectations. For example, it is not unusual that one member of the couple gives her/his partner that which s/he her/himself would like. S/he then feels discounted by her/his partner when her/his gift or contribution is not appreciated. The therapist can help the partners unveil their expectations and bring into view their individual hopes and desires. When couples create sand trays, especially if they portray their hopes or views of a relationship, the partners, as well as the therapist, can see the discrepancies and similarities in their expectations. They can then act out of knowledge rather than presumption. If their goals are similar or complementary, this knowledge can enhance their relationship. If their goals are divergent, they may decide to end the relationship.

For example, one couple, Nancy and Ted, came to us for premarital counseling. Initially we took about 15 minutes for them to discuss their relationship. Both were enthusiastic about their imminent marriage and revealed no immediate problems. They felt, on a conscious level, that sandplay would be an interesting, explorative experience. As they created their worlds they discovered that there were issues of which they were unaware. Following our suggestion, they created separate trays and took each other through their respective worlds. At that time it was clear to us that each had different views about what they wanted to include in their life together.

We then instructed them to create a conjoint world, bringing in objects from their individual trays as well as any other objects of their choice. One issue that became evident related to having children. Nancy brought the rocking chair she had in her individual tray into the joint world. When Nancy described the rocking chair she stated that she hoped they would have a baby shortly after they got married. Ted appeared surprised. Although they had discussed the possibility of having children, this was only addressed on a hypothetical level. They had not been in touch with or communicated their deeper inner desires. As they further explored the world, it became evident to them that this could be an irreconcilable difference. Ted was not sure he ever wanted children and was definitely not interested in having them now. The sandplay provided them with an opportunity to explore this issue prior to marriage. For Nancy and Ted, the experience led to a dissolution of the relationship. Of course, sandplay also offers a format for resolving differences and achieving compromise.

Fourth, partners interact with each other from different aspects of themselves. Eric Berne's paradigm of the child, parent, and adult ego states within each individual is one viable approach to viewing the roles partners play within the relationship (see Berne, 1964). Individuals often play out the early scripts they learned (Steiner, 1974). Sandplay provides an excellent medium through which to gain insight and work through the conflicting roles within the relationship. In addition to playing different roles within the dyad, each partner also serves many capacities other than being a partner. At times the outside roles complement the relationship. Sometimes one member may experience a role of her/his partner as interfering with the integrity of the relationship. This brings to mind a couple we were seeing whose marriage changed dramatically once the woman worked outside the home. The man felt abandoned when the woman directed her attention and energy toward her job.

Fifth, in working with couples the potential for triangulation is present. Although many believe that the therapist can stay out of the triangle, to some degree the therapist's very presence creates a triangle. Bowen proposed that "[t]he most uncomfortable participant in a dyad, or two-person system, predictably draws a third person into the twosome when sufficient stress occurs in the two-person relationship" (Hall, 1991, p. 23). Because of this, you must be vigilant of countertransference and of being pulled into the dynamic of the relationship. One way to minimize this possibility is to view the couple, not the individuals, as the client. Confidentiality issues also may arise if the therapist sees the partners individually. The therapist must be clear and direct with the couple about how individual sessions apart from the partner are handled.

In couple therapy, helping clients become aware of patterns of relating that are helpful, as well as those patterns that are destructive, is key to assisting them in making constructive changes. Sandplay provides a medium through which each partner can "reveal relevant history, visions of ideal self, goals, hidden parts of self, social self and roles, as these pertain to the current situations that brings the couple into therapy" (De Domenico, 1991, p. 3). We concur with De Domenico that sandplay gives the couple an opportunity to witness and explore in a tangible way how the individuality of each partner does or does not contribute to the relationship. It increases self and other understanding, helping couples discover the behaviors, patterns, and perceptions that have led to the difficulties they are working to resolve (De Domenico, 1991).

Stages of a Sandplay Session with Couples

Because there are several different approaches to using sandplay with couples, depending on the couple's dynamics and issues, we describe the stages through which we generally proceed. We were first introduced to the following procedures of having couples work in a joint tray or simultaneous individual trays by De Domenico (1991). We have directly adapted her 10 phases, terminology, observations, and directions for both the couple's communication tray and the individuation trays. Our methods evolved as we experienced the needs of our clients. The stages follow a pattern similar to working with individuals, moving from more nonverbal, unconscious to verbal, conscious work. In this chapter we specify the stages for *spontaneous* trays both for couples working toward enhancing communication and for those working toward individuation. In spontaneous trays the therapist does not suggest the content or structure the building process, but only gives general directions. In chapter 6, where we describe more directed trays (i.e., where the structure is greater and the directions more specific), the recommendations vary from these guidelines. When we address communication issues, we have couples work in a joint tray. Some couples create separate worlds in different parts of the tray; some create one shared world interactively; some do not allow interference with their objects; and some move, adjust, or remove their partner's objects without consent. When we address individuation issues, we begin with separate trays.

De Domenico's original phases were (1) introductory phase, (2) choosing the trays, (3) building phase (she described a variety of procedural possibilities for using one or more trays [see 1991, pp. 9–16]), (4) experiencing and revisioning phase, (5) sharing-with-the-partner phase, (6) reflecting-on-the-process phase, (7) sharing with the therapist phase, (8) understanding phase, (9) photographic documentation phase, and (10) reviewing phase (De Domenico, 1991, p. 8). The stages for sandplay with couples as we have adapted them, whether the partners construct one conjoint tray or individual trays simultaneously, are:

Stage 1: Creating the world
Stage 2: Experiencing and rearranging
Stage 3: Communicating with the partner

Stage 4: Therapy
Stage 5: Documentation
Stage 6: Transition
Stage 7: Dismantling the world

These stages are suggestions. All stages are not always experienced, nor are they always so delineated. What you do with your clients in a session depends on your own therapeutic orientation and the applicability to that particular couple. The stages, as you can infer from the designations, are very similar to the parallel stages for individual clients. However, there are a few distinctions. In the creating the world stage, the partners are introduced to the sandplay process and construct their separate worlds or a conjoint world. This corresponds to De Domenico's "introductory phase," in which she familiarizes the couple with the sandplay room, the trays, the materials, and the directions, and the "choosing the trays phase," when she directs the couple to decide together the tray(s) they wish to use. Often each partner has previously experienced using the sand tray. If this is the case, a brief reintroduction is sufficient. In the experiencing and rearranging stage each builder silently experiences her/his own individual or their conjoint world. Any changes they wish to make are welcomed by the therapist. They reexperience their own world and then experience their partner's world if separate trays have been used. The communication with the partner stage is a divergence from the procedure in individual sandplay. This corresponds to De Domenico's "experiencing and revisioning phase." In this stage, combining De Domenico's "sharing-with-the-partner phase" and "reflecting-on-the-process phase," each builder takes her/his partner into the completed world(s). The partners then reflect on what this creating and sharing has been like for them. The therapist continues to remain quiet and, for the most part, inactive. S/he facilitates the communication by assisting the partners to share with each other, by both listening respectfully and describing their perspectives.

The therapist moves into a more active role in the therapy stage. Through questions that arose for the therapist, reflective responses, and other therapeutic interventions, the therapist promotes experiencing, understanding, and resolution focused on the dynamics portrayed in the tray. In De Domenico's "sharing with the therapist phase," each partner takes the therapist on a tour of her/his/their world(s), and helps the therapist understand it. As with individuals and in De Domenico's photographic documentation phase, the documentation stage is the time when the therapist suggests to each partner that s/he may photograph the world(s) from her/his perspective. In the transition stage, when the clients move away from the sand tray, the therapist encourages the couple to make sense of the world(s), the issues contained in it(them), and how the session relates to current problems. Clients are also helped to transition into the world outside the therapy room. De Domenico's "understanding phase," when she explores with the couple how the tray relates to their current issues and the messages they glean from the sand tray, precedes her "documentation phase" and is completed at the tray, unlike our transition stage. In the dismantling the world stage, the therapist disassembles the scene(s) after the couple has left the room. Occasionally, when this is not possible, the partners are each asked to remove one object from the tray, which breaks the energy pattern. Then the therapist and the couple put away the rest of the objects. After the couple leaves, the therapist takes time to reflect on and record the experience. In De Domenico's final phase, the "reviewing phase," she reviews any photos or videos with the couple either in the session or in a subsequent session. Although there is considerable overlap between the stages for doing individuation work with couples (i.e., each member of the couple constructing her/his own sand world simultaneously, then, if appropriate, bringing their worlds together) and doing communication work with couples (i.e., constructing a conjoint sand world), we discuss the two formats separately for clarity.

When to Suggest Sandplay and What Approach to Use

Sandplay is introduced at varying times during the therapy process, depending on the reason couples have entered therapy. There are several indicators for choosing sandplay as an intervention early in therapy. Because sandplay is an effective assessment tool, it can be used after the first intake session during your initial evaluation of the relationship. Some couples may have been self- or other-referred to you specifically for sandplay therapy. In these cases, you will probably employ sandplay in the first or second session. Some couples may come for short-term therapy and/or for a single issue. For example, a couple may have compatibility in most areas of their relationship but have one issue with which they are struggling. After meeting with them once, you may believe that sandplay would break the verbal pattern that is keeping them stuck; therefore, you would suggest sandplay for the next session. Some couples come specifically for brief premarital counseling. Sandplay is a facilitative tool to determine areas the couple may wish to explore further. In these cases, you can forego a period of therapeutic trust-building. However, we have found that, unless couples have been referred to us specifically for sandplay or for assessment, a brief period of trust-building promotes greater comfort with the disclosure that sandplay evokes. When you schedule a couple's sandplay session, you may wish to reserve one and a half to two hours.

Once you conclude that sandplay is fitting, there are two options for initiating the sandplay: either (1) you will choose whether the couple works in one or two trays or (2) the couple will make that choice. If you determine from the couple's dynamics that you will make the choice, decide if the couple should work in one or two trays. If the partners are distant from each other or have difficulty connecting or communicating, the creation of a sand world in the same tray can help them learn to interact productively and resolve issues in their relationship. We call this a *communication sand tray*. Working in one tray also provides information regarding the couple's communication skills and patterns and reveals to the couple, as well as to you, the dynamics in the relationship.

Using trays independently is advisable when the couple is enmeshed or overly symbiotic. The separate trays promote movement toward individuation, due not only to the autonomous construction of the sand worlds but also to the witnessing of each other's creations and explanations. We call these *individuation trays*. This work helps each partner recognize the other as having an identity apart from their union. Constructing individual spontaneous sand worlds simultaneously also is pivotal when one or both partners feel unable to freely express themselves without fear of criticism, control, or some other negative consequence. "When the couple builds Worlds simultaneously, they may learn to create or tolerate an environment where they can work and function as individual human beings" (De Domenico, 1991, p. 10). Withhold using a joint tray until the partners have developed sufficient ego strength to maintain their individual identities. They are then able to work conjointly in a constructive manner.

If significant detachment or enmeshment patterns are not present, the couple may make the choice of whether to use one or two trays. Also, during the initial assessment, the decision whether to create together in one tray or construct worlds separately should be left to the partners, because their choice conveys information to you about their perspective on their *I/we* identity.

Where therapist instructions would be redundant, explanations are less detailed than in the previous chapter. In such cases you can refer back to chapter 3. When something specifically refers to couple work, we illustrate more thoroughly. To emphasize the importance of specific instructions, we reiterate that you must remain present and attentive to the choices, placement, and sequence of placement of objects; the pace, style, and deliberateness of constructing the world; the verbal and nonverbal expressions; and the many other observations you would make during individual sandplay therapy. But now you must also attend to the interactional dynamics of the couple. Although we do not describe working with families in this chapter, the considerations specified below can be applied to families. Spontaneous sand tray work with families is addressed in chapter 5.

COMMUNICATION SAND TRAY
Stage 1. Creating the World
INTRODUCING SANDPLAY TO THE COUPLE

This world reflects the couple's joint reality. In your first session with the couple you will have introduced sandplay as one of the modalities you sometimes use with individuals and couples. You will also have briefly introduced the couple to the therapy room, including the sand trays, the miniatures, and the materials available. Now that you and the couple have decided to do sandplay, you might introduce sandplay by saying, "You know we have just been talking about something that has been causing difficulty for the two of you. We really don't know exactly why this is so, or what some of the underlying issues and solutions are. These are often hidden, even from ourselves. Sandplay is a way that many couples have found very useful in uncovering their hidden issues and gaining insight into themselves and each other. It's a way to communicate with each other in a different manner. Somehow in doing a tray the wise inner aspect of themselves knows what is happening and can show them how to resolve the issue. I was wondering if you'd be willing to try it."

Observe how each partner thinks about and responds to your suggestion. Observe how they come to the decision to participate. Notice who takes the lead and if coercion/submission or discomfort is present. If you are aware of reticence, check it out. Often clients feel that this is child's play. You can reassure them that couples sometimes feel this way, but once they begin they experience the natural flow of this kind of expression.

One or both of the members of the couple may already have experienced sandplay in individual therapy. In that case, a brief reintroduction to the trays and materials is sufficient. If you have a larger tray for couple work, introduce them to that tray, displaying the blue bottom and reminding them that they may create anything with the sand, miniatures, and water. The couple may choose to use this tray or any others you have. If neither partner has done sandplay before, a fuller explanation and opportunity to peruse the shelves will be necessary (see creating the world stage in chapter 3 for more details). Tell the couple that there is no right or wrong way to construct a joint world, although the partners need to come to some agreements. For example, they need to decide (1) the tray they will use, (2) if they will use miniatures, and (3) if they will use water. They may agree to proceed in any way they choose. Let the couple know that they may talk or be silent. They may change anything they wish at any time. Remember to let them know that you will be silent unless spoken to. Also, with the couple's input, determine a position in which to place yourself to observe them as they build their world. If you plan to take notes, photographs, or a video of their world as they build, ask them if it is all right for you to do so. Explain that it will help you and them remember what happened during the process.

CONSTRUCTING A CONJOINT WORLD

Some behaviors and attitudes are essential for you to remember as the couple builds. It is important for you to hold the psychological dynamic of the couple as a unit. This diverges slightly from work with individuals, where you are the container for what one person is experiencing. Accept, without judgment, all the couple's dysfunctional and functional behavior. In our culture people tend to focus on the individual as opposed to the couple. This may be the first time that the members of the dyad have been in a setting where they are not judged separately but viewed as a unit functioning together. When they are viewed as a unit, partners are able to express who they are without fear of being blamed or compared to the other. Also remember, during the session, that you must stay outside the tray both physically and emotionally. If at all possible, remain silent. However, after your initial assessment, if one or both partners repeatedly show disrespect or try to control the choice or placement of objects in the tray, you may wish to intervene and either point out this behavior or suggest more respectful conduct. Later, discuss this in the transition stage.

There are many behaviors to which to attend. The following is a list of some of the observations you will want to make, based on suggestions introduced in our training with De Domenico (1991) and observations we made in our work with dyads. Notice the couple's verbal communication. Do they converse about what is to come and make decisions together? Once the tray is chosen, do they independently choose objects and begin placing them in the tray or do they talk about what should go into the tray and how it should be divided or shared? Are their decisions made agreeably or do they argue about what goes into the world? Do they verbally evaluate or criticize what the other has done? Is a rationale or explanation given for the choice or placement of an object? Do they ask permission of each other in regard to possible interference with placement of an object near the other's object? Is there considerable talking or are they silent?

Notice how the partners communicate nonverbally. Notice the differences in their style, pace, and need for immediate resolution, as well as distancing and pursuing patterns in the relationship. What does their body language convey? Is there distance or closeness? Does one partner watch and follow the lead of the other? Is there nonverbal evaluation in the form of facial expressions, sighs, or physical movement? Do they follow or ignore each other's themes? Do they change each other's contributions to the world and, if so, how does the other react? Do they undo or accept each other's work? How able are they to be flexible? Do they support each other's journey? What emotions are they willing to disclose and what do they withhold? How much joy, pleasure, and humor do they share? Where is the emotional outpouring? Notice moments when the couple's energy is bringing them together, blocking interaction, or when there is mutual creativity. Notice the differences in their intensity. Do they complement or interfere with the creative process? Do their approaches change during the course of the building? Do they become more involved with or alienated from one another as the building proceeds? These questions address only some of the behaviors to observe. The totality of the couple dynamics as they construct their world is a microcosm of their relational interaction. Your observations, coupled with the dyad's later explanations in the communicating with the partner stage, serve as the foundation for exploration in the therapy stage.

Although the period of time differs from one couple to the next, allow about 30 minutes for the constructing phase. If you wish to record, you may videotape, take notes, and/or take several photographs or slides during the process, with the couple's permission (see chapter 8). Remain present, constantly observing the couple and their verbal and nonverbal interactions.

Stage 2. Experiencing and Rearranging

EXPERIENCING

This is a time for quiet reflection and deepening the couple's experience of the world they have created together. As opposed to your work with individuals, do not respond to or verbally reflect on emotional expressions of either partner. This will interfere with the other partner's immersion into the world. Encourage them to experience the entire world, not just their own objects. Let them know that all the meanings the objects have evoked for them are valid, including their divergent feelings or interpretations of the world. Advise the couple to remain silent. Suggest that they walk around the tray and view the world from different perspectives. You might say, "Now that you have completed building this world together, I'd like you each to experience it individually. Allow yourselves a few minutes to silently be in all parts of this world. Remember that the entire world belongs to each of you. Imagine yourself there, what it is like, how it feels. You might even imagine you live in it together. After a few minutes, you might want to walk around the tray and see it from all angles."

Observe the couple's reactions to the completed world. Notice if they have responses to particular objects or areas of the tray. Notice if they are able to experience the creation independently from each other or if they observe each other's nonverbal behaviors. Allow at least five minutes for this phase. Pay attention to each member of the dyad, tuning in to when each seems finished. Nonverbally signal the one finished first that you are aware of her/his completion and that the two of you can wait until the other is finished. You may quietly suggest that s/he take a little more time to reenter the world.

REARRANGING

As in your work with individuals, provide the couple with an opportunity to make changes as evoked by more deeply experiencing the completed world. Because there are two people responding, different feelings may be elicited, summoning the desire to make distinct alterations. Welcome any changes, deletions, and/or additions. Also let the couple know that they may leave the world as it is. You might say, "Now that you have both spent some time in this world, it may seem just the way you want it or you might have found that there are some changes either one or both of you might want to make. I asked you to refrain from talking as you experienced the scene, but now, if you'd like to, you are welcome to talk with each other. I will, however, remain silent. When you are finished, let me know." Notice how the revisions are made. Do the partners move or remove only their own objects or also the other's objects? Do they ask permission? Observe the couple's reactions as changes are occurring. If you are recording the process, you may want to take a photograph of the world as they first completed it and one of the changed world.

Stage 3. Communicating with the Partner

GUIDING THE PARTNER THROUGH THE WORLD

At this time, ask each member of the dyad to guide her/his partner through the world as s/he experiences it while you quietly observe. You might say, "The two of you have constructed a wonderful world together, each bringing into the world your own objects. You certainly have some ideas of what this world feels like and is to you. You may even have some ideas about what it is for your partner. If you would, I'd like you to give your partner a tour through the world as you see it. You may just talk spontaneously about whatever experiences are contained within the scene for you, or you may wish to talk about the objects and the terrain in detail, or you might even choose to invent a story. As you describe the scene, you might want to imagine all the objects as inhabitants of this world, and give your accounting in the third person. The objects that your partner placed in the tray may have a similar or a different meaning to you than to her/him. That's all right. Just as in real life, we each have our own perspectives and look at things in different ways. As one of you guides your partner through the scene, the other one will quietly listen and respectfully allow for the unique story that is being told. You'll want to dispense with any of your ideas and be present to what your partner is saying. You will then have an opportunity to relate your story." Once you give these instructions you may either have the partners determine who will go first or direct one of them to begin. If an imbalance of power exists, one partner is more verbally assertive than the other, or one partner generally follows the lead of the other, ask the more passive partner to begin.

Help to facilitate or deepen the connection. This may be done by modeling total presence, by empathic listening, and/or by asking for clarification. Give equal time to each partner. If one partner is naturally more verbal than the other, you can ask more questions of the quieter one. You can avoid a lengthy explication of the scene by the more loquacious partner by suggesting an amount of time before either partner begins. For example, you might say, "Why don't you each take about five to ten minutes to describe the world to your partner?" There are several things that you will want to notice as communication transpires. Observe how present the listening partner is. Is s/he distracted by her/his own thoughts? Does it seem difficult for her/him to not interrupt? Does s/he seem really interested? Notice if the partner giving the narrative looks to her/his partner for approval or watches the partner's reactions. Does the narrator direct her/his remarks to you as opposed to her/his partner? How much does the speaker seem willing to divulge? How much is the second partner describing the tray influenced by the first rendering of the scene? Notice the language the speaker uses, the emotion-laden areas or objects in the tray, and other specifics delineated in the touring the world phase in chapter 3. If you notice objects that are not addressed, remember to comment on them in the therapy stage.

REFLECTING ON THE PROCESS

After each member of the couple has recounted her/his description of the world, encourage the partners to talk with each other about what this experience was like for them. At this point you are bringing them even more into a conscious, analytical mindset than in the guiding phase and out of the tray for the moment. You might say, "As you can see, each of you has your own view of this world. Would you tell each other how it felt when you played together and constructed a united scene? The feelings may have changed at different stages in the development of the world. For instance, you may have felt one way as you chose objects, you may have felt a different way as you placed objects in the tray, and yet another way once the scene started to take shape."

Again, encourage the more passive partner to begin. If the couple seems to have difficulty knowing how to start, you might ask specific questions. For example: "What were you aware of as you were choosing objects?" "What was your reaction when your partner (state the person's name) began to place things near your objects?" "What did you notice about how the two of you added objects to the same tray?" Ask them about their divergent perspectives on the scene and the process or, if it is the case, the similarity of their views. Continue to observe the dynamics between the partners.

If either of the partners directs her/his discussion toward you while s/he describes the world or relates her/his feelings and observations on the process, instruct her/him to address her/his partner. You might say, "Perhaps you could describe this world as you see it to (name the partner) or discuss your feelings about what you just did. When you do this, you are taking the opportunity to practice talking with each other in a new way." This discussion of process allows the partners to clear up any possible presumptions or mind-reading they may have been doing, provides an avenue for open verbal communication of feelings, and helps deepen their understanding of each other. Allow several minutes for them to share their reflections.

Stage 4. Therapy

You have learned the clients' language and interpretations of the world via the tours/narrations that they shared with their partners. Until now they have been communicating with each other and you have remained silent, except to give directions. You will now take a more interactive role. Join the couple on their side of the sand tray with their permission. Remember to stay outside of the couple's sand world, use the clients' language, address both partners, pay attention to nonverbal behaviors, and maintain regard for both partners' needs. You might say, "You have described the scene to each other and discussed what this experience has been like for you. I wonder if it would be all right if I explored this world further with you." As with individuals, ask questions about the world that deepen the experience, provide insights, and help the partners better understand each other. If there are objects that have been buried or glossed over in their narrations, inquire about these items. Encourage the couple to explore the world in the third person (not the first or second person), using the objects as the inhabitants of the world. You may use therapeutic interventions (such as Gestalt, psychodrama, communication skills, imaging, or any techniques familiar to you) to facilitate understanding and resolution. Many of the approaches are similar to ones that you use with individuals. See the therapeutic intervention phase in chapter 3 for more detailed explanations.

When you are finished with the therapy work or when the time is approaching to end the session, have the couple arrange the world as they would like to leave it for today. You might say, "It is now time for us to finish. Would the two of you please leave the world as you would like it for today? You may want to keep it just as it is or you may want to move objects, take an object out, or include an object that seems to be needed. I'd like you to decide together how you want the final scene to look." At this point you want them to collaborate on a final decision. This is an opportunity, no matter how much conflict they have in their relationship, to reach an agreement cooperatively.

Stage 5. Documentation

Have each partner take a photograph of the final world from whatever perspective s/he chooses. You might say, "This world is one you have created and played in together. This is the end of your journey for this session and, as I do whenever people create something in a sand tray, I give them the opportunity to take a photograph of their final scene. If you wish to photograph the world, each of you may take a picture from whatever angle you choose. You may wish to take your photos from the same or different perspectives." As with individuals, ask the couple for permission to take a photograph for yourself. For more details regarding the methods, purposes, and value of photographs, see the documentation stage in chapter 3.

Stage 6. Transition

After they photograph the sand world, ask the couple to move with you away from the tray to your consulting area. So far the focus has been on the symbolic representations in the tray. Although the partners have been interacting on a verbal level, they have not been directly applying their sandplay experience to their relationship in the first person. During this stage a transition is made from the sand world and the characters in that world, to the real world and the couple's personal relationship.

MEANING-MAKING

There may be times when either one or both members of the dyad are confused about why they have chosen the same object repeatedly in worlds they have created. They may wonder what the personal and archetypal meanings are of the object. As with individuals, the couple may look up the meaning of an object in a symbol or mythology dictionary. However, it is important to let them know that they must determine for themselves if that interpretation is relevant for them.

CONNECTING THE SANDPLAY EXPERIENCE TO THE COUPLE'S REAL WORLD

Encourage the couple to link what transpired as they created, experienced, and explored their sand world to their current relationship. Have them elaborate on any issues that were represented or played out in the tray that reflect dynamics or occurrences in their life. Explore the significance of any of the objects, groupings, or dialogues that provided insight and taught them something about themselves, their relationship, and their growth possibilities. You might say, "Sometimes we can see ourselves or things about ourselves in the worlds we create. Do any of the figures in the tray represent either of you? If so, which ones?" Investigate solutions to dilemmas that were revealed in the tray. You might say, "Some things changed in the course of your exploring the world. Did the dialogue between the characters and the resolution they came to give you any ideas about what you might want to do after you leave here today?"

If appropriate, make comments about what you saw. You may want to delve into some of the ways the partners interacted with each other. For example:

1. Did they seem to be close or distant?
2. Was there a pattern of aggression/submission?
3. Did one or both partners appear open and revealing or secretive and concealing?
4. What was their pattern of orderliness; did they differ on how orderly or chaotic they were?
5. Were there differences in their level of activity or passivity?

Posing these questions helps the couple see patterns that exist in their relationship. If complex issues arise, a therapist might wish to use more than one session to process a tray. If unresolved, the same issue will reappear in new trays.

Slides, videotapes, photographs, or reconstruction of the world may be useful to continue processing the sand tray. Review any photographs or videotape you have taken with the couple, on the same day, if you have time during the session, which is rare. If not, wait until the next session. Between sessions review the photos or videotape, on your own, to ascertain what photographs or sections of the tape illustrate behaviors, issues, and patterns you wish to show the couple. The photos and tapes may also be used at a later time to review their impasses, their journey, and their progress.

You might decide to give an assignment to reinforce the couple's insights from this experience and to change the dysfunctional dynamics in the relationship. You may wish to suggest an activity for them to complete out of the office to facilitate positive change. Here are some suggestions for outside follow-up:

1. To explore what the world was about, have each partner use the created world as a foundation for writing a story.
2. Talk with each other about why they chose particular objects and what those objects represented about them or their partner.
3. Have them think about how the world portrayed them/their partner/their relationship.
4. Ask them to think about whether there were objects, themes, scenes, or formations that they would have included but didn't because of expressed or anticipated objections from their partner.
5. Have them practice pattern changes discussed in the office.
6. Any questions or intuitions not covered in the therapy stage may be posed as possible topics to think or write about or explore together.

Between sessions the couple will have an opportunity to act on the insights gained on both conscious and unconscious levels. Encourage the partners to share any dreams, thoughts, or writings, if it feels safe to do so. Help the couple create a plan of how they will use the events and ideas from the session.

Stage 7. Dismantling the World

As with individuals, disassemble the scene once the couple has left the office, unless they indicate that they wish to dismantle it or your schedule constraints demand that the objects be replaced before the couple leaves. It is unusual for couples to choose to remove the objects from the tray prior to leaving. However, if they do, instruct each partner to remove one object from the scene and replace it on the shelf. Notice which item each removes. Then ask if you may help them put the objects away. The reasons for this are detailed in the dismantling the world stage in chapter 3.

UNDERSTANDING THE WORLD

If you are dismantling the world after the couple has left, use this as an opportunity to reexperience all that transpired in the session. Recall which objects each partner brought into the world and what the items seemed to mean to her/him. Recollect how the other partner responded. Call to mind the dynamics between the couple and the transformations that occurred. Because you are now alone with the sand world, your attention is not drawn to other aspects of the process. The tray now has your undivided focus. Additional insights can be gleaned. Apply what you observe to what you know about the dyad. See what the sand world reflects about them and the direction in which the couple is headed.

CLEARING THE WORLD

This is the time to replace objects on the shelves and continue to reflect on the couple's work. Complete your notes. If something puzzles or confuses you, you may wish to recreate the world at a later time, role playing each of the partners. As with individuals, time or circumstances may have precluded completion of all the stages. However, the building together has necessitated a new kind of interaction between the partners and has opened avenues of communication. By building a world together, they have created a unified product and gained greater understanding of their dynamics. And by sharing their perspectives, they have learned a little more about their individualities within the couple unit. Being held and respected as a couple has also conveyed a new viewpoint on coupledom.

Example of Couple's Communication Sandplay

We'd like to relate an example of sandplay therapy with a couple who had difficulty communicating. They had been living together for approximately two years before they came to us for therapy. Their tumultuous relationship was becoming unbearable, though they still loved each other and wanted to stay together. They had each worked individually in the sand tray but not together. Their strong wills and disregard for each other's space was evident as they constructed and rearranged the sand world. As they chose objects, they frequently observed each other. They occasionally made judgmental comments on the other's choices. At one point during the construction of the world, Jessica placed a three-headed dragon on a rock on the side where Matthew was working. Immediately afterwards Matthew placed a ferocious-looking monster on Jessica's side of the tray. Then, as they were silently experiencing the scene, nonverbal cues revealed to us that both were non-accepting of some of their partner's objects. As they were rearranging, they verbally expressed disagreements and moved the other's monsters away from their own spaces. During the communicating with the partner stage they clearly attributed divergent meanings to the objects and found it difficult to accept each other's differences, especially the presence of each other's monsters.

When we arrived at the therapy stage, we suggested that the two monsters, which were clearly antagonistic toward each other, dialogue. The two figures advanced toward each other and began screaming and fighting. The fight persisted until it was obvious that there would be no resolution. Responding to the physical tension we observed, we intervened and suggested that the partners stop and notice what they were experiencing in their bodies. Both described a lot of tension in their arms. Jessica felt tightness in her chest, throat, and jaw. Matthew felt a knot in his stomach and tension in his hips and legs. Recognizing that the session was almost over, we briefly had them experience the bodily sensations. We then suggested that they take some deep breaths, breathing in relaxation and exhaling the tension. As we could see their bodies relax, we suggested that they return to the tray and place their objects where each figure would feel safe for now.

After the couple arranged the world as they wanted to leave it for that day and took their photographs, we moved into the transition stage. We explored how each of the figures in the tray related to them. We encouraged them to discuss with each other what the experience was like for them, including their thoughts, emotions, and bodily feelings. Before we ended the session we asked them how they could apply what they had learned. With our coaching, they determined that any time a disagreement arose, they would (1) agree to remove themselves from the situation, (2) feel their feelings and notice their thoughts, (3) take deep breaths as they did during the session and visualize the monsters becoming relaxed.

We devoted their next session to teaching communication skills and sent them home to practice. The following week we moved back into the sand tray. We suggested that they each choose an object to represent the part of themselves that was like the monsters used in the previous tray. We let them know that they could choose the same objects (monsters) or different items. Having experienced the first tray and having practiced the breathing and communication skills, they chose less fierce objects. We proceeded to have the couple give voice to the objects, utilizing their new communication skills. Then we asked the couple to move away from the tray. We suggested that they physically push against each other, trying to move their partner. They both seemed to have equal strength and stayed virtually in the same position. Then we asked them to dance together, taking turns leading. They moved around the room with ease. After these exercises, we discussed the differences in their body sensations and the disparate outcomes between pushing against and cooperating. To end the sandplay we had them return to the tray and decide if the objects were still appropriate. They then chose even less aggressive objects and placed them side by side. During the transition stage, they discussed their reactions and revelations.

INDIVIDUATION TRAYS
Stage 1. Creating the World

There are many commonalities between the stages of couples doing a communication conjoint tray and individuation separate trays. In order to avoid redundancy, we describe only the ways the sessions differ. As we discussed earlier, we use separate trays when a couple is overly symbiotic or enmeshed, when one or both have difficulty freely expressing themselves with the other, or when for some reason they are unable to maintain individual identities within their union. This method of doing sandplay provides an opportunity for each to move toward individuation and to learn to respect and value each other's and their own uniqueness. Also, building worlds in separate trays offers an occasion to experience their own and their partner's ability to function in the other's presence as independent individuals. Although there are a variety of ways of conducting sandplay with couples using separate trays within the session, we focus on strengthening individuality and enhancing respect for the unique entity of each member of the dyad. We mention some alternative ways of directing the session with separate trays in the therapy stage of this section.

INTRODUCING SANDPLAY TO THE COUPLE

If one or both of the partners have not experienced sandplay before, give a complete introduction of the sandplay experience and materials (see the introducing sandplay to the client phase in chapter 3). If the clients have done sandplay, you might say, "This might be a good time for each of you to create your own scenes in the sand. As you well know, sometimes things get rough within a relationship and it is hard for one or both of you to express how you are feeling or to understand how the other person is feeling. Creating worlds in the sand can be a fun and different way to help you discover more about yourselves and each other and new ways to address those things that seem to get in the way of understanding and resolution. You may each choose whichever tray you want to work in and whether or not you want to wet the sand. Then each of you may build your world." If this is not an assessment tray you might add, "I only ask that you attend to what you are doing and not what your partner is doing. You'll have an opportunity later, if you wish, to share with each other what you have done." You may omit the *sharing* aspect if you believe the prospect of sharing will inhibit one or both of the partners.

In the event that they choose trays that are in close enough proximity to watch each other as they build, move one of the trays to another part of the room. To allow for greater freedom of creativity and independent construction of the worlds, we have found that it is best if the trays are not side by side. Allow from 20 to 40 minutes for them to construct their worlds. You might say, "You'll have approximately a half-hour to complete the creation of your scene. Sometimes one person finishes before the other. If one of you does so, then I encourage you to remain in your own space so that you do not disturb your partner. You might want to immerse yourself into your creation, just being with it. You may find in spending time with it that you will want to add, move, or remove one or more of the objects. Or you might find that it is exactly as you want to leave it. I will let you and your partner know when it is time to complete the constructing for today."

CONSTRUCTING SEPARATE WORLDS

Because the partners are working independently, there is less opportunity to follow the other's lead than there is when couples create a conjoint world. Encourage the couple to work/play without verbal communication and with no intrusion into what the other is doing. Be available to help them locate objects if they need your assistance. Discourage them from talking or looking at each other's trays during construction, both while each is building and once one partner has finished. As each partner creates her/his individual scene, there are many things to observe. Because the members have not yet established their separateness and are influenced by the other, it is important that you watch for signs of dependence, interference, sabotage, and influence.

Place yourself in a position that is comfortable to both builders and from which you are able to observe both of their trays. Notice each partner's choice and placement of objects; the pace, manner, and intention of her/his construction; and the world as it is coming into wholeness. Attend to each person's nonverbal expressions, movement, emotional tone, etc. This requires a great deal of focus, because you must be present to two separate operations simultaneously. If you wish, take notes of the concurrent events to help you remember all that is transpiring. See chapter 8 for details on recording couple sandplay sessions. Obviously, you cannot be attending completely to two events at one time. However, with total presence, you will be able to take in the important aspects of each partner's process. When one partner finishes, observe the patience and respect this person exhibits toward the one still working, and note whether the partner still building feels pressured to hurry. When the allotted time has elapsed, let the couple know that it is time to arrange their scenes the way they would like to finish them for now.

Stage 2. Experiencing and Rearranging

EXPERIENCING

Have each member of the couple immerse her/himself into her/his own world. Instruct each to silently reflect on the world s/he just created and to fully be in all aspects of her/his own world. You might say, "Please take a few minutes to fully experience all parts of your world. After spending a little time with the scene, you might want to walk around the tray and view the world from different angles. You'll find that things look different from the other sides of the tray." Allow sufficient time for both partners to completely experience their sand worlds even if one finishes before the allotted time. Although you cannot observe everything each of them is doing, remember to remain present and observant. Remain silent during this phase.

REARRANGING

Let the couple know that they may make any changes in their worlds. You might say, "Often when people immerse themselves in the world they see things that they may want to change. They may wish to move one object, remove another, or add something that they feel is missing. Or they may wish to leave it exactly as it is. You may each do anything you wish with your world."

EXPERIENCING THE PARTNER'S TRAY

This is an opportunity to further practice mutual respect and acceptance of differences, as well as to recognize presumptions they may have made about their partner. You might say, "If it is all right with both of you, could your partner take a look at your world?" If both respond affirmatively, continue, "Now take a few minutes to fully be in your partner's world. I ask you not to make any comments or touch anything in the tray. Take it in respectfully, knowing that it belongs to your partner." As you remain silent, observe any reactions each is having to her/his partner's world. Notice any looks of concern or confusion and any apparent desire to change something.

Stage 3. Communicating with the Partner

Instead of a conjoint world, the partners have constructed two completely different worlds to share. Although each partner may have divergent interpretations for each world, it is the meaning that the creator gives to the scene that must be honored and respected.

GUIDING THE PARTNER THROUGH THE WORLD

Instruct each client to take the partner on a tour of her/his world. Remind the observer to be silent, to listen attentively without responding verbally or nonverbally or adding any of her/his own interpretations. Advise her/him that this is her/his partner's world and is imbued with the meaning her/his partner gives to it.

REFLECTING ON THE PROCESS

After each partner has recounted her/his description of her/his separate world, encourage the couple to talk with each other about what sharing their worlds and experiencing each other's world was like for them. You might say, "As you can see, you were both given the same instructions and you created your own unique worlds. Would you tell each other how it felt constructing your own scenes with your partner in the room? Would you tell each other what it was like as you described your world to your partner and what it was like viewing and listening to your partner's explanation of her/his creation?" Again, encourage the more passive partner to begin. If the couple seems to have difficulty beginning, you might ask specific questions. For example: "How did you feel as you were each creating in your own tray?" "Were you curious about what your partner was doing or were you focused entirely on what you were doing?" As you have throughout the process, observe the dynamics between them. If they direct their comments to you, remind them to speak to each other. Allow several minutes for them to share their reflections.

Stage 4. Therapy

Having witnessed the tour each member gave her/his partner and having explored what the process was like for each of them, you now become more interactive. There are several different approaches from which to choose, depending on the couple and the situation. When working on individuation, we prefer to work therapeutically with each of the partners in her/his own world with the other partner observing and remaining silent. Deepen each person's exploration and understanding of her/his own world by asking questions and making therapeutic interventions evoked by the descriptions each shared.

For example, a couple with whom we worked had created two very different worlds. The woman had a very quiet world, sparsely filled with objects of nature and fanciful and celestial items. The man's tray was more abundant and active, filled with vehicles, people, and objects of nature. As we worked with the woman, we asked her if she was willing to move the star, which she described as magical, around the world. When she did so her partner clearly saw how the star brought a sense of comfort and peace to each figure and area of the tray that it touched. Observing respectfully and nonjudgmentally, he learned how important the stillness of nature was to his wife's well-being on a level he had not experienced before. He understood that her resistance to the hectic life he had thrust upon her was not obstinacy or unwillingness to interact with him.

As each partner's ego strength increases and partners become more individuated, there are several other ways to use separate trays. After each has given the other a tour and they have discussed what that was like for them, you may inquire if they would like to have the other enter their world and experience it more as a co-inhabitant and co-explorer than as an observer. Explore how they can share each other's world and the experiences they can have. The creator of the world maintains primary authority over her/his world, but the other partner may express feelings, ask questions, and interact. Have both partners first explore one world fully. See what it is like for them to inhabit that world together and what experiences they could have. Once they have done this they can move to the other's world. This interaction occurs only if the partners are individuated enough to maintain their identity and a sense of safety.

Another option is to have the partners place their trays side by side. Have them verbally explore how the worlds relate to each other. As the therapist, feel free to ask questions that investigate the similarities and differences between the issues arising in the trays. Also identify how each dealt with those issues in her/his sand world. Explore any theme or message that the worlds convey to each member of the couple. A third option is to suggest that they each take things from their separate worlds and bring them together to form a united world, moving from individuation to communication work. We leave these decisions to your discretion. Just be sure to conduct the session based on the couple's needs.

Stage 5. Documentation

The documentation stage is similar to the parallel stage with individuals and with couples building a conjoint world, except that each partner has the opportunity to photograph her/his own world and, with her/his permission, you photograph each world. (See the documentation stage in chapter 3.)

Stage 6. Transition

MEANING-MAKING AND CONNECTING THE SANDPLAY EXPERIENCE TO THE COUPLE'S REAL WORLD

Help the couple make sense of their worlds and connect the sandplay with their life outside of therapy. Facilitate exploration into the similarities and differences in their views of each other's worlds and what they learned about their partner. Have them check out any misconceptions they had. Have them examine how they can reinforce their individual identities. Encourage the couple to use what they learned from today's experience by following some of the suggestions presented in the transition stage in the communication sand tray section.

Stage 7. Dismantling the Worlds

After the couple has left, dismantle the worlds with the same level of awareness as described in earlier dismantle the world stages. You may gain additional insights about each member of the dyad as you attentively disassemble her/his tray. With this heightened awareness, some things may strike you about the etiology of the dissension within the couple or may reveal a key to enhancing the couple's relationship. As you reflect on the couple's work, you may wish to devise an organized way to think about what has transpired.

As you can see, there are alternative approaches to working with couples depending on their needs. In chapter 6 we provide further options of working with individuals and couples in a more directive manner.

. . . .

Stages of a Couple's Communication Sandplay Therapy Session

Communication trays are used when the partners are distant from each other or have difficulty connecting or communicating.

STAGE 1: CREATING THE WORLD

- *Introducing Sandplay to the Couple:* Briefly reintroduce sandplay. Let the couple know that they can break old patterns, learn new ways of communicating, and gain insights.
- *Constructing a Conjoint World:* Direct the couple to create a world in the same tray. Psychologically hold the dynamic of the couple unit. Remain attentive both to each individual and to the relationship.

STAGE 2: EXPERIENCING AND REARRANGING

- *Experiencing:* Remain silent as the couple quietly reflects on the world they created together. Instruct them to view the entire world, not just their own objects.
- *Rearranging:* Inform the couple that they may leave the world as it is or change it. They may consult with each other during this activity.

STAGE 3: COMMUNICATING WITH THE PARTNER

- *Guiding the Partner through the World:* Observe silently as each partner sequentially guides the other through the world. Remind them that each person's perspective is valid for her/him, although they each may have different ideas of what the objects represent.
- *Reflecting on the Process:* Encourage the couple to discuss the experience of creating a world together and what they noticed about their individual perspectives.

STAGE 4: THERAPY

- Become a more interactive part of the process and explore the world with the couple. Utilize a variety of therapeutic interventions, keeping the focus in the tray as much as possible.

STAGE 5: DOCUMENTATION

- Give each partner an opportunity to take a photograph from her/ his perspective. With their permission, take your own photograph.

STAGE 6: TRANSITION

- *Meaning-Making:* Help the couple recognize that the final word on interpretation is unique to the individual.
- *Connecting the Sandplay Experience to the Couple's Real World:* Encourage the couple to link what transpired in the tray to their relationship. Investigate patterns, issues, and solutions which were revealed in the sandplay. If process photographs were taken, review them. Suggest follow-up activities.

STAGE 7: DISMANTLING THE WORLD

- *Understanding the World:* Dismantle the world after the couple has left, recalling which objects each partner selected, the responses of each partner, and the dynamics within and outside the tray.
- *Clearing the World:* Continue reflecting on the couple's work as you replace the objects; record your notes.

. . . .

Stages of a Couple's Individuation Sandplay Therapy Session

Separate trays are used when partners are enmeshed and need to individuate or when they have reservations about expressing themselves with each other.

STAGE 1: CREATING THE WORLD

- *Introducing Sandplay to the Couple:* Briefly reintroduce sandplay. Let the couple know this can help them learn about each other.
- *Constructing Separate Worlds:* Instruct the couple to create their own worlds simultaneously in separate trays without intrusion. Psychologically hold the process of each partner and the dynamic of the couple unit. Remain attentive both to each individual and to the relationship.

STAGE 2: EXPERIENCING AND REARRANGING

- *Experiencing:* Remain silent as the partners quietly reflect on their own creation. Encourage them to view their own world from different perspectives.
- *Rearranging:* Inform each partner that s/he may leave her/his world as it is or change it.
- *Experiencing the Partner's Tray:* If both partners agree, direct each to view and immerse her/himself into her/his partner's world without comment or encroachment.

STAGE 3: COMMUNICATING WITH THE PARTNER

- *Guiding the Partner through the World:* Observe quietly as each partner sequentially guides the other through her/his world. Instruct each to respectfully and silently attend to the tour, allowing for personal interpretation.
- *Reflecting on the Process:* Encourage the couple to discuss what it was like creating their worlds with their partners in the room. Ask what it was like sharing their worlds and experiencing the other's world.

STAGE 4: THERAPY

- Become a more interactive part of the process. Explore each partner's world with her/him as the other silently observes. Utilize a variety of therapeutic interventions, keeping the focus in the tray.

STAGE 5: DOCUMENTATION

- Give each partner an opportunity to take a picture of her/his own world. With permission, take your own photograph.

STAGE 6: TRANSITION

- *Meaning-Making/Connecting the Sandplay Experience to the Couple's Real World:* Encourage the couple to link what transpired in the trays to their relationship. Suggest possible follow-up activities to implement pattern changes. Invite them to explore the meanings of the objects for themselves.

STAGE 7: DISMANTLING THE WORLD

- Dismantle the worlds after the couple has left, recalling each individual's approach, the responses of each partner, and the dynamics within and outside the trays. Reflect on the couple's work as you replace the objects; record your notes.

. . . .

Things to Remember with Couples

Issues particular to couple therapy:

- Avoid triangulation.
- See the couple as a unit.
- Have partners address each other, not you.
- Encourage couples to respect their different perspectives.
- Also review the summary "Things to Remember during the Creating Stage" in chapter 3.

. . . .

Things to Observe with Couples

- The individual as well as the couple dynamics.
- The couple's dysfunctional as well as functional behavior.
- The couple's verbal and nonverbal communication.
- The interaction with each other's objects.
- Disclosing and withholding behaviors.
- Balance/imbalance of power.
- Each partner's contribution to the creative process.
- The variations in the roles each takes.
- The partners' differences in pace, style, intensity, etc.
- The partner's reactions to and observations of each other.
- The ability of the partners to listen attentively and tolerate divergent ideas.
- The degree to which one partner is influenced by the other.
- Also review the summary "Things to Observe" in chapter 3.

·· 5 ··

SPONTANEOUS SAND TRAYS WITH CHILDREN AND FAMILIES

Sandplay with Children

Our focus thus far has been on detailing the many aspects of sandplay work with adults. Many therapists, however, work with children (younger than 11–12 years of age) and adolescents (12–13 to 18 years of age) and would like to expand their repertoire of play modalities. Others would like to develop their practices to include children and/ or adolescents. We have found that many psychotherapists are deeply concerned about the fact that they have had very few courses and very little guidance in working with youth. Then, after graduate school, they are suddenly faced with numerous child clients and few skills to deal with them.

Frequently, parents, schools, and family service organizations refer troubled children and adolescents to therapists. These referrals will no doubt persist or continue to increase as children and adolescents become even more saddened, angry, and violent in a culture that tends to emotionally ignore and dispossess its youth. Play, specifically sandplay, is an ideal approach to working with troubled children and adolescents. It allows them to access their innermost thoughts and feelings and resolve issues unconsciously, without being deliberately confronted and alienated.

As Lowenfeld (1935) first realized, play with sand, water, and objects is an ideal way for a child to objectify her/his ideas of the world so that s/he can define them, confine them, and eventually master them. Children and young adolescents tend to be more concrete than older adolescents and adults and so often need physical form to express themselves. Just as with adults, there appears to be at least two layers of meaning in a child's sandplay, the surface meaning and the symbolic meaning. Sandplay can be a powerful medium to enable a child to communicate both the conscious and unconscious material s/he seems unable to clarify. Weinrib aptly stated, "Sandplay therapy is essentially an unconscious, or at some stages, a semiconscious process. It has an almost magical attraction for children and a powerful efficacy" (1983, p. 87).

We experienced the magical attraction of sandplay when we worked with 9-year-old Maria. According to her parents, she had been reluctant to come to therapy. Maria hesitantly walked into the therapy room. Her eyes widened with wonder as she viewed the many objects that lined the walls. And then she saw the sand trays. She immediately drifted to the tray with the fine coral sand and sifted the sand with her fingers. When we mentioned that the surrounding objects could all be used in the sand trays, her eyes opened wider and a smile began to appear on her face. This wonderland of symbols and sand trays disarmed Maria. Children's natural attraction to play and to the sand make sandplay an ideal therapeutic tool.

Although work with children in sandplay is somewhat similar to the work with adults we have described in chapter 3, there are some differences. Unlike in adults, language and abstract thinking are limited in children. Not until adolescence does the transition to abstract thinking occur. In sandplay, however, children are able to express their innermost conscious and unconscious thoughts and ideas without communicating them verbally. Contrary to what usually occurs with adults, children often have no conscious knowledge of what is happening inside themselves or what the sand world is about, even after the play has been explored. Children more frequently choose not to talk about their play but wish to merely experience it. However, something transformational does occur. The unconscious mind is able to resolve issues, often quickly, that it has placed into physical form through play. Changes in behavior occur spontaneously as a result.

Sandplay with children takes more varied forms than with adults. These variations are usually governed by the child's imagination and creativity and your direction. Sometimes a child's session looks much like an adult session, in that it advances through the stages described in chapter 3. More often the activity level in the tray is greater, either due to the child's creation of a moving/action tray on her/his own or to her/his invitation to the therapist to be a player in the sand world. Although adults may use more than one tray, especially upon your direction to amplify an area in the tray that seems significant to them (see chapter 6), children may spontaneously use multiple trays. Children frequently instigate games, such as hide and seek, in which they include the therapist. Usually they develop the rules as they play.

Because the children we see in therapy are at different stages of ego development, it is vital to remember that the ego strength of many children may be very tenuous and their defenses may not yet be in place. Ego strength and conscious awareness of oneself develop slowly, growing throughout childhood and adolescence. It is therefore important to be much less confrontive than you might be with adults. When challenged, children often become extremely anxious and refuse to cooperate. Anyone who has children or has worked with children no doubt has experienced these phenomena. In order to reduce resistance and apprehension, we usually speak to children about anxiety-provoking topics in the third person. For example, we might say, "Many children find it hard to talk about what happened to them," instead of, "You seem to be having a hard time talking about what happened." Or we deal with upsetting subjects with play therapies only.

In sandplay with children we keep the play in the tray and consistently use third person references. This is not always the case with adults who frequently make the connection between objects and themselves or someone else in their lives. Adolescents see this connection less frequently than adults. Children rarely do. For example, adults often identify objects as themselves or people in their lives, whereas children usually do not. Remember, it is not important for the child to see the connection. The unconscious mind will do the work. We do not press for any verbal understanding of the tray unless the child addresses the topic on her/his own. Children more often than adults complete only the creating stage and then do not wish to talk about their sand worlds. Adolescents are more likely to explore the world and its significance than younger children.

A story told to us by one of our workshop participants illustrates how unconscious resolution does happen for children in its own way and time. Jeff, a young school counselor who had limited experience working with play techniques, spent most of his sessions talking to his clients. He became increasingly frustrated by his inability to work with Adam, one of his fifth grade students, who had been referred to Jeff by Adam's homeroom teacher for severely disruptive behavior in class. Whenever Jeff questioned Adam or confronted him with his behavior, Adam withdrew into himself. Adam spent most of the sessions sitting quietly twiddling his fingers while Jeff talked. His behavior in class did not change. Upon talking to a colleague who had taken our workshop, Jeff decided to use sandplay for some of his clients. Although he knew very little about sandplay therapy, he read our workshop materials, bought a sand tray, and collected some objects. The next week, when Adam entered the room, he immediately headed for the sand tray. Over the next several weeks Adam played in the sand, creating many battles. Jeff sat silently by and watched. Even without any verbal intervention on Jeff's part, Adam's behavior began to change. The teachers and parents were pleased because Adam was less disruptive and appeared happier. In this instance the healing process was clearly nonverbal and nonconfrontive. Jeff was so impressed with the results that he decided to attend sandplay workshops to better understand what was happening in sand tray work and how to effectively facilitate the process.

Although there are many aspects of the sandplay that no doubt impacted Adam, one of the benefits was probably that the sand tray served as a transitional object for him. When the ego is ready to emerge, the sand tray enables the child, as Winnicott described, to begin to differentiate between the *I* and the *not-I* in the development of the ego. This differentiation normally occurs in early childhood, which distinguishes work with children from adults. We have noticed that in some cases, as Weinrib suggested, the sand tray replaces the therapist as the transitional object, since "the transition moves at least partially from the person of the therapist to the sandtray as it becomes an independent object" (1983, p. 52). We concur with Weinrib that the sand tray cultivates independence at the same time it provides security. Even later, when the ego is already developed and the person is more consciously aware of her/himself as a separate entity, the sand tray may serve as a transitional object when unresolved childhood issues are addressed.

We have found that working with children can be both satisfying and challenging. To therapists who are not familiar with child therapy, the disorder or mess that children tend to create can be disturbing and/or time-consuming. Children often use a multitude of objects, several trays, and an excess of water during sandplay. Additionally, children's lack of insight and limited ability to verbalize what is occurring internally may be disconcerting to the therapist. When there is neither verbalization nor immediate behavior change, the therapist might wonder if any progress is occurring. In addition, children frequently repeat the same behavior for several sessions. This is yet another time that self-doubt may creep into the therapist's mind, provoking questions about her/his effectiveness. Also it is necessary to create and enforce rules with children, especially those who are developmentally immature, who act out, or who are destructive. This need sometimes feels antithetical to the therapist's stance as an unconditionally accepting helper. Furthermore, play therapy requires that the therapist be willing to play on the child's level. You will want to consider these factors when you decide whether to work with children.

If you decide to work with children, the following information about what you might see in sandplay at different developmental levels, patterns of sandplay you might encounter, and therapeutic interventions you might use will help to prepare you for this endeavor.

Developmental Stages in Sandplay

It is helpful to have a framework from which to assess the child's stage of development in her/his sandplay. Understanding what to expect and what the child's play may mean from a developmental perspective can assist you in evaluating the child's level of functioning and facilitating and guiding the process. "When such an analysis occurs . . . it may provide input for the adoption of a therapeutic stance" (Stewart, 1990, p. 42) and give you information to speed up the process, a benefit in this era of managed care and brief therapy.

We keep the discussion on development brief, because it is beyond the scope of this chapter to recount developmental theories in depth. We assume that if you are working with children, you know the most highly regarded developmental theories, such as those proposed by Erik Erikson and Jean Piaget. Those working in the field should also be aware of more current research that pays attention to gender differences and issues of cultural diversity.

While noticing the individual's progression in her/his own sandplay is of greater benefit than finding her/his place in a developmental paradigm, familiarity with generally accepted developmental stages is valuable. We have chosen to provide information gleaned from Dora Kalff's and Charles T. Stewart's writings because they are both experienced sandplay therapists and have shared their findings regarding the type of sandplay children exhibit at different stages. Our goal here is to increase your awareness of behaviors you might find in sandplay therapy that reveal the stage at which the child is functioning and that signal progress. The child's maturational level and development lags are frequently revealed by the different types of play, the objects chosen, and themes in the tray.

According to Kalff, whose perspective on stages of ego development concurs with Erich Neumann's theory, "in the first phase [up to approximately 6 or 7 years of age], the ego expresses itself chiefly in pictures, [in] which animals and vegetation predominate. The next stage [up to approximately 11 or 12 years of age] brings battles, which appear again and again, especially in puberty. By now the child is so strengthened that he can take upon himself the battle with external influences and he can come to grips with them. Finally, he is admitted to the environment as a person and becomes a member of the collective" (1980, pp. 32–33). Many sandplay therapists find this to be a fitting model (e.g., Bradway & McCoard, 1997; Dundas, 1990; Stewart, 1990). Although we have seen some of these patterns emerge in our clients' trays, we agree with many sandplay therapists that these motifs of animals, then battles, and then community do not always appear. However, we find that the rhythms and patterns that we do see help shed light on our understanding of the client's process. We observe that the scenes frequently move from chaos (in earlier stages of development) to order (as children mature and develop a greater sense of identity).

Charles T. Stewart (1990) has devised a method for the evaluation of sandplay synthesizing Neumann's, Erikson's, and Piaget's developmental stages. Although he has acknowledged the limitations of his method, we present it here to encourage you to explore it in the sandplay work you do with children. In our experience, while we concur with his findings, we observe that the child's type of play sometimes does not fit this chronological model. Furthermore, our experience has not been broad enough, to date, to ascertain if this model applies across cultures.

In Stewart's paradigm, games of appearance and disappearance, such as peek-a-boo and hide and seek, occur in the first stage, Infancy II, which spans the ages of 7–10 months to 2 years. We generally do not do sandplay with children under the age of 2½ years because of developmental limitations. However, there may be times that older children are functioning psychologically at this stage due to childhood trauma or neglect that arrested their development in separating from their mothers and beginning to build trust in themselves and the outside world. We need to pay attention not only to the child's chronological age but to how the play discloses the maturational level at which the child is functioning (see chapter 9 for more detail). Children functioning in the Infancy II stage often fill the tray with all the objects at hand. They may also focus on making things happen, like moving, sifting, watching, and listening to the impact of the sand within the tray. In addition, they may push or fling objects into the tray to see how they fit and may bury and uncover objects in the sand.

Stewart's second stage, Early Childhood I (EC I), covers ages 1–2 to 3–4 years. The ages overlap with Infancy II because of differences in development that occur. In this stage games of order and disorder appear. Children are striving to acquire autonomy. This brings about internal conflict, because they are struggling against the parents who have given and continue to give them nurturance. While rebelling against their parents' control, they are conflicted between dependence and independence. The sand tray provides a safe, limited space where children can begin to develop their autonomy. This is a time when you might observe them dealing with issues of retention and elimination (i.e., to hold on and to let go, confrontation of opposites, building and destroying). Our experience supports Stewart's observations that there is a great deal of chaos as well as creating and annihilating. For example, a 4-year-old client created sand trays, building and destroying chaotic scenes with a multitude of objects, for several consecutive sessions. As time passed, he began to be more discriminating as to which objects he chose and began lining them up across the tray. He spent several sessions repeating this activity. Although the objects did not form a coherent pattern, he was beginning to bring greater order to his world, in the tray and outside of the office.

Stewart's third stage, Early Childhood II (EC II), spans the ages of 3–4 years to 6–7. In this period the child is the central focus in the games s/he plays. Actions that involve being attacked and/or having to escape are manifested frequently in the tray. According to Stewart, the emphasis here is not on being the attacker but on flight from danger. Children's aggression or conflict tends to be less organized than the battles exhibited at an older age. Conflicts appear, but there is more evidence of a central figure portrayed in the tray (e.g., a house or person under attack, a fenced-in area, an island or a pool of water in which a central figure appears). This is a transitional period when the child experiences anxieties about exercising independence as s/he moves away from parents toward peers. During this stage, children also test the limits with behaviors such as allowing sand to fall to the floor and resisting ending the session at the appropriate time.

We find that as the child transitions from EC II to Stewart's Middle Childhood (MC), which spans 6–7 to 11–12 years of age, s/he moves into an oppositional stage, with dualities displayed in the tray across or apart from each other. At this *fighting* stage, we are often invited into the tray as an opponent in the battle, corroborating Bradway and McCoard's experiences (1997). According to Stewart, MC games of peer sexual differentiation appear. Male and female trays begin to differ significantly, although for both genders there is greater integration of the self than at earlier stages. Whereas fighting or danger may occur for both sexes, boys are more likely to portray battle scenes between cowboys and Indians or soldiers, while girls are more likely to portray individual struggles with opposing forces and often use dangerous animals instead of armed forces. Girl's trays are commonly more sedate and peaceful.

During this oppositional stage, land masses may be separated from each other (e.g., by walls, fences, gullies, rivers). Signs of gaining ability to set boundaries and deal with internal and external conflicts appear, for example, with the use of fences providing protection and a limit. But gradual removal of the barriers or inclusion of bridges made of a variety of materials permits connections between areas in the tray. This may indicate that the client is linking opposing parts of her/himself. During this transition, as integration and acceptance of opposing sides of the self occur, the objects tend to become balanced and centered in the tray. They may come closer to each other, touch, or form a circle in the center. The circle may be the unconscious attempt of the psyche to heal and unify itself. According to Bradway and McCoard, "Sources of energy, including wells, food, or gasoline pumps, [also] often appear during periods of transition" (1997, p. 112). It is not unusual to observe children beginning to include nurturing activities as well as sources of energy in their trays. When a 9-year-old client's trays began changing from our being opponents fighting in the tray to our having a tea party where she prepared and served our meals, it was evident that a shift was occurring. The shift back and forth happened several times, complete with accidental spilling of the sand.

Stewart's paradigm ends when the child reaches approximately 12 years of age. It is at this time, according to Kalff's model, that adaptation to the collective commences. The adolescent's perspective of her/his place in society begins to shift, as the ego has developed to the point where the adolescent is gaining enough strength to become a member of "the collective." Although teenagers are often secretive and are hesitant to trust adults, they are beginning to understand their place in the adult world. It is a time to master new tasks that arise and resist the pull toward the comfort of the familiar. Not only are teenagers dealing with the dilemma of moving from being children to becoming adults, but they also receive mixed messages from their parents about their roles. They often feel that they must show the world (and the adult therapist) that they are grown up. Because they perceive sandplay as childish, adolescents are often hesitant to play in the sand. However, if framed invitingly, sandplay can be seen as an opportunity to assert their dominance or control at a time when they are struggling with separation issues. Sandplay allows the *child aspect* of themselves to be active even while their *individuating self* gains autonomy and takes the leadership role with the adult therapist. This period is evidenced in the tray by scenes portraying real-life situations and a sense of social perspective. Gender differences continue to be apparent. Males are more likely to build outdoor scenes, while females tend to build indoor ones.

Julie, 12 years old, was referred to us because her parents felt that she was having difficulty adjusting to her parents' divorce and her father's remarriage. Her father had recently married a woman with two daughters of her own. Julie lived part-time with each parent. In therapy, Julie spent several weeks creating the interior of a house in the sand tray. There were two parents and three children figures. Each week the activity in the sand tray house changed, moving from conflict between the children and between the parents to greater harmony within the household. It seemed initially that Julie was struggling with the disharmony between her biological parents at the same time she was adapting to the situation with her stepsisters. She continued to recreate her situation in the sand until she began to internalize the equanimity between her father and stepmother and began to adjust to having siblings. The household within the tray mirrored the changes she was making outside the therapy office.

Patterns in Children's Sandplay

There are idiosyncratic patterns that often appear in sandplay with children. Because most children are less able than adults to filter out unwanted stimuli and to set their own internal limits, you may need to establish clear limits and avoid overstimulating them with a profusion of objects. When you are furnishing your sandplay therapy room, your intent is to provide an extensive language for the unconscious and conscious mind of the child to have at her/his disposal, not to create the semblance of a toy store. Remember, with children who are easily overstimulated or distracted, you can cover the shelves or limit the number of exposed objects.

It is not unusual for children to dump an abundance of objects into the tray or build very chaotic scenes. This most often occurs with clients who are very young, either chronologically or developmentally. Also, children who have very little impulse control or are awash with emotion that needs release will indiscriminately empty objects from the shelves into the tray. You may wish to allow this excess to persist for several sessions (if you can tolerate it), to determine the purpose of the behavior and to see if it changes naturally over time. Children often will repeat a pattern until it no longer serves a purpose. At that time a shift occurs and the behavior changes. If you determine that the child needs external limits set for her/him, you may limit the number of objects s/he takes from the shelf (see "Limiting the Number of Objects" in chapter 7). The opposite can also be true; children sometimes create overly ordered or vacant worlds. It is important to assess the meaning of these behaviors by reviewing the child's psychological history and current situation (e.g., deprivation/neediness, chaos in her/his life, perfectionism), developmental stage, and impulse control.

Just as some children use an overabundance of objects, some children use multiple trays. Because this is not an unusual occurrence, it is advisable to have at least three trays available if you frequently work with children. Children seem to compartmentalize different aspects of themselves. An example of this is an 8-year-old who created three worlds. During the transition stage of the therapy session she stated that the worlds were like different things in her life that she liked. Sometimes a child's imagination propels her/him to continually expand the world and s/he needs additional trays for different parts of the world. We worked with a 6-year-old who needed another tray for the pet store and another for his grandmother's house.

Children and adolescents frequently play out transference issues in the tray, especially if they see you as someone to rescue them or to take control over them and/or over what happens to them. One 11-year-old with whom we worked came into the session after an altercation with her teacher. She constructed a sand world that reflected issues of power and control. When the session was close to ending she frantically added many objects to all three trays she had created. As she did this she said, "You sure are going to have a lot to clean up." In essence, she created a situation in which she was punishing us instead of the teacher by increasing our clean-up time. This complex response of projection and self-empowerment was not conscious.

Unlike most adults who wet the sand in the tray, some children flood the tray with water. If the child floods the tray, you will have to decide whether you are comfortable allowing this to happen again. If you are not, but the child repeatedly seems to want to create a body of water in which to float, sink, or drown an object, you can provide an empty tray for such purposes. The child is free to fill the empty tray with water or place a small amount of sand in the bottom of the tray that can provide a base but will not absorb all the water. The child is then able to sink items, drown people or other figures, bury objects under water, and have articles move through the water. If you are not disturbed by the repetition of flooding the tray, you may allow this behavior to continue. If this is the case, you might wish to alter one of your trays to accommodate this flooding behavior (see "Sand Trays" section in chapter 2). You may also wish to provide bowls or other receptacles that can be inserted in the sand-filled tray. The containers should be large enough to hold objects, so that the child can float or move things in a body of water surrounded by land.

Some children repeatedly fill containers with sand and then empty them. This seems to give them a sense of power and control. Children may even want to empty the sand from the tray and then refill it. This is another reason to have an empty tray available. The emptying and refilling may be kindred to the repetition of building and destroying, another common activity for children. They often create recurring sequences of building and destroying in one session and usually in one tray. Although all change in the tray, for both the child and the adult, is a form of building, altering, and destroying, the blatant building of structures with sand or objects and then smashing and destroying them is more common with children than adults. This pattern generally reflects a release of anger or need for empowerment. It also confers on the child the knowledge that s/he has the ability to create and destroy and then create again. In addition, some children need to put away their objects at the end of the session. This further demonstrates the child's need to have power over her/his world and allows her/him to recognize that s/he has the ability to create, then break down and recreate or repair the world.

Children also bury and hide objects in the tray. For very young children this may reflect experimentation with object permanence. For older children there are often issues that they are either unaware of or choose not to explore. Often the hidden objects represent aspects of themselves that they do not accept. The uncovering of objects is frequently evidence of greater willingness to see or work on unresolved issues.

There are other patterns particular to children. The types of objects children select and the way they use them often differ from adults. Children use fantasy and movie figures, prehistoric animals, cowboys and Indians, and army figures more frequently than do adults. They often create idyllic scenes in the tray. Certain themes frequently appear in children's trays, such as battles, power struggles, and conflicts with authority figures. Often the child brings into the sand tray an object that is a power or authority figure and one that is powerless. This behavior is readily understood, since developmentally there are both internal and external struggles for power and control in children's lives as they move toward individuation and self-empowerment. In addition, adolescents tend to play out themes of identity and individuation.

Some behaviors dictate that sandplay be avoided and another modality chosen. When children throw sand or try to climb into the tray, you may opt for another activity. These actions reflect an inability to adhere to the limits that sandplay requires. If you determine that the child is not developmentally or emotionally equipped to play in the sand (see chapter 9), you will need, at least temporarily, to choose another therapeutic modality.

Because of the limited scope of this chapter, we have discussed briefly the significance of all of these patterns and their implications. However, if the child exhibits repetitive patterns and her/his verbal and nonverbal communication, behavior, and history fail to give you sufficient clues about what is happening, you might wish to consult with a child therapist or professional in child development and/or read some of the sandplay books or symbol dictionaries listed in appendix 3.

DIVERSE MODES OF SANDPLAY
Spontaneous Static Trays

Similar to adults, when children create spontaneous static trays, they build a scene or world in which there is no ongoing action. The stages and directions you will give parallel the ones described in chapter 3. As mentioned previously, this material was adapted from De Domenico (1989). However, there are variations that need to be addressed before you work in the sand with children. We have found that many children are immediately attracted to the objects/toys and sand trays when they enter the room and frequently initiate play in the sand, sometimes on their first visit. We give children permission to play with the sand and objects whenever they ask or appear interested, if it is appropriate. Because play is a natural process in a child's life, because the child is usually unaware of symbolic meanings, and because you will not be confronting the child, it is not as necessary as with adults to create a trusting relationship prior to sandplay. Instead, trust usually develops as you hold and honor the creations. Sessions for older children and adolescents are usually limited to an hour unless you find that an hour tends not to be enough time to complete the sandplay process. If this is the case, you can schedule a 90-minute session. Young children may not be able to concentrate for extended periods and may become restless and distracted. If you find that the child you are seeing has a short attention span, you might reduce your session to 30 or 40 minutes.

During the introducing sandplay to the client phase, only brief explanations about why we use sandplay are given to children, especially young ones. For children who are reticent to play in the sand, we might say, "Sometimes children have a hard time putting their thoughts and feelings into words. People often think in pictures. So frequently they find that it is easier to make a picture of something they are thinking about and feeling than to talk. In this tray you can use the sand, the water, and/or any of these objects on the shelves to make the pictures. This will help us find out what is happening inside of you that creates those problems we just talked about. Then, we can find a way of making it better." Reluctant children are often shy, perfectionistic, or afraid of doing something wrong. It is vital that you spend extra time acquainting them with the environment and that you give frequent permission. If they are still hesitant and uncomfortable with the process, let them know that you can find other ways than sandplay to communicate. Tell them that they may use the sand whenever they wish. Very often these children will come back to the tray in subsequent sessions.

Before the child begins to play, let her/him know that s/he can make anything in the sand s/he wishes and that there is no right or wrong way to play. Show her/him the sand, water, and objects. It is then necessary to explain your rules for play in your office. Each one of you will no doubt develop your own rules. We tend to make no more regulations than necessary for productive play. Our first rule for all play is that the child may not hurt her/himself or us in any way. We ask that the child keep the water and sand inside the sand tray, and we let her/him know that s/he may use as many objects and as much water as s/he wishes. We allow all objects on the shelves to be placed in the sand trays. Prior to the arrival of a hyperactive or destructive child, we remove the objects that we are concerned might be broken. Except in extraordinary cases, guidelines such as these are not required for adolescents and adults.

The introducing sandplay to the client phase with adolescents is similar to adults. What we note with adolescents is that they tend to disdain play because they believe sandplay is for "kids" only, not for "grownups." Let the adolescent know that it is always her/his choice whether to use the sand trays. It may, however, be necessary to stress that these materials are not only for children. Tell the adolescent that many of your adult clients use the sand trays regularly and find them very helpful in resolving what is happening in their lives. Inform the adolescent that you too use the sand tray to help you understand and solve your problems. It is even more important with adolescents than with adults that you model putting your hands in the tray. Sift or move the sand, thus showing the adolescent that you as an adult and a therapist enjoy the sand and feel comfortable using it. You might suggest that it would be okay for your adolescent client to merely doodle or write in the sand if s/he wishes, while the two of you talk. This activity creates familiarity and comfort with the sand and serves to produce a mild altered state. It also distracts adolescents enough so that they are able to talk more freely during the session.

As with adults, we suggest sandplay to adolescents when it might benefit them. It may, however, take longer for adolescents to gravitate toward the tray than it does for children or adults. We do not pressure adolescents to play in the sand, but frequently, as trust develops, they respond favorably to our suggestion to do sandplay or even turn automatically toward the tray to play out their issues.

When the child or adolescent is finished creating the world, proceed to the experiencing and rearranging stage as you would with adults. You might say, "This picture is just like a world. It is a special place. Take a little time to pretend that you live in this place. You can get up and walk around the tray if you like and see this world from all the different sides." Young children spend very little time in this process because their ability to sit still and reflect is limited. Older children and adolescents take a longer time, using their imagination to pretend they live in the world. At this point some children spontaneously begin to talk about what it is like to live in the world. If this is the case, do not stop them but let the dialogue flow naturally into the therapy stage.

Young children, as well as some older children and adolescents, may resist talking about their worlds. If this occurs, do not pressure clients to continue but instead end the play after the experiencing and rearranging stage. Let them know that they can talk with you about this or any other world they create at any time, if they wish. Often older children and adolescents begin to talk about their sandplay as they become more familiar and comfortable with the process.

If the child or adolescent is willing to talk, proceed to the touring the world phase. Ask the child if s/he can be your guide or teacher and tell you all about the world and what is going on there. Giving the role of guide or teacher to the adolescent has particular value, because it puts the adolescent in the position of power and knowledge. This is especially important during this period of individuation. Before the client begins to guide you through the world, inquire if it is all right for you to ask her/him some questions as s/he talks.

If you are seeing a young child, you might wish to follow Lowenfeld's technique to elicit more extensive responses. She asked children to pretend that she was a visitor from another country who knew nothing about the children's way of life. She would then request that they explain everything about their world so that she would be able to understand what everything meant and what it was like to live there. We have found that, because of the times we live in, children are more prone to explain in detail if we suggest that we are a friendly alien from another planet. We make sure we enter into the play and pretend we know nothing and don't understand this strange planet. So that the play is less threatening, especially for young children, we sometimes use a special alien puppet named Poaweil who is wise and kind. Usually the children address all their answers to Poaweil. Most children are comfortable and enjoy pretending in this manner.

If children are hesitant to describe their sand world or don't know where to start, you might ask them to use their imagination and tell you any story they want to make up about the world. We saw an 8-year-old boy who had been physically abused by his stepfather. When asked to talk about his world he would become very anxious. However, he loved to tell stories and often regaled us with lengthy tales of

Bob, the innocent bunny, who was beaten, tramped on, and eventually killed and eaten by the wolf. Each week he would create a new sand-play episode in the life of Bob. These stories seemed to parallel his own life and fears.

During the therapeutic interventions phase, as with adults, you can ask the child or adolescent to have objects talk to each other. Older children and adolescents are capable of dialoguing fairly extensively. You can also use psychodrama effectively. Ask the child to show you what is happening. For example, you might say, "Show me how the bunny runs away" or "Show me how the wolf hits Bob." Then take the action out of the tray into the therapy room. You might say, "Pretend you are the wolf and this teddy bear is Bob. Now show me how the wolf hits Bob." This exercise can be adapted to anger release when the child is ready. Imaging, or using the imagination, is another effective technique, because fantasy is a normal part of a child's daily play/work. You might say, "Pretend that I have come to visit the hunchback that you said lives in the castle. Would you ask him if he would be willing to take me on a tour of the castle?" If the child says that the hunchback is willing, you might ask the child to have the hunchback tell you exactly what all the rooms look like and what is happening in them. These techniques keep the play and communication with you nonthreatening and enjoyable for the child. At the same time, you are able to elicit valuable information and help her/him resolve unconscious matters.

Most children want photographs of their worlds. During the documentation stage, ask a young child from what position s/he would like you to take the photograph. For children capable of taking their own pictures, the actual taking of the photograph with a Polaroid camera is frequently an adventure and a learning experience. Make sure you teach the child how to take the photo, but then give her/him the option of taking it from any perspective s/he wishes. Children often treasure their photographs and use them as transitional objects to connect them to therapy and to you when they are not in session. We have found that some children like to take the photograph of the tray that we keep for our files as well. If you are comfortable with this and think the child is capable of taking one that is adequate for your files, allow her/him to take the picture.

For older children and adolescents, proceed with the transition stage as you would with adults, but less in depth. If the child or adolescent has explored her/his world, you might ask, "How was that, making the world?" or "In what way is your life like that sand tray at times?" or "What in the sand tray do you want to remember?" If there has been some resolution in the tray, you might ask, "How can you make that happen in real life?" Some children and adolescents are willing to explore these questions; others are not. Take your lead from the child. Again, remember that it is not important for the child to consciously know what the tray means or what is happening inside of her/him for sandplay to be effective. Trust the unconscious mind of the child.

The following is a case example of an 8-year-old girl who resolved many of her inner conflicts by creating spontaneous trays. Molly was referred to us by her school principal for outbursts of anger and hurting other children by tripping or shoving them. According to her parents, there was nothing happening in the home that might explain her behavior. They felt that the problem originated in the school. When Molly arrived at our office she was immediately drawn to the tray and began to play in the sand. She built frantically for a while, and when she was finished she spontaneously told us a highly animated story. Throughout the course of therapy she told the same story many times. She created many sand worlds where figures (sometimes animals and sometimes people) were forced by a male figure to do a variety of acts that they did not want to do. If they refused they were beaten and humiliated. When questioned about the world, she refused to talk and instead changed the subject. After a few sessions with the parents, the mother admitted that the father was very controlling and would at times become violent with Molly when she refused to obey. The principal also stated that Molly's teacher tended to be authoritative. After playing out being dominated for some time, Molly suddenly shifted and began to play being the one in control. Sometimes Molly would take this theme out of the tray and act out the role of the one who could tell us exactly what to do. Usually she would play house or school. We would follow her demands. Our only rule was that she could not hurt herself or us. Shortly after this shift in play, her behavior in school changed. With continued work with her parents and teachers, Molly once again became the cheerful little girl she had previously been.

Spontaneous Moving Trays

According to De Domenico (1988), there are two types of worlds that children frequently build spontaneously. The spontaneous static world that we just discussed is usually built by older children and adolescents, while the spontaneous moving world is most often created by younger children and by children who need to release excess energy. In moving worlds, the sand tray becomes the stage on which the child acts out her/his self-created drama. The drama often incorporates much energy and constant change. Usually there are several cycles of breaking down the old and creating the new as the story progresses. Sometimes children will ask you to join them in this play. De Domenico (1988) stated that the player in a moving world actually builds many static worlds, one after another, and then explores the relationship between these worlds. The builder is most interested in the shifts between the worlds and the focus is on transformation, not on the outcome.

It has been our experience that boys, more often than girls, create moving worlds. Chris, a 6-year-old boy we saw, created many moving worlds. He had been referred to us by his physician. When Chris first arrived, his parents were very concerned about him. Since a car accident in which the mother had been seriously injured, Chris, a very active boy, no longer played with the other children and did not want to go to school. Frequently he kicked and screamed when he had to leave his mother. Chris spent his first sessions industriously building roads and driving cars and trucks from place to place. His cars often got stuck in the saturated sand and had to be rescued by a truck. This was accompanied with a great deal of noise and activity. Then one day he began to crash his cars into each other. Shortly after this session, he brought a helicopter into the scene. The helicopter rescued the occupants of the cars and took them to the hospital, where the doctor sewed them up and bandaged them. Chris continued to recreate this scene for several sessions, until one day he concluded the play with everybody being well and going home. When he arrived for his next session, Chris stated that he did not want to play in the sand. He said that sandplay was boring. He decided instead to play a game with us. At this point his mother reported that he was again playing with the other children and was less hesitant about leaving her.

If a child begins to create a moving world after you have introduced her/him to sandplay, it will not be possible for you to record the sandplay process unless you have a video camera. You will also not follow the stages we have discussed previously. The child will automatically progress through whatever changes s/he needs to make to resolve her/his inner issues. Most children accompany their drama with sounds. Some children create a running dialogue or story of the play as it evolves. It is best not to interrupt the play to ask questions, because this often suspends the process. However, you might wish to try a technique that De Domenico (1988) uses to help children process their moving worlds. When you see significant developments, and/or notable sounds and speech occurring during the play, you might wish to comment on them or reiterate them verbally to bring them to the attention of the child as s/he is playing. This tends to help the child observe and become aware of her/his own process. If a child creates a car crash similar to the one that s/he experienced in real life, as Chris did, you might state what you saw and heard in the child's play. For example, you might say, "That child screamed when the cars crashed." Or you might repeat what the child said using her/his emotional content in your speech (e.g., "Oh no, oh no, we're going to crash!"). Always take your lead from what is happening in the tray. Do not project your own ideas or interpretations onto the child's play. After the drama is finished, you may wish to examine the final world and explore the last positions of objects and patterns the child has created. This may be helpful to the client, but because the continuing creative process yields most of the information and work, the end picture is of limited importance.

To help the child recall the drama, you might ask her/him some questions. For example, you might ask the child to remember what it was like for the figure or figures in the tray to be in the car crash. You might even ask her/him to reenact the accident outside the tray, allowing for greater expression, large muscle movement, and decreased limits. If you assess that it is timely to have the child deal with the accident more fully, you might ask the child to bring the figures in the crash back into the tray and have them dialogue with each other. You might say, "Remember when the cars crashed? Could you bring the cars back into the tray and have the people talk to each other about what they think and how they feel and what they want to say?"As an alternative you might have the child place the figures into a new tray to bring the dialogue between the figures into greater focus, without distractions.

After you have completed the exploration of the world, ask the child if s/he wishes to take a picture of the final world. Although you and the client can take a photograph of the final world, remember, the significance of the world is not in this image but in the process. When the child leaves, write down the important events and patterns you saw during the development and at the completion of her/his moving world. It is unlikely that you will be able to record or recreate exactly what happened unless you have videotaped the session.

Interactive Sandplay

It is not unusual for a child client to invite the therapist to take an active role in the sandplay, just as they do in other play therapy modalities. In our experience, many children, especially children under the age of 8 years, request our participation. Occasionally adolescents do the same. It is the child who is *in charge* of her/his sand world; therefore, acceding to her/his request for your participation is prudent.

We learned an important lesson early in our work with children, relevant both to sandplay and to other play methods that require an active role on the therapist's part. Our desire to help the child change, coupled with what we thought would be most helpful for the child's adjustment to the society in which s/he lived, often led us to model behavior that we wanted the child to learn. It eventually became evident that it would have been more therapeutic to accurately follow the attitude representative of the child's inner and outer world at the time. After admonitions from several child clients that we were not doing it *right*, that "we were supposed to be the bad guys and act bad," we learned our lesson. Although there is an appropriate time to model the desired behavior, it is important to be attuned to what is relevant for the child at that particular time in the child's developmental process. Be careful not to impose your values on the play (e.g., making the bad guy nice). Your responses must facilitate personal growth. Unless teaching/modeling is in the best interest of the child at a particular time, do not teach morality or rightness. You want to provide the opportunity for the child to experience what s/he needs, to move toward healing. One way to avoid this pitfall is to ask the child how s/he wants the figure to act or what the figure should say. We have found that most children are willing to give us direction. However, some resist, letting us know that it is our job, not theirs, to create the role of the figure.

We recall a 7-year-old boy, Simon, with whom we worked. He was struggling with his parents' separation and was rebelling against all authority figures. Simon was attracted to the sand and began setting up battles from the beginning of the therapy process. Initially he played both the aliens and the good guys. He eventually engaged us in alien invasions in the tray. We were always assigned the part of the aliens, who were frequently destroyed by the end of the session. As the weeks passed, the objects he chose for the good guys began to change. Simon selected stronger-looking, larger figures. He empowered those figures and at the same time himself. His mother and teachers reported that his behavior was less disruptive in school and he was less rebellious at home.

Although we do not generally suggest that you request to be included in the sandplay, there are exceptions. If a child needs direction and her/his play seems immobilized during a spontaneous moving tray, you may ask the child if you can help or take the part of any of the characters in the tray. If an ongoing battle in the child's life needs to be played out with another person, you may inquire if the child would like you to play that person in the tray. If the child has already created a scene that clearly portrays this conflict, you might say, "Would it be okay if I played with you in the tray? Maybe I could be that lady (the figure that is the child's opponent)." You may also choose to request playing the figure that represents the child. If you want to model behavior to facilitate the changing of a pattern within the child's sand world, you may wish to ask the child if you can move or be the object that represents the child in the tray. It is essential to always get permission from the client before entering her/his world.

SANDPLAY WITH FAMILIES

Because children live in families with adult authority figures and are not capable developmentally, emotionally, and physically of fully taking care of themselves, they have much less control over their lives than do adults. In fact, a young child's survival depends on the adults in her/his environment. It is probable that many child and adolescent dysfunctions are related to unresolved issues in the family and community. It is therefore more important than with adults to include the parents and other members of the family or environment (e.g., teachers, social workers, probation officers). These adults may have the power to change the situation and ongoing dynamics the child faces. We have found that change occurs much more rapidly in children and adolescents if family members and significant people in their lives are included in therapy, at least as an adjunct to our individual work with a child. Always ask permission from your client to include others in therapy prior to arranging the sessions. With adolescents it is essential that you include them in all family sessions or get their permission to work separately with their parents or teachers so that trust is not destroyed. Dyad, family, and/or group sandplay is a very effective way to aid communication and to alter dysfunctional dynamics. Remember, however, that you need the willingness and cooperation of all family members, especially the ones with the most power.

Sometimes families come to you for family therapy. More often, however, the parents bring a child whom they have identified as the problem and, consciously or unconsciously, have used as the scapegoat. Because "the vast majority of human behavior seems to be determined by the functioning of the system" (Allen, 1988, p. 11), it is difficult to deal with clients' problems when you see only the individual. Since a change in one part of the family system is followed by a compensatory shift in other parts, members of the family must cooperate to ameliorate the identified child client's symptoms. Allen wrote that "children and most adolescents do not have enough power in their families to make significant impact on the systemic dynamics, so that individual work with them is pointless" (1988, p. 217).

We have found that working with the child individually coupled with working with the family leads to more complete resolution of the child's presenting issues. However, there are times when we do work with the individual child and meet with the parents separately. This occurs when there is a pending separation or divorce and the child needs her/his own space and time to work out her/his feelings. Further, it is often not appropriate or helpful to let the child be privy to antagonism existing between the parents. In addition, when a parent has been abusive, it may be too threatening to include the perpetrator in the same session as the child. Also, when you are teaching parenting skills, it is valuable to see the parents apart from the child(ren).

We assume that if you are doing family therapy, you have a basic knowledge of family dynamics and systems theory. Anytime you find family therapy appropriate, using play provides a mode of communication and interaction relevant for the child. Play is a child's natural mode of communication. As Eliana Gil stated, "My basic contention is that adults must stop inflicting adult interactions on children and making demands that children participate in ways they cannot successfully negotiate. Instead, I encourage clinicians to enter, and direct parents to enter, the world of children, thereby offering them opportunities for rich and reciprocal emotional contact with the adult world"

(1994, pp. 37–38). It is important to help parents not only to accurately observe and empathize with their children, but also to learn to play with them.

The major differences between working with individuals and working with families are that the members are of diverse ages and varying developmental levels and abilities. Also, interaction, communication, and power issues increase exponentially with the added members in the family. Because of the number of people involved, there can be logistical difficulties in getting all family members scheduled together. The benefits of including the family in therapy, however, outweigh the possible difficulties. Furthermore, we advocate sandplay with families because we feel that it is important for the family members to relate on a level understandable to the child. Below we present three possible procedures for using sandplay with the family.

Sandplay as an Assessment Tool

Sandplay can serve as an excellent diagnostic tool with families. We concur with Gil's position that "Assigning a joint task . . . [sandplay in our case] affords the clinician a first-hand view of how parents organize themselves to enter a joint task, what verbal and nonverbal communication skills they use, and how parents and children negotiate fairness, boredom, limit-setting, and so on. The clinician can also detect issues of relatedness and attachment and other interactional dimensions" (1994, pp. 40–41).

It has been our experience that the parents are our first contact when working with children. The initial referral usually results from (a) parents who are concerned about their child who is experiencing some sort of distress either at school, with peers, or at home, (b) the court system because the child/adolescent has gotten into legal trouble, (c) family services due to reported abuse or neglect, or (d) school personnel. Occasionally, a child or adolescent will request counseling her/himself. For young children, we generally talk with the parents first to get an overview of the current situation and the history of the child and the problem. We then meet with the child to establish rapport and trust. For adolescents we rely on the expressed desire of the family members, especially the teenager. If it is the adolescent's preference, we meet first with her/him subsequent to a brief phone call with the parents regarding the reason for the referral. This sequence allows greater trust to evolve in the therapy with the adolescent. If we determine that the situation is best served by working with the family, we have found that sandplay is more revealing of family dynamics than talk therapy.

Where family therapy seems fundamental to the process, we let the parents and the child know that we would like the family to come in together to help us learn more about the functioning of the system. We might say to the child, "You know that you have been unhappy with how things have been going for you at home. There seem to be a lot of things that you would like to be different. Is that true?" The child usually responds affirmatively. You might then say, "Would you like it if we could work together to see if we could make some of those changes?" Again the child usually responds affirmatively. You might then say, "I have a way to help that happen. When I have the whole family come in together, I can learn how to help the family make things better. What do you think about that?" By now you not only are offering the child what s/he wants but have also established a "yes" set (i.e., a positive mindset that occurs in the client after making several assenting responses).

The approach is somewhat similar with parents. We have found that some parents are reluctant to change their perspective from seeing the child as the problem to recognizing the family system as dysfunctional. If you assess that the parents are invested in maintaining the child as the identified patient, you might wish to form an alliance with them. Let them know that they have greater knowledge of the child than you do and you need their help. You might say, "This is your child and you know her/him better than I do and are the most invested in her/his getting well. It would be very helpful to me if I could work with you all together as a family." Because parents generally are looking for relief of their child's problem and/or alleviation of the disruption it is creating in the family, they are willing to do what is needed. You will also want to educate them about the use of play and how it both helps provide information to you and allows the child to communicate on her/his level. Sometimes parents resist the opportunity for the family to play together. This may be indicative of their lack of playfulness with the child outside the therapy room. Or it may suggest that the parents feel threatened in some way. They may be fearful either that they will not do it *right* or that hidden material will be revealed.

If the family members agree to use the sand tray, you are ready to begin. If possible, schedule an hour and a half to two hours for the family sandplay assessment session. The process of doing an assessment tray with a family is similar to the spontaneous communication tray with a couple (i.e., doing a conjoint tray). Proceed through the creating the world, experiencing and rearranging, and communicating with family members stages. The therapy stage is often omitted when assessment is the objective. The documentation stage provides valuable information, as do the transition and dismantling the world stages. If all of the family members have not yet experienced sandplay, you might say, "I know that you all want things to work better in the family and you want everyone to be happier. You haven't created a world in the sand tray together before and, as we planned, today you can do that. Sometimes families make a scene in the tray together and they learn things about themselves and each other. It's a new way to play or interact with each other." A brief introduction to the trays and objects will be required if this has not been accomplished previously (see the creating the world stage in chapter 3 for details).

We have a large sand table for use with families, but a traditional size tray (approximately 20″ × 30″) is adequate. If you have more than one tray, you can allow the family to choose the tray they want to use. Impose no rules. Indicate that there is no right or wrong way to build a scene or world. Since they have already been primed to play together in the sand, you are ready to give them specific directions. You might say, "Here is the tray you will be working in today (or choose a tray you would like to use today). You can each choose whatever objects you want to use and place them in the sand in any way that you wish. You can decide how you want to create the world. You can talk about it together or you can do it without talking. As the world comes into being, you may want to move objects that are already in the tray or you may leave them just where they are." If you plan to take a series of photographs, take notes, or make a videotape, be sure to ask their permission and explain that it will help you remember how the world came about. It is usually not feasible to take detailed records with a family. If something noteworthy occurs in the dynamics that you want to make sure you remember, you might briefly jot it down. Inform the family that you will silently watch them as they play together.

Observe how they begin and how each member proceeds. The observation with a family becomes even more complex than with a couple because the number of people has increased. Obviously, you will not be able to see exactly what each member is doing, except when they are all at the tray creating together. It is the family dynamics you need to observe. Notice the roles that each family member takes. How are the parents interacting with each other? How does each parent interact with the child? Does triangulation occur, such as two colluding against the third? Is enmeshment (symbiosis) or distancing apparent? Is there evidence of one or both parents projecting their own sense of self onto the child? What is the power differential and how is it handled? Is the child free to play as s/he wishes? Does one or both of the parents or the child take over? Do either or both of the parents set limits if what they consider to be inappropriate behavior is demonstrated? How attentive are they all of each other? Do they work independent of each other or try to lead or follow each other? Do they work cooperatively to build a unified world in the tray or do they create separate scenes and use only their own sections within the same tray? Do they ask each other permission to place an object close to someone else's object or ask if they can move someone else's object? Do they feel free to do this without asking? Do they accept or do they reject and criticize the others' contributions to the scene? How much tension or ease does each family member exhibit? You will not be able to observe everything, but pay attention to the dynamics that you are most interested in assessing. This will vary depending on the circumstances in the family. Allow as much time as is needed for the family to create the scene.

When doing sandplay for assessment, you can stop after the creation is completed, although sometimes, if time permits and you want to pursue further observations of family interaction, you may continue to the next stages. If you choose to continue the process, give the family several minutes to experience the scene silently. Suggest that they may leave the tray just as it is or make some changes. Following the experiencing and rearranging stage, give each family member an opportunity to take the other family members on a tour of the world. Notice the respect and attentiveness each member of the family receives and gives as the narrations proceed. In your directions, do not stress respectful and attentive listening. Do not instruct them not to interrupt. If inattention, disrespect, and/or interruptions persist and you have already ascertained the pattern, you may then intervene. Because this is an assessment tray, your objective at this point is not to effect change but to gather information. Although you do not intervene with therapeutic techniques, the potential for change or at least heightened awareness may occur in the transition stage.

Subsequent to the building of the world (if the sand tray work ends here) or the communicating with family members stage, give the family the opportunity to take a photograph. Observe how they choose which family member takes the picture and from what angle. Do they cooperate? Does one person take over? All decision points in this process provide you with information regarding the family dynamics.

After the photograph is taken, ask the family members what the experience was like for them. In this transition stage, inquire if they learned anything about themselves from the way they created the world. Ask the parents if they can identify any patterns in the way they played in the tray that reminded them of interactions in their families of origin. This is often best done in a follow-up session with the parents. As with individual and couple work, dismantle the scene thoughtfully, remembering what transpired during the session.

Individuation Sand Trays

If you are working with a child from an enmeshed family where members are not able to maintain separate identities or are unable to express themselves freely, family individuation sandplay sessions can be invaluable. In the first sandplay session with the family, you might wish to confirm your suspicions that the family is enmeshed by having them complete an assessment tray. During the next family session, you might wish to have the family come in together but have each member work in an individual tray. In order to complete the process, schedule two hours for this session if possible, especially if there are more than three individuals in the family. Since the process and stages are very similar to the couple's individuation sandplay discussed in chapter 4, here we will delineate only the differences.

To introduce the family to individuation sandplay you might say, "Sometimes families, even though they spend a lot of time together or think they are pretty close, don't know very much about each other as separate people. They may not know what each person likes, dislikes, what makes each one happy or sad, or even what her/his interests are. This exercise will help you get to know each other better." Then it is time to explain the sandplay experience and materials if you have not done so previously, and state your rules for play. In an enmeshed family, rules for play are essential. We have found that rules must be rigorously enforced if patterns such as interrupting each other, speaking or doing things for the other, or making negative comments are to be broken. You will no doubt develop rules that fit your practice. We first discuss respect. We then let all members know that they will be building their own worlds and that they need to remain with their own trays even if they finish before the others. Emphasize that it is important to respect each other's privacy. We also urge everyone to build quietly so as not to disturb someone else. Family members are requested not to talk to each other, make any comments, or look at each other's trays during the creating stage.

The problem you may face with this exercise is that, depending on the size of the family, you may not have enough trays. If you conduct family sessions frequently, you might wish to buy extra trays and sand. We have found that the smaller Rubbermaid plastic trays (roughly 15″ × 21″), which are approximately $5.00 each at discount stores, are large enough for members to build their worlds. Ask each person to select a tray and begin. Let the family members know that they have about 20 minutes to create whatever they wish. Keep the trays as far away from each other as possible to eliminate the temptation of looking and commenting. As with couples, observe the family and watch for signs of dependence, interference, sabotage, and influence. If the rules are broken by anyone, walk over to the person immediately and gently remind her/him. If necessary, move that person's tray to a separate area. If one person is finished before the others have completed their worlds, ask her/him to quietly experience her/his tray. However, because you deal with varying ages and developmental levels when you work with families, remain especially mindful of individual needs. For example, if children are young or have limited attention spans, we set aside toys for them to play with quietly in case they finish early. We let the children know that they may play with these toys as long as they do not disturb the others who are still creating their worlds.

During the communicating with the members stage, let the family know that they will all get a turn to talk about their creations for approximately five minutes. Give each person an equal time to talk. Ask all the members to gather around one of the trays and request that one of the individuals take the others on a tour of her/his sand world. Begin with the member who has least power in the family or the one that is most easily influenced by the others. If this is too threatening for the selected person, choose the most benign member to go first. When you are concerned that one of the family members (often the most powerful one) might sabotage therapy, is not invested in therapy, or might end therapy if s/he is not permitted to maintain power, you may give the family the choice of who speaks first. You might do this for one or two sessions.

Ask each member to speak directly to the family. If this is too intimidating, let her/him know that it is okay for her/him to speak to you for now. Reiterate the rules. Let the family members know it is now all right to look at each other's worlds, but they may not comment or disparage others' creations in any way (e.g., make faces, roll their eyes). Ask them to listen attentively to the person speaking. If members are not capable of respectful behavior, request that they quietly watch while you model the behavior. Encourage each person to reveal as much as you deem appropriate at the time. In some cases it is important to be cautious, especially when there is a possibility of emotional or physical abuse by a member of the family. In a case such as this, if a member begins to speak about an issue that you know may create problems (e.g., an adolescent dating a person of whom the parents do not approve), redirect her/his attention elsewhere. You might say, "I realize that what you are beginning to talk about is an issue for you, but this might not be the best time to talk about it. Let's go on with the tour for now and we will address this when you are all ready to deal with it." Note the subject in your file and return to it when you determine that the family is ready. When members are finished taking each other through their sand worlds, ask them to share with each other what it was like to create their own worlds and how they felt about telling the rest of the family about their creations. If the family is unable to communicate respectfully, eliminate this step until the members are able to honor each other's differences.

During the therapeutic intervention phase, work with each person separately as you would if you were conducting individual sessions. However, remain mindful of the rest of the group, not only by observing reactions but also by remembering to be careful with what you ask each member to divulge. Allow each member of the family to take a picture of her/his own tray and to take the photo home. During the transition stage ask each person what s/he learned about each of the others and about her/himself that s/he did not know prior to the session. In order to break old patterns of faultfinding, request that family members keep their comments positive, at least until they learn how to communicate without constant criticism. Ask each one what s/he personally can do to encourage her/his own and others' individuality during the following week.

You might ask family members to continue creating individual trays for a period of time until you assess that they are ready to work together as individuals. When therapy progresses to the point that each member's self-esteem becomes less entangled with the others and communication becomes safe, the family is ready to create a communication tray.

An example of an individuation sandplay session follows. A family with whom we worked in therapy illustrates the need for individuation sandplay in a system where cultural principles are deeply established. Mr. and Mrs. Lee came to see us shortly after the death of their oldest son, Wang. Wang had committed suicide after his first semester at a prominent university. Although he had been performing above average, Wang seemed very distressed when he received his grades. He had told his brother, who was in high school, that he felt that he had disgraced the family by not excelling and that he could not face his parents. The Lees were devastated by Wang's death and could not understand what had happened. They stated that the family had always been close and that they loved their children very much. They had no recollection of ever telling Wang that he had to get top grades. Since the family had arrived in America from Cambodia eight years ago, Mr. and Mrs. Lee had worked extremely hard to provide their children with the best America had to offer.

Upon our request, the Lees brought their two sons, Chen, age 15, and Liang, age 12, to family sessions. During the sessions the boys confirmed the family's closeness and stated that they could not understand why Wang had done this to all of them. Chen said that he, like Wang, was at the top of his class academically. Liang reported that he was struggling to remain in the top 10%. Although, in time, the Lee family moved toward resolution of their grief, it was apparent to us that the members were unable or unwilling to speak for themselves. We therefore asked if they would be willing to create separate sand worlds. It was difficult for them to see the benefit of this kind of play. But, by this time, they trusted us as therapists so they agreed.

During the communicating with the members stage, Liang went first. He had built a scene with several people working very hard in the rice fields. A road ran through the middle of the fields. At the end of the road he had placed a large rock with a Buddha on top of it and some houses down below. A young boy, carrying an enormous sack of rice on his back, was walking down the road toward the village and the Buddha. Liang stated that the boy was exhausted and wanted to put down the sack but couldn't because the other people would be very disappointed. They were depending on him to get the rice to market and return with the money. His failure to complete his task would bring shame on him and poverty to the others, so he had to continue on his journey without complaint.

As we asked Liang more about the sack of rice, he suddenly said, "It's like all the things I feel I have to do right. I just don't want to hurt or disappoint my parents. They've done so much for us. I know they just want us to be the very best we can be, but it's so hard. . . . "At this point Chen looked anxiously at his parents and at us and then asked if he could say something. He placed a hand on his younger brother's shoulder and stated, "I know just how that boy feels." When it was Chen's turn to talk about his tray, he further explored the feelings that Liang had so honestly expressed.

Although Mr. and Mrs. Lee had difficulty understanding their children's feelings, the family was finally able to speak openly about the issues. In time, Mr. and Mrs. Lee were able to talk about their life in Cambodia and the expectations they had carried from generation to generation and from one country to the next. They could acknowledge that they did not want their unresolved problems from the past to haunt their children.

Communication Sand Trays for Families

If you perceive via an assessment tray or interview that family members are distant from each other or have difficulty communicating, spontaneous family communication sandplay (all members building a world in the same tray) is appropriate. Communication sandplay can facilitate healing for the child and other family members. Since this procedure is conducted very similarly to the communication sand tray for couples discussed in chapter 4, we refer only to the differences. When family members are distant from each other, family interaction and communication tend to be infrequent. Each person spends most of her/his time without connecting to the others. The family rarely performs tasks or spends time together as a unit. We have found that patterns of behavior and communication in distant families can often most easily be changed during a project that includes the entire family. When all family members build in the same tray, they must learn to communicate and interact just to complete the exercise.

It is much more difficult for you to observe and interact with several people than with only one or two. Unless you are videotaping, recording becomes laborious and unproductive. When you are working with a family, note that you are working with several individuals but you are also interacting with the family as a unit, a whole that is greater than its parts. As with couples, you become a part of that system to some extent. This is unavoidable but can be beneficial at times. However, in most cases the extent of your involvement in the family system is kept to a minimum if possible. Probably sandplay, more than most techniques, allows you to remain on the periphery, especially during the building process.

Once you decide to have the family do a communication sand tray, you might say, "Sometimes families become so busy that they spend very little time together and forget how to talk and interact with each other. This exercise will help you get along better as a family." Make sure to allow two hours for a session when the family is larger than three. As with families who create separate sand worlds, it is necessary to introduce the group to sandplay in such a way that each one understands what you are asking her/him to do. It is also important to have rules that all members must follow. We usually ask all members to remain quiet throughout the building period, except during the time they need to interact to make decisions about the sandplay (e.g., where to place their objects). Members may not make derogatory comments to each other or make faces or hurt each other. Again, respect is emphasized and enforced. Now ask the family to select a tray together and decide whether they will use water and objects. If you are working toward a more democratic system in the family, you might give each person a vote. Tell them that they may build any scene or world together that they wish.

If members have no idea how to communicate appropriately with each other, stop the process and model new behavior. For example, if you see a parent repeatedly move some of her/his child's objects, you may intervene. You might say, "Johnny looks a little upset that you keep moving his objects. Perhaps you could ask his permission. For instance, you might say, 'Johnny, would it be okay if I moved this rock to the other side of the tray?' Then wait for Johnny to respond." This prompts both asking respectfully and listening to the child's reply. Remain aware of the dynamics that are occurring as the family is building so that you can refer back to specific situations during the therapy stage. Have each person first experience and then talk about the sand world, claiming the entire scene as her/his world. As with families doing individuation sandplay, ask the least powerful member to go first during the communicating with the members stage, if appropriate.

Make sure that members speak directly to each other. Ask those not conducting the tour to listen in silence and try to view the world from the speaker's perspective, setting aside their own biases. It is important to stress that each person's perspective is perfect for her/him, even though other members may see the same world differently. Usually five minutes is adequate to delve into each narrator's viewpoint of the jointly constructed world. Then explore with each person what it was like to create a scene together and to explain it to each other.

During the therapy stage, address the strengths as well as the weaknesses of the family. Use the objects in the tray to reveal and help change the dynamics. As with individuals and couples, you can use the therapeutic interventions discussed in chapters 3 and 4. If you choose to direct the client to have the objects dialogue, ask the person dialoguing to take the role of both objects. To bring in other perspectives, you might have each individual who brought in the object give voice to her/his own figure during the dialogue. Then have members change roles. If the members of the family are unable to negotiate the world together, invite them to bring in a helper or wise one. If they are still incapable of communicating or problem-solving as a family, ask if it would be okay for you to take the role of the helper.

In a communication tray, request that the family cooperatively find a place from which to take the photograph and decide who will take it. Make sure each person has a vote. During the transition stage ask the family what each one learned about the way the family interacts. Then inquire about what pattern they would like to change and how they want it altered. Have each one indicate what s/he can do and what s/he thinks others could do to change the family pattern of interacting. Form a plan with the family that they can implement during the following week. Make sure to follow up on any assignments you give.

Distinctions Between Child &
Adult Sandplay

- Play is a natural form of expression for children.
- Children tend to be more concrete and need physical form to express themselves.
- Language and abstract thinking are limited in children and therefore there is less outward evidence of progress.
- Children generally have no conscious knowledge of what is happening inside themselves after the play has been explored.
- Children often choose not to talk about their experience.
- Sandplay with children takes more varied forms. Frequently the activity level in the tray is greater.
- The ego strength of children may still be very tenuous and their defenses are usually not yet in place.
- The sand tray is a transitional object for children that fosters independence and at the same time provides security.
- There is a need to enforce rules and limits with children.

Developmental Aspects of Sandplay

DORA KALFF
- First phase (up to 6–7 years of age)
  Animals and vegetation predominate.
- Second phase (6–7 to 11–12 years of age)
  Battles and conflicts occur.
- Third phase (11–12 through adolescence)
  Scenes showing real life and a sense of social perspective appear.
  Integration into the collective

CHARLES T. STEWART
- First stage: Infancy II (7–10 months to 2 years)
  Hiding and finding; burying and uncovering
  Filling trays with an abundance of objects

- Second stage: Early Childhood I (1–2 to 3–4 years)
    Chaos, creating and destroying
- Third stage: Early Childhood II (3–4 to 6–7 years)
    More organized battles than second stage
    Central figure in conflicts
    Testing limits
- Fourth stage: Middle Childhood (6–7 to 11–12 years)
    Dualities displayed
    More organized battles than third stage
    Differences in male and female trays
    Appearance of fences signifying formation of inner limits
    Connection between previously separated areas

· ·

Common Patterns in Children's Sandplay

- Becoming overstimulated by a multitude of objects
- Filling the tray with an overabundance of figures
- Using multiple trays
- Playing out transference issues
- Flooding the tray with water
- Filling containers with sand and emptying them
- Building and destroying
- Burying and uncovering; hiding and finding
- Playing out battles, conflicts, and power struggles
- Creating moving trays
- Throwing sand
- Climbing into the tray

Spontaneous Static Sand Trays with Children

Similar stages to adult sandplay session except

- Play in the sand in their first session
- Reduced time for young or easily distracted children
- Rules for play and limits set
- Resistance in some children to talk about their world, completing only the creating and experiencing stages
- Photographs as transitional objects

Spontaneous Moving Sand Trays with Children

- No delineated stages
- Often created by younger children
- Cycles of breaking down the old and creating the new
- The process, not the final scene, is significant

Interactive Sand Trays

CHILD INITIATED
- Allow children to initiate interaction with the therapist.
- Permit children to direct the play in the sand.
- Follow the child's lead; don't teach morality.

THERAPIST INITIATED
- Request inclusion in the play if the child is stuck.
- Ask permission before entering the sand world.
- Model behavior when appropriate.

. . . .

Assessment Tray with Families

Similar to couple's communication sandplay except

- Prior to beginning the sand tray, educate the family about the use and value of play.
- Proceed through all stages, except the therapy stage, if time permits.
- Set no rules or limits after giving initial directions.
- Be attentive to family dynamics.

. . . .

Individuation Trays with Families

Similar to couple's individuation sandplay except

- Respect and attentiveness for all members is emphasized.
- Various developmental levels exist among the family members.
- Communication issues increase exponentially with added members.

. . . .

Communication Tray with Families

Similar to couple's communication sandplay except

- It is more difficult to observe and interact with several people of varying developmental levels.
- Cooperation among all members is necessary when building in the same tray.
- Respect and attentiveness for all members is emphasized.
- Agreement among members is required when taking the photograph.

·· 6 ··

DIRECTED SAND TRAYS WITH INDIVIDUAL ADULTS AND COUPLES

In this chapter we describe several applications of sandplay other than the spontaneous creations that we discussed in chapters 3, 4, and 5. Although the interventions detailed are mostly for adults, some of them can be applied to work with children, especially adolescents. (To learn more about directed trays specific to children and families see chapter 7.) With directed trays, as with nondirected trays, you accept and hold the client's creation and remain attentive, noticing the client's nonverbal and verbal expressions, behaviors, and emotions. You continue to remain non-intrusive and outside of the tray. Unlike spontaneous trays, you direct clients either in subject matter or technique to help focus on the issue at hand. Although you direct the client to a greater extent in methodology and subject matter than in spontaneous trays, it is the unconscious and conscious of the client that guide the content of the tray.

There are several techniques that you can use and innumerable topics (e.g., specific traumas and problems, relationship issues, dreams, hopes, needs, fears, or past experiences) that you might suggest to clients as the focus for sandplay. When it is your professional opinion that a client requires focus in a particular area, which is intruding on her/his life and hindering forward movement, or the number of sessions is limited and rapid resolution is required, a directed tray is effectual. In a time of reduced mental health funding and managed care, the number of sessions you will have with a client may be few. Directed sandplay techniques can often increase your effectiveness and bring about change more rapidly.

In this chapter we elaborate on techniques we learned about subpersonality integration and family of origin work in sandplay from Donna Linn and about the slowing-down process and amplification work in sandplay from Gisela De Domenico, who brought to our awareness the concept of directed trays. We have found these techniques to be very useful in our practice. We also describe some additional procedures we have developed with the help of our clients, which we find particularly valuable to move clients through pertinent issues. Once you become an experienced sandplay therapist, you will likely find yourself conceiving alternative ways of proceeding with clients. You will also know intuitively when it is time to suggest a topic or use a specific method that would serve your client.

REDESIGNING LIFE SITUATIONS

There are many situations and events in people's lives that create problems for them. When a client has experienced a situation that s/he was unable to deal with appropriately, or has developed a dysfunctional pattern of relating, thinking, or behaving that is preventing her/him from obtaining specific goals in life, a sandplay session utilizing this technique can rapidly change her/his perception and behavior. It can also teach problem-solving and new coping skills.

The technique we call redesigning life situations is based on the theory that the mind is literal and that memory and emotion of an event can be altered by imagining one is reliving and erasing the old way and creating a new one. The process changes one's perceptions and reactions. We have found that sandplay, because of its physicality and its ability to create a natural altered state, is particularly well suited to this approach. Although mostly used with adults, this exercise can be used with older children and adolescents who are capable of problem-solving.

It is best if you have at least an hour and a half to complete this exercise so that you won't be rushed. We do not usually recommend directed trays until a client has completed at least one or two spontaneous trays and is familiar with sandplay. It is also important for you to have gained the trust of the client, so that s/he will feel safe in following your suggestions. When you determine that this method might be of value to your client, discuss the pattern/behavior that is unproductive for her/him or that you have observed with her/him. Then you might say, "This pattern seems to be causing you a lot of problems. Are you committed to changing your actions/thinking in such a way that this won't continue happening?" With a child or adolescent you might begin by saying, "You have told me several times now that when the teacher tells you not to do something at school, you blow up at her and then you get in trouble and you get punished. This seems to happen when you are with your parents, too. Would you like to find a new way to handle those situations?" It is essential to receive a sincere affirmative answer. As we all know, change seldom occurs without a commitment. If the client is willing, you may proceed.

At this point you might say, "Are you willing to try something a little different in the sand tray today than you've done before? People I've worked with often find that this way of playing helps them break old patterns or ways of behaving that have been so hurtful for them." If the client agrees, tell her/him a little about how directed trays are different from spontaneous trays and something about what you will be asking the client to do in this particular session. This usually alleviates some of the anxiety of using a new approach. Also inform her/him that if s/he does not understand your directions at any time, to please ask and you will explain.

Now ask the client to recreate in the tray the situation that produced the problem for her/him, using any objects s/he needs to show you what happened. If it is a recurring pattern, request that the client recreate the event that is most recent or most prominent in her/his mind. When s/he is finished, ask the client to take you on a tour of the world, telling you exactly what happened during the incident. Briefly process this tray as you would a spontaneous tray, but in less detail. By now the client will probably see fairly clearly what created the problem and, if it is a recurring pattern of thought or behavior, the reason s/he has kept it in place. Do not ask the client if s/he wishes to take a picture of the tray. A photograph might reinforce the old patterns and behaviors.

Ask the client to select the object or objects in the sand world that represent(s) that part of her/himself s/he perceives as central in creating the problem. You might say, "There seems to be at least one figure/object in this world that represents the part of yourself that creates the problem. Can you show me which one that is?" Have the client bring the object(s) to the center of the tray. Invite the client to find one object on the shelves (or make an object) that symbolizes a wise and loving entity and place it in the center close to and facing the figure that symbolizes her/himself. Ask the client to have the two figures dialogue. If the client is unable to have the wise one be loving with the figure that represents her/himself, or come to any solutions and more productive ways of behaving or thinking, ask the client if it would be okay for you to take the role of the wise one. Occasionally, especially during a crisis, a time when a client is very self-critical, or when a child is not yet capable of coming up with productive solutions on her/his own, it is impossible for the client to work out the situation and s/he needs the modeling of the therapist. When the dialogue is complete and the client understands what changes s/he wants to make, ask the client to bring in a figure that symbolizes her/himself and is able to act and think in this new way. You might say, "Can you find an object or figure on the shelves or make something that could act in this new way? When you've done that, put the object in the middle of the tray with the other two." We frequently encourage the client to make an object so that we can send that object home with her/him later.

Now ask the client to deliberately remove all the objects in the world and place them on the table beside her/him. Direct her/him to remove the central three objects last, thus clearly reinforcing the dialogue and the solutions. Stress that s/he is now undoing all the old and will start with a clean tray. You might say, "You are removing the old ways of behaving from your tray. They are all gone now and you can start new." When the client is finished, have her/him take some deep breaths and visualize all the old patterns and thoughts disappearing in any way s/he needs to. For clients who have difficulty producing their own images, you may wish to be more directive and have them close their eyes and pretend that they put each object in a trunk and lock the trunk. Then request that the client rebuild the world in the way s/he wishes a similar situation would evolve next time, doing, saying, and thinking the things s/he thinks would be more productive. You might say, "Now you can start fresh. Make a new world in the tray, and you can make what happened to you happen just the way you would like it to." Let the client know that s/he can use the same objects s/he used in the last tray or select different ones. The only object that you ask the client to reuse is the one that symbolized the client capable of changing the behavior, so that the object can actively help create a new pattern in the world. When the client is satisfied with the new world, have her/him briefly give you a tour of the current tray and talk about the changes.

Direct her/him to take a photograph or, if s/he wishes, you may take it. Contrary to your instructions for taking a picture of a spontaneous world, do not give the client a choice in this exercise because you will use the photograph as a part of the homework assignment. During the transition stage, ask your client to put the image of the world that symbolizes the *new way of being* in a prominent place where s/he will see it frequently so that s/he will be constantly reminded of the changes. This photograph, which the client can touch and see, will help anchor and reinforce the new pattern. You might also ask the client to make an object, use the object s/he has already made, or find something in her/his environment that reminds her/him of the new way s/he is going to act. Then have the client carry the object in her/his pocket so that s/he can touch it many times a day and remember. When you are working with adolescents or adults, you might ask the client to rerun the process of her/his last tray in her/his imagination at least twice a day, preferably just as s/he is waking and immediately before s/he goes to sleep. These are the times that the unconscious is closest to the surface and is most easily influenced.

We describe the case of a young adult client to illustrate this approach. Richard was a 25-year-old Native American client who came to us because he was having difficulty getting along with his coworkers and with his boss. This was not an isolated situation for him. In his past job he experienced several outbursts of anger in reaction to what he felt was prejudice against him. Richard was fired from that position. It seemed that, wherever he worked, he was surrounded mostly by Caucasians who he felt were not respectful of him. After several sessions, including one spontaneous sandplay where he created an idyllic world, Richard remained frustrated. Although he realized that his perceptions were somewhat irrational, he continued to react in anger to subtle looks and comments.

At this point we suggested a redesigning life situations tray. In response to our instructions he portrayed in the tray his last angry reactions with a coworker. After briefly processing the scene, he brought in a bear, his animal guide (or spirit totem), to help him change the pattern. Following his dialoguing process, Richard chose a smooth solid rock to represent himself. After identifying with the rock, he removed all the objects from the tray. He then created a new scene using the rock as himself. In this scene Richard had the rock face each direction, starting with the east. He stated that this helped the rock remember who he was and the strength within himself. When he was centered he could refrain from personalizing or irrationally interpreting what others around him did and said. He replayed his interactions with his coworkers, this time actualizing more harmonious relationships. When Richard went home he found a very smooth dark rock to symbolize this new self. He carried it with him wherever he went to help him center when he felt anxious or angry.

EGO-STRENGTHENING AND SKILL-BUILDING

Although ego-strengthening and skill-building often result from spontaneous sand trays, there are times when a more directed tray is advantageous. When clients are dealing with specific fears or anxieties, have explicit tasks with which they are struggling or skills they wish to enhance, or have low self-esteem, this more directed intervention is beneficial. Because sandplay can move the client to an altered state of consciousness and a greater focus, this technique is akin to ego-strengthening hypnotic techniques. It is also similar to role playing in the therapy office, with the additional benefit of objectifying with symbols the actual behavior (e.g., having figures practice being more assertive). We usually use this modality with adolescents and adults. We also utilize it with children once they are capable of problem-solving.

Postpone this directed tray until you have established a trusting relationship with the client and s/he has had some experience with spontaneous sandplay, unless the client has come expressly for the issues stated above or has come for brief therapy. The initial instructions are simple and will vary between clients experienced in sandplay and those who have not previously used sandplay. For a new client, describe the way sandplay works and introduce her/him to your sandplay materials (see the introducing sandplay to the client phase in chapter 3). Then instruct the client to put the *problem* in the tray. For an experienced client, suggest that s/he may want to try a slightly different way of approaching sandplay. For example, you might say, "You really seem to be struggling with talking with your boss about the promotion you feel you deserve. I think that creating a scene in the sand tray would be very helpful for you. But instead of just choosing any objects that attract you, why don't you choose whatever objects seem to summon you that relate to the problem you are focusing on today. How would you like to try that?" With a child you might say, "Boy, you keep getting in trouble for not doing your homework. It might be fun today to make up a story in the sand tray about someone who gets into the same kind of trouble."

Because the client has been struggling with this particular problem and may have some conscious or unconscious resistance or fear of experiencing what may arise when s/he allows her/himself to deal with it on a deeper level, it is important to emphasize and establish a feeling of safety. This brings to mind a client with generalized anxiety, who had previously done spontaneous sandplay in which difficult hidden material had been disclosed and strong emotions had been evoked. He carried with him fears stemming back to childhood, including fear of being possessed by the devil and anxiety that he could not perform up to standard. Although we had explored these fears, discovered their etiology, and found ways for him to intervene when the fears arose, he was hesitant to allow himself to address them on a deeper, more emotional level. He was afraid that if he really felt them, he would lose control and plummet to the depth of his fear as he had in the past. Therefore we made a plan. We agreed that if his feelings started to become too intense, he would remind himself that he was currently feeling much better about himself and his life and that the fears were fallacious. He would remember that in his everyday life he was able to see the irrationality of these thoughts and was able to control his frightening feelings when they came. We decided that if he needed support in doing this, we would assist him. He also wanted to be assured that no matter how emotional he became, before leaving the session he would be *brought back* to a more grounded place and have tools he could use after he left the session. This preparation made it easier for him to proceed with his directed tray.

Once you and the client have established the *safety net* and the client has created the initial scene in the tray, advance through the experiencing and rearranging stage and touring the world phase (see chapter 3). Then proceed to have the client find ways to help alleviate the fears and/or solve the problem. This can be done by bringing in objects that represent helpers, such as a wise guide, a strong part of themselves, or someone they admire and trust. For example, when a client has low self-esteem, you might suggest that s/he create a tray where someone reminds her/him of all of her/his capabilities and strengths or of how s/he has solved similar problems in the past. Moving objects to other positions and dialoguing between or with objects are some other facilitative interventions that can be used.

There are times when the client may place in the tray only the problem symbols and not her/himself. For example, an agoraphobic client created a metropolis with tall buildings, a shopping area, and automobiles in the tray. After she described the world as a dangerous place, we asked her what it would be like if she were in that world. She shuddered and said that it would be scary. We explored ways that she could feel safe, reminding her that she could stop at any time and reiterate to herself the fallacy of her fears. She was reassured. She complied with our suggestion to first choose an object that represented her frightened self and then choose one that represented a part of herself that is strong and aware of the invalidity of her fears. The strong self figure was less afraid but still had some trepidation. The two figures were, however, able to travel around the city in the tray together, exploring the various shops and buildings, becoming more relaxed as they walked through the city scene.

In the next session the client again created this scene, this time bringing in only a figure that represented a strong part of herself who added strength and wisdom. This time she felt even more relaxed. Often, it is propitious to have clients practice their newfound skill in several trays over time to enhance and internalize their renewed sense of themselves. After several trays and rehearsals both in and out of the office, gradual amelioration of this client's fear occurred.

As in spontaneous trays, offer the client an opportunity to take a photograph. Most clients do take a picture. Some, however, decline. This may imply residual fear, uncertainty, or anxiety. It may also indicate that there is more work to be done regarding this issue, especially if the client's body language reveals discomfort. This may be something to explore. One client we saw said that she felt resolved with the issue but that she would rather not have a photograph of the tray. She didn't want a reminder of it and would rather put it behind her. We inferred from her statement that resolution had not yet been attained. In a subsequent tray, she found greater resolution but still didn't want a photograph; however, this time she appeared more comfortable and stated that she had already integrated a sense of inner peace about her fear. Although this client chose not to photograph her sand world, other clients who may initially resist taking a picture do take a photograph upon resolution of the problem in a later tray.

Once you have moved away from the tray, ask the client what the

experience was like for her/him and how s/he could use what transpired in the sand tray. Reinforce the positive movement that has been
gained. Fortify the feelings and tools for establishing a sense of security
outside of the office by providing suggestions. Give the client the task
of using the confidence s/he has gained in her/his daily life. For instance, in the previous example we suggested that the client, knowing
that the wise, strong, relaxed part of herself was with her, gradually
take more and longer walks in a populated part of town.

NEGOTIATING OPPOSITES

We live in a world of dualities and oppositions. We, like other therapists, have found that throughout therapy, regardless of the techniques
we use, clients continually work with opposites inside and outside of
themselves. Such conceptions as love/hate, light/dark, free/trapped,
strong/weak, good/evil, and victim/aggressor frequently surface in
therapy sessions. Clients search for resolution and integration of these
opposing forces. In De Domenico's workshop, she presents the concept of opposites being revealed in the tray, emphasizing exploration
of the intersection of the personal and archetypal realms of experience.
Usually integration of opposites occurs gradually and naturally over a
period of time. If, however, you have a limited time frame to work
with a client or s/he avoids bringing up these issues either verbally or
in the sand tray, you can ask your client to do a directed tray dealing
with the relevant opposites. This method can be used with children
and adolescents as well as with adults. The sand tray lends itself well
to working on dualities, both because of the objects clients choose and
the positions in the tray they place their objects.

The technique we describe here came out of therapy work with a
client, who, without direction, selected a bear and an infant to symbolize her issue of strength versus vulnerability. She then proceeded to
create a tray using these objects. Over the next several sessions she
continued using symbols for this issue, but the objects and the story
she created changed over time.

If the client is willing, give her/him two objects that you have previously selected. The two objects must symbolize the duality that you
assessed the client needs to resolve and eventually integrate. You may
choose the objects using information gleaned from the client in your
previous discussions, or you might choose objects that are recognized

as symbolizing this duality (e.g., angel/devil) and are culturally relevant for the client. If the client is willing and ready to do so, you might instead ask her/him to find objects that symbolize the duality s/he will be exploring. Regardless of how the objects are chosen, direct the client to create a world in any way s/he wishes using these and any other objects. Then process the sand world as you would during a spontaneous sandplay session, with an emphasis on the identified duality. In the transition stage ask the client to notice how these opposing forces manifest in her/his life during the following week. It may be necessary for the client to create more than one tray, using objects that symbolize these opposites, in order to progressively facilitate resolution of the conflict. If you decide to ask the client to create another world focused on this duality, make sure you ask her/him to choose the objects. Objects that represent the duality may change as the client works through the issue.

We used this approach with Jamie, a 21-year-old woman, who came to us to address sexual harassment from her boss. He would make lewd remarks or pinch or slap her buttocks whenever they were alone. This had been going on for almost a year. She had not reported the problem because she was afraid of losing her job. She felt extremely helpless but was afraid to talk about the situation, because she had been taught at home that she should never show signs of weakness. Because Jamie had no health insurance and had limited funds, she was able to attend only six sessions. In the third session we explained directed trays and asked her if she was willing to create a directed world. She said she was, and we gave her a wolf and a rabbit as the symbols for the aggressor and the victim. When she processed the tray she realized just how helpless the little rabbit was when the wolf, fangs bared, loomed over it.

In the next session she was able to rescue the rabbit from the grasp of the wolf and place the rabbit in a safe location. In the fifth session she selected a man as the aggressor and a woman as the helpless one, and had the two objects dialogue with each other. The woman figure was able to tell the male figure that his actions were unwanted and very inappropriate. In the last session Jamie stated that, although she had still been afraid, she had confronted her boss and resigned. She was presently looking for another job and felt certain that she would not allow a similar situation to develop without confronting it immediately. Although Jamie was emotionally not at a point to file a complaint, other clients often do.

SUBPERSONALITY INTEGRATION
IN THE SAND TRAY
FOR ADULTS AND COUPLES

Although we have done extensive ego-state work with clients outside of the sand tray, and clients have spontaneously represented many aspects of themselves and have revealed themselves in the tray, we are indebted to Donna Linn for this invaluable technique. The following subpersonality integration strategy is a more directive way to explore ego states or parts of the self. Because clients more often than not have self-doubts, self-criticism, or lack of acceptance or understanding of their shadows, creating subpersonality trays provides an excellent opportunity to reintroduce diametrically opposed, hidden, or rejected parts of themselves and facilitates exploration, acceptance, and integration of those attributes. This approach is very well suited to most clients, but is especially useful in bringing to light internal conflicts and the denied aspects of the self. We have found that once individuals reach a developmental level where they are able to use abstract thinking and are capable of identifying different aspects of themselves, this intervention can be very effective.

Estelle Weinrib wrote, "Sandplay therapy accelerates the individuation process—at least to some extent—resolution of complexes, integration of the shadow, and the differentiation of the negative and positive aspects of the animus/anima. It seems to move in a more direct line toward the constellation of the Self and the renewal of the ego" (1983, p. 87). We agree, but wish to emphasize that for some clients directive sand tray work can more readily achieve resolution of complexes and more directly focus on integration of the shadow than spontaneous trays. People often project *negative* or shadow aspects onto others, especially those to whom they are close, for example, peers, spouses, siblings, parents, and coworkers. Therefore, dyads (e.g., spouses, adolescent and parent, coworkers) can also benefit from this intervention. Subpersonality trays reveal people's shadow aspects in a nonthreatening way and facilitate recognition of their projections. With this growing awareness clients can find ways to have the shadow parts of themselves cooperate with other aspects of self and with their partners. We have seen clients learn to honor those aspects of themselves that they did not want to see and learn to have those parts function more compatibly. Their new self-knowledge also helps partners respect their differences as people and enables them to better explore how their various parts interact, complement, and aid each other.

There are several segments to a subpersonality integration sandplay session:

Introduction and choice of objects
Statements of feelings about the objects
Animation of the objects
Identification with the objects
Interaction among the objects
Documentation
Transition
Dismantling the tray

Introduction and Choice of Objects

INTRODUCTION

When working with individuals or couples, introduce sandplay as you would with a spontaneous tray. However, add a statement indicating that this experience will differ from the creation of previous trays because you will be giving more specific directions. In order to avoid biasing the client, we give no further rationale or explanation prior to the process. You might say, "Today I am going to ask you to do your sand tray a bit differently. I think that this way of playing in the sand will be very interesting to you. Others who have done this have found their experiences very enlightening." If you are working with a couple you might add, "Not only will you gain understanding of yourselves and each other, but you might find ways to resolve some conflictual issues." Have the client choose a tray in which s/he would like to work. When working with a dyad, you may initially have them choose a joint tray or separate trays in which to work. This will depend on their degree of individuation, as discussed in chapter 4.

CHOICE OF OBJECTS

Once the tray(s) has been selected, instruct the client to choose six objects, three that s/he finds appealing or attractive and three that s/he finds aversive. For a dyad, each person will choose six objects and place them either in their separate trays or in a divided single tray, keeping their objects separate from the other's objects. To the individual client you might say, "In choosing your objects for today, I'd like you to find three objects that are very appealing to you because you find them attractive or are drawn to them in some way. And I'd like you to choose three items that are aversive to you, objects you find unattractive, ugly, or offensive in some way. You can place them in a row in the tray you have chosen." Notice if there seems to be greater ease in choosing aversive or attractive objects. Although we may recommend that clients place the objects in a row, this is not necessary. However, starting with the objects in the straight line allows the changes to be more obvious as the therapy progresses. Give similar directions to couples who have selected a joint tray, but begin with a suggestion that they divide the sand in two parts any way they choose. Direct them to place their objects on their own side of the tray.

Because each object that a client chooses, whether it is in a spontaneous tray or a directed tray, is coming from the client's unconscious and conscious, it has significance to the client. As Dundas writes, "objects may represent images of the individual's deep psyche, and not just the immediate expression of a conscious thought" (1990, p. 4). By directing the client to choose three objects that s/he likes and three that s/he does not like, we are in fact directing the client to opposites within her/himself. Often opposites spontaneously appear in trays. But in subpersonality integration trays, we are essentially *forcing* the issue.

Statements of Feelings about the Objects

Once the items have been placed in the tray, have the client (or each member of the dyad) make a few statements about why s/he likes or does not like her/his objects. Such descriptors as, "It is really pretty and soft," or "It is really ugly looking and mean," are typical. At times clients will describe objects in terms of what the objects remind them of in their lives, for example, a memory, a person, or an experience. Remind the partners in a couple that whatever each partner attributes to her/his objects is accurate for her/him. Just as the partner makes no judgment or comment on the client's statements, neither do you. There may be times when you find something attractive and the client finds it distasteful or vice versa. Remember, you are there to hold and accept the client's convictions. Give no verbal or nonverbal messages. The client's descriptions of the objects give you a clue as to what those objects mean to her/him. The descriptions also reveal her/his view of aspects of her/himself.

Animation of the Objects

Have the client animate the objects. You might say, "Pretend that you have a magic wand or are a magician and can make these objects come alive. What would each object say?" Ask the client to have each object speak. This allows for verbal active expression. The client's articulation reveals more about what the object is *thinking*. This process inevitably shows an additional side of the object or confirms or contradicts your perceptions so far.

We have found that clients are generally willing to bring their objects to life and give them voices. However, if clients are reticent, be patient and encouraging. They are usually successful at having the objects *speak*. Notice which objects the client more or less easily gives a voice. Sometimes the aversive objects speak first and more clearly; sometimes the appealing objects more willingly speak. Remind couples to respectfully observe, without interference, as their partners complete this task.

Identification with the Objects

Until now the sandplay has focused on the objects. At this point direct the client to associate the objects with her/himself. Ask the client what aspect of her/himself each object would represent. You might say, "If part of you is like that object, what part of you would it be?" or "What aspect of you is similar to that (naming the object)?" or "How is that like a part of you?" Prior to giving these instructions, we sometimes choose to summarize how the client described each object and what each object said. We find that doing this helps to make the connection between the dissociated characteristics and the internal aspects of the person. When working with a dyad, emphasize the importance of giving full nonjudgmental attention to one's partner. Have one partner complete the discussion about all her/his objects before moving on to the other.

Interaction among the Objects

INTERACTION AMONG THE CLIENT'S OWN OBJECTS

The goal for individuals is to help the client recognize her/his internal dynamics. In this process the client can detect the possible value of all her/his parts and find ways that some aspects of her/himself can interact in a cooperative way with other parts. This results in a more integrated, balanced, and self-accepting state, moving toward resolution of complexes. Instruct the client to move objects and place them in a position that creates a harmonious scene. Suggest that the client pair all the articles in such a way that one object can help another object. An alternative direction you might give is to have the client place items in groups so that one or more objects can be helpful to other objects. For example, one client we worked with placed an angry beast in the tray. She found that the beast needed the crystal and the teddy bear to reduce the beast's uncontrollable rage. Direct the client to have the objects dialogue with each other, much as you would do in the therapy stage for individual spontaneous trays. Base your instructions on the language and issues revealed by the client in the earlier segments of this exercise. You might say, "How can these objects (name objects as the client has named them) negotiate with each other to get along better?" or "What kind of help does this object need? Who in here can help her/him/it?" or "What does she/he/it need to say to, or ask, or communicate to her/him/it (identifying different objects)?" Similar to the therapy stage of spontaneous trays, there may be much movement in the tray. As the end of the session approaches, encourage the client to leave the scene the way that feels best for her/him. Although we do not generally suggest bringing in other objects, if the client is having difficulty finding any consolation or cooperation among the discomforting objects, this recommendation can be advantageous.

With couples we sometimes use other procedures during this interaction among the objects segment. The couple may proceed as described for individuals, i.e., each partner consecutively engages in her/his own therapy, while respectfully and silently observing the process. This allows for some individual *intra*-integration, resolution, and clarity prior to *inter*-integration work between the partners. After each partner has had an opportunity to do her/his personal integration in her/his own tray or on her/his separate side of the shared tray, the two individuals begin to synthesize their objects and find means to have their opposing parts work together. Another option is to forego the individual integration work and do couple therapy with their respective objects. We decide based on the individuals' levels of ego strength, as well as the intrapersonal work that seems to be needed in order for the partners to do interpersonal work. When one of the partners is mildly dissociated or has a great deal of internal conflict or non-acceptance of aspects of her/himself, we find that it is essential for the couple to complete the individual therapy process first. This facilitates attainment of sufficient internal harmony among her/his own subpersonalities so that s/he can interact safely with her/his partner's subpersonalities, which may be in opposition. The greater the internal assistance, understanding, and harmony, the greater the ability to find resolution externally.

INTERACTION AMONG EACH OTHER'S OBJECTS

The goal of having the couple's objects interact with each other is twofold. First, this interaction helps the couple recognize the value of all aspects of themselves and each other. Second, it assists them in discovering how these aspects interact positively and negatively within the relationship; it can also demonstrate how certain aspects can aid in resolving relationship conflicts. For example, if one partner has an aggressive side, a nurturing or patient aspect of her/his partner may be available to show understanding. This is a powerful method to help clients identify what is needed, honor their differences, recognize that there are possibilities for acceptance of each other, and notice the aspects that are in direct conflict.

Once you are prepared to have the partners work together, suggest to them that they erase the line separating their objects or, if they have worked in separate trays, bring their objects into separate sides of a joint tray. Then have them pair or group their own objects with their partner's so that all of the objects are now integrated, creating one scene instead of two. Suggest that they create a world with all their objects in a way that represents their relationship. You might say, "You have chosen to share a life together. Now I suggest that you have these objects share the same space. We're going to look at how these various objects interact with each other and what they need to make a compatible life together. What characters (objects) of yours can be paired or grouped with those of your partner? Which ones seem to go together?" Direct these questions to both partners. Once the figures are placed in the tray, observe the pattern the couple establishes within the tray and the acceptance or non-acceptance of each other's objects. Notice if they match like objects (e.g., aversive with aversive, appealing with appealing) or objects of a dissimilar nature (e.g., aversive with appealing). Observe how the partners negotiate and consult with each other, if one takes the lead or tries to control, and if they seem able to cooperate in this endeavor. We sometimes find that the strengths of the relationship, or those aspects that brought them together, are placed in the center of the tray, and difficulties and conflicts are placed on the perimeter. Occasionally there is an object that doesn't seem to fit, and the couple needs to work to find a place for it. Frequently this exercise evokes laughter or tears. You often witness the parts that partners hate about each other or that are in direct conflict with each other.

Prior to engaging the partners in the therapy stage, ask each of them to describe the scene that has evolved from the joining of their objects. Then perform interventions similar to those you would use in the therapy stage of working in spontaneous trays. You may begin by having them identify the aspects that they placed in the tray that are in conflict with the other's objects. Instruct them to have the conflicting objects dialogue. Then suggest that the couple determine together how they can pair or group the objects that seem to go together in a way that makes the interaction among the objects work best for the whole picture. For example, these are some questions you might direct toward one or both of the partners: "What does that figure (naming the object) need?" "Who can help her/him/it?" "What does that object feel about that (partner's) object?" "What can help these two get along?" "What problems do these objects have with each other? How can they resolve those problems or negotiate their differences?"

When the end of the session is approaching, there are several alternative ways of concluding: (1) Have the couple arrange the scene the way they would like to leave it for the day. You might say, "How would the two of you like to leave the tray as you end today? You may arrange the objects in any way you wish." (2) Have the couple leave the scene in a way that would most depict how they would like to see the sand world for the day. You might say, "How would you like to leave this tray if you wanted to have a good feeling about the relationship in the tray?" or "Who needs to feel better in this scene and how could you leave the tray with that object feeling better?" (3) Have them leave the tray in a way that represents how they are feeling as the session ends. (4) Have the couple arrange the objects in a way that would connote a positive outlook for change.

Documentation

Have the client or, in the case of couple work, each partner take a photograph from the perspective s/he chooses. Ask permission to take a photograph for yourself.

Transition

Direct the individual or the couple to discuss any insights, thoughts, and feelings s/he or they have and how s/he or they would like to apply the sandplay experience after s/he or they leave the session. These are some possible questions you might ask: "How does this reflect your situation/relationship?" "How can you use what happened in the tray today to help you in your life/relationship?" "What did you learn from this sandplay today?"

Dismantling the Tray

After the client has left the therapy room, thoughtfully dismantle the tray and make your notes. By identifying both the troublesome areas and the strengths discovered in the sandplay session, you can structure subsequent sandplay work to address these issues.

Case Illustration of Subpersonality Integration Work

Marika and Chuck came in for therapy because of their discomfort in their relationship. They reported that they frequently found fault with each other and felt criticized by the other. They felt stuck in an argumentative pattern of communication that often ended in a stalemate. Each of them had created spontaneous trays in the sand previously in individual sessions and had found the sandplay enlightening. When we suggested that creating a tray together with more directions from us would be very helpful, they consented.

Following our instructions to divide the tray in half and choose three attractive objects and three aversive objects, the couple separated the sides of the tray by drawing a line down the middle of the sand. Marika chose an eagle, Yoda, and a smooth rock on which was engraved "wonder" for her attractive objects. For her aversive objects she chose a hunter pointing a gun, a broken horse, and a Chinese dragon. Chuck chose as his attractive objects a Native American hand symbol made of metal, a bridge, and a silhouette of a girl with a wand in a picture frame. His aversive objects were a multiheaded dragon, a gray figure of a person with its hands bound behind it, and an army tank with a man aiming a gun appearing from the top of the tank (see illustration #10). Marika described the eagle as being free and strong, Yoda as being wise and accepting, and the rock as holding the wonder

Illustration #10. Couple's Subpersonality Tray,
Introduction and Choice of Objects Stage

of life. She described the hunter as being destructive and egocentric, thinking he was better and more valuable than the animals he was killing. She described the broken horse as damaged and weak, and the dragon as fierce and dangerous. Chuck described the hand as outreaching and protective, the bridge as a path to understanding and connection between people and places, and the girl in the frame as a free creative child full of hope. He described the dragon as an angry, fire-breathing monster, the bound figure as someone who was confined and restricted from doing what it wanted to do, and the tank as murderous and destructive. As they continued to give their objects voices and identify the parts of themselves the objects represented, they listened respectfully to each other. They were intrigued not only by the parallels between the objects they had each chosen but also by the aspects of themselves that were apparent in their dynamics.

We next had them erase the line dividing the tray and couple or group their objects as they chose. We decided to proceed to this step without each one pairing their own objects with each other because they seemed ready to integrate their objects. With little disagreement they grouped the dragons together, the hunter with the tank and the broken horse with the bound figure. It took more thought and negotiating to join their attractive figures. They placed the wonder rock, the girl in the frame, and the eagle together. They joined Yoda with the hand but had difficulty placing the bridge, which they ultimately placed in the middle of the tray. At our request, Marika described the world as it looked to her and related what this experience of creating a conjoint world was like for her. Then Chuck did the same from his perspective. Although the intensity of symbols of anger and aggression in the tray was notable, Marika and Chuck were able to listen to each other without confrontation.

We encouraged dialogue among any of the figures they wished to give a voice. Both jumped right in and had the monsters shouting and fighting. As the therapy proceeded, we asked if the monsters wanted to continue to battle. At first the couple was unsure, then indicated that the world with all this aggression was not a very pleasant or safe place to be. With our suggestion to find a way to alleviate this disharmony, Marika and Chuck began to rearrange the objects. Different groupings were made and changed until they arrived at a culmination (see illustration #11). They felt that the destructiveness of the hunter and the tank could be soothed and given understanding by the "wonder" rock and the hand. The dragons needed a bridge between them so that they could communicate in a way that messages could reach each of them. The strength and freedom of the eagle could help move the broken, weak horse to health and reclamation of its power. The bound figure needed to regain the hope and freedom the girl in the frame exuded. The couple both realized the power of Yoda's wisdom and ability to accept all the inhabitants of the world, so they placed him overlooking the tray, with his outstretched arms encompassing it all.

They each then took a photograph of the world. In our discussion after we left the area of the tray, both Marika and Chuck were able to apply the drama of the sand world to their relationship. They could see the positives and negatives they each contributed. Marika agreed that when the hunter or dragon in her felt like it was emerging or she experienced Chuck's dragon attack, she would honor the dragons and remember that the bridge was in place. Chuck agreed that when Mari-

Illustration #11. Couple's Subpersonality Tray,
Interaction among the Objects Stage

ka's hunter attacked him, he would also remember the bridge and the girl in the frame who could be helpful and hopeful. Both liked the image of Yoda above the world and stated that he would be in their minds when they felt critical or criticized. The symbols of the aspects of themselves and the focus on the drama in the tray helped them to disrupt the reactive dynamic in which they had been stuck.

FAMILY OF ORIGIN TRAYS

Many of the patterns, beliefs, and issues that emerge in sandplay are rooted in past experiences. Legacies are handed down from generation to generation. When these messages can be identified and their effect recognized, an individual comes to understand her/himself better and achieve greater influence over her/his life journey. Often it is helpful for clients to unravel the stories, recognize the messages, and identify those aspects of themselves that have been influenced by their families, either overtly or covertly. Therapists can utilize a variety of techniques to help clients discover acquired patterns and belief systems, e.g., family trees, autobiographies, and multigenerational therapy.

We have found that creating a family of origin sand tray, which we learned from Donna Linn in a workshop, not only visibly exhibits the family heritage but also allows the therapist to become acquainted with the client's family members and their belief systems, behaviors, and idiosyncrasies. In addition, it permits the client to experience symbolically what each family member represents to her/him and allows for therapeutic work among the family member symbols, providing the opportunity for discovery and denouement of unresolved relationships and insidious familial patterns. Positive supports and strengths within the family are also recognized, and issues that brought the client into therapy are clarified.

We do not divide this procedure into stages, though it does follow the same general progression as spontaneous sandplay, that is, from more unconscious, non-interactive work to more conscious, interactive work. We begin with an introduction and choice of objects. The client then describes what is in the tray. We follow this with greater interaction with the client via therapeutic interventions. As in spontaneous sandplay, we conclude the session with documentation and a brief transition period.

First, introduce the client to sandplay as you would with a spontaneous tray. Amend the directions to the client by letting her/him know that you will give more specific instructions than in spontaneous sandplay. However, other than these directives, s/he is free to make whatever choices s/he wishes. Emphasize to the client the relevance to her/him of exploring family relationships and messages. Let her/him know that your suggestions will facilitate greater understanding in this area. Direct the client to choose an object for each member of three generations of her/his family (i.e., grandparents, parents, and siblings). You might say, "You may choose whatever object seems appropriate to represent each member of your family. It may be any object that symbolizes or calls forth a feeling about that person. Perhaps you could line up your grandparents here (designating the top of the tray). Beneath them, place your parents, and beneath them, you and your siblings." The parents' siblings may also be included if this is not too cumbersome and is relevant to the client's issues (e.g., a history of alcoholism, depression, mental illness). However, because you want the focus on the immediate nuclear family and because time is limited, we recommend that you not include the extended parent generation. If there are relevant familial patterns, these will probably emerge in the session without symbolic representation. You can then confirm the impact of these patterns on the client.

After the objects have been chosen, ask the client to describe what it is about each of the objects that reminds her/him of that person, beginning with the oldest generation. Encourage the client to relate any memories that come to mind. Frequently clients choose objects other than people. For example, one client chose a large rock to represent his maternal grandfather. In describing the rock it was clear to him and to us that his grandfather played an important role in his life. He described the rock as solid and strong. The client indicated that his grandfather was always there for him and that he felt very secure and safe with his grandfather. He even stated that the rock connoted a gentleness that, similar to his grandfather, was hidden.

Taking your lead from the information the client has shared while describing the objects/family members, begin appropriate therapeutic interventions as described in the therapy stage in chapter 3. We recall one client who was struggling in her current relationship, the latest in a series of relationships that she had terminated. She realized that when a relationship became too serious she found some reason to end it. She was dissatisfied with and confused about this pattern. When she did a family of origin tray she chose a woman carrying a serving tray to represent her mother. Initially, the client was unaware of the significance of this choice. As she described all the objects, she indicated that her mother was someone who prepared the meals and took care of the family. When we later suggested that the figure that represented the client (a dancer) speak with someone in the sand world, the client briefly hesitated and then had the dancer approach the woman with the tray. The client gave voice to the figures and had them dialogue with each other. The dancer asked the woman why she was always carrying the tray. The woman responded that it was her job. As the dialogue proceeded the client realized that, although she appreciated her mother's availability when she was a child, she generally saw her mother as subservient to her father. She realized that she did not want to give up her freedom and independence and that she viewed marriage as a sacrifice. This insight not only helped her move to a greater self-understanding but facilitated a transformation of perspective on the definition of marriage. She recognized an unconscious fear that was related to her inability to commit to a relationship.

As the end of the session approaches, instruct the client to leave the scene as s/he wishes it to be for that day. Provide the opportunity for a photograph and ask permission to take one for yourself. Discuss the insights the client has gained and how the experience can be applied outside of the therapy office. If apropos, suggest some follow-up activity to put into action what the client has learned. After the client leaves, dismantle the tray thoughtfully and make notes.

AMPLIFICATION

Amplification, as the word implies, is a process that allows the client to elaborate on one issue, topic, or object in the created world. This technique was taught to us by De Domenico, and we have found it fruitful for use with children and adolescents as well as adults. The client may choose the focus of amplification, or the therapist may do so. Sometimes, when a client has created a spontaneous or directed world and has completed the therapeutic intervention phase, one object, a group of objects, or a section of the tray may present itself as significant or needing further resolution. The area that touches you may not always be the same one that moves your client. Although the area often portrays an unresolved issue, it may also reveal a strength. Occasionally an object that represents spiritual or emotional strength and peace to the client is of greater value at that moment than one that represents an unresolved conflict. It is therefore important to give the client a choice as to what part of the tray s/he wishes to explore.

Prior to engaging in the amplification process, give your client the opportunity to take a photograph and, with her/his permission, take one yourself. Then instruct your client to choose the area of primary importance to her/him. You might tell the client, "If you are willing, I would like you to try something a little different for the rest of the session. I will have you choose a figure or an area in the tray that you would like to specifically work on or would like to take time to appreciate." If you are working with a child you might say, "It might be fun for you to find something you have put in this tray and give it a completely new world in another tray. You can make the new world in any way you want it." Most often the client will have objects or an area that s/he is interested in exploring, but if this is not the case, move into the transition stage. If your client agrees that further emphasis is beneficial, direct your client to select another tray of her/his choice, build a new terrain if s/he wishes, take the objects of her/his choice from the previous tray and place them into the new world. If the client chooses, s/he may add other objects to complete the scene. Allow a brief period of time to process the new world. If time does not permit for both trays to be fully experienced, you can ask the client whether s/he would like to rebuild the amplified scene in the next session. You might say, "We don't have time now to spend with this new world and I notice that there are many things here that could be explored further. If you would like, you can rebuild this tray the next time we meet and delve into it in more detail. Since we have a photograph and I have recorded your process, you should be able to rebuild it easily."

To illustrate amplification, let's look at a therapy session with Jessie, who had come to us to deal with stress and anxiety attacks. As a divorced mother of two, working full time at a demanding job, she found herself out of balance and anxious much of the time. When Jessie built her world she worked rapidly, bringing in a multitude of objects. In one corner of the tray she buried a coffin with a male figure inside, whom she later identified as her ex-husband. She then placed a figure of a child on the sand on top of the buried coffin. In the center she placed two children and a mother screaming at each other. It seemed obvious to us that these groupings of objects represented issues she needed to investigate further. However, when it was time for Jessie to choose the area she wanted to explore, she immediately selected the corner of the tray that contained a solitary Buddha sitting near a large cluster of crystals. In the new tray she built a beautiful alter of large rocks near a lake and placed the Buddha near the lake in the hollow of the rocks. Then she placed a woman, whom she later identified as herself, on top of the rocks overlooking the scene. Her body began to relax and the tears flowed. She sat there for several minutes breathing in the scene and the peaceful feeling. Then she turned to us and said, "Thank you. This is the first time I have felt inner serenity since my husband walked out on me." When Jessie returned the following week she said she had used the image of the scene and the feeling it elicited to relax whenever she felt herself becoming anxious.

Sometimes you might decide not to give the client a choice of the area to be amplified. If you have a client who tends to avoid issues or who is experiencing a powerful emotional response to an aspect of the tray, you may want to ask her/him to amplify that area or issue. This can be done either during or after the therapeutic intervention phase. The instructions you give to the client are similar to those just described, with the exception that you identify the initial focus.

TRAUMA TRAYS

Because most therapists frequently work with clients who have experienced trauma recently and/or in the past, we include a short section on how to use sandplay to remember and resolve emotional wounding. The trauma work described here comes from years of work with clients using hypnosis, imaging, and Gestalt to help them relive their trauma and thus, over time, release it and then reframe and integrate it. We wish to thank Gisela De Domenico for suggesting the concept of replaying the trauma in the tray. Traumas that have seriously threatened the emotional and/or physical integrity of people (e.g., being involved in or witnessing physical and sexual abuse, neglect, school shootings, homicide, war, accidents, or natural disasters) often lead to distressing symptoms, such as fear, terror, and helplessness. Sometimes clients reexperience the traumatic events and begin to avoid any stimuli associated with the trauma. At times they become hypervigilant or dissociate and become numb. They may be unable or unwilling to speak of what happened. Occasionally clients come to therapy with a feeling of general unease, anxiety, and depression without realizing the source of the problem. In any case, most clients who have experienced severe trauma, whether they remember it or not, have difficulty functioning in a normal fashion and need help to resolve their issues and memories of the event.

When a client has forgotten or is unable to speak of her/his traumas, you might assess the client's possible unresolved issues by suggesting the creation of a spontaneous sand world early in therapy. Sandplay may reveal unconscious memories of past traumas that have not been addressed. Often, however, clients come to you with the explicit purpose of dealing with a trauma that has occurred recently or one that they remember and that is creating fairly severe symptoms. Under these circumstances sandplay can be used as soon as the client and you have developed a trusting relationship. Directed trauma trays can be used with clients as young as 7 years old if they are maturationally capable of understanding your directions. If your client feels threatened by guided play focused on the trauma, allow her/him to create spontaneous worlds for as long as s/he needs to before you proceed to directed trays.

For the initial directed tray at least, you might ask your client to recreate the incident as it occurred but as if it were a play. Include all the characters, actions, reactions, thoughts, and feelings. Direct the client to tell the story as it evolves in the tray. Although the creation of a static picture is of value, more information can be gleaned if the' client creates a moving world. This process allows the client and you to focus on changes as they occurred during the trauma. You might say, "As you recreate the situation, show me and tell me exactly what happened during the incident with you as the main character. Describe it from your perspective. Start at what you consider to be the beginning and follow the events as they unfolded to where the incident ended." For children, you might say, "Find a person or animal on one of the shelves and pretend that the object is you. Show me in the sand tray just what happened to you. You can use as many objects as needed to make it very real."

Portraying the incident in the tray and focusing on the building process often distance the trauma and allow the client to reveal the details of the story in the tray with less intimidation. Directed trauma trays are different from spontaneous trays in that you encourage the client to relate the story in the first person instead of the third person. If the client has difficulty relating the incident in the first person, you might suggest that s/he create a story in the third person, possibly using fictitious names. You might also suggest that s/he become the director of the play and relate the story from the director's perspective. Children particularly find this latter technique less threatening and will often reveal more if they speak in the third person. You might say to a child, "Pretend that what we were talking about happened to one of the objects on these shelves (point to the shelves and let the child choose an item). Now show me what happened to her/him/it and tell me a story about it. Make it happen in the sand. You can use anything on these shelves you need." If there is an area of the tray that needs further exploration after the client has completed the moving tray, ask your client to amplify this portion. This may be done during the same session if there is time, and if not, during the following session.

Not only does the client reexperience the trauma as s/he recreates it, but s/he also frequently moves stuck emotional and physical energy as s/he uses her/his hands to move the sand and manipulate the figures in the tray. When the client actually sees what occurred during the trauma from this perspective and explores the experience verbally, a release of emotion and a change of perception frequently occur. Many clients have relived their traumatic experiences only in their minds and have spoken very little about them to others.

Depending on the trauma and the issues, it is often valuable to suggest specific aspects of the trauma for sandplay during subsequent sessions. In addition, directed trays for redesigning life situations and ego-strengthening and skill-building, as described earlier in this chapter, can be used to help clients resolve traumas.

Another way to address trauma in the tray is to ask the client to create a scene, bring in all the people with whom s/he needs to resolve this issue, and then bring in a figure that represents her/him. Have the client process the tray using the stages already mentioned. During the therapeutic intervention stage, ask the client to have the figure that represents her/him dialogue with each one of the figures symbolizing people with whom s/he feels unresolved. If need be, have the people dialogue with each other.

Ask your client to amplify any area of the above trays that needs resolution. For example, Terry, who had been raped during a date, brought in a symbol of the man who raped her, as well as symbols of her mother, father, and present boyfriend, when we asked her to build a world that included all those with whom she needed to resolve the issues resulting from this incident. During the session it became apparent that Terry was still very angry at the man who raped her. She realized that she needed further resolution with him before she could leave the incident behind and trust men again. Terry chose to amplify the section in the tray that included the rapist. She placed an aggressive figure of a woman representing herself across the tray from him and then had the figure of the woman scream at the offender and pound him into the sand. She later revealed that it had been important to have the figures of the man and woman alone in the tray because she felt the parent figures would have disapproved of the woman's anger. With the judgmental parent figures present in her tray, the woman could not fully express herself. After the session, Terry realized how important it was for her to remove the introjection of her parents' voices of judgment so that she could finally be as angry as she needed to be.

Partners/families of the client are often affected by the trauma, even though they may not be aware of what happened. It may, therefore, be important to work with the client's partner and/or family. However, include the perpetrator of the trauma in the therapy only if s/he has already done or is doing her/his own personal work and the client and other family members agree to inclusion. When your client has resolved the trauma for her/himself and wants to find resolution within her/his partner/family unit, suggest couple/family therapy. There are several ways to work with couples and families involved in trauma. Again, you can begin with individual spontaneous sandplay sessions to acquaint the couple/family members with sandplay. Once they are comfortable with the process and you have assessed that they are ready, have each member build a separate world showing the trauma from her/his perspective. Then, as in the guiding partner through the world phase in chapter 4, have each member tell the story to the others, including their feelings and their thoughts. Often new perspectives are revealed, and members gain new insights and resolve old bitterness or misunderstandings. If you have time after they have shared their worlds and you feel they are ready to do so, have them take the objects that they would like to include from their first world and bring them into a new conjoint world of the couple's/family's choosing. You can then explore the new world together.

The following is an example of this approach. We worked with a couple who was having difficulty resolving a recent trauma. The young woman had been assaulted during an evening run in the park. Although her partner, an older man, seemed very solicitous, the woman felt that he carried resentment. They were no longer close. During the therapy stage her partner revealed that he believed that no self-respecting woman would go out running in the park after dark. He admitted blaming her for being "at the wrong place at the wrong time." As he focused on the area in his own tray that portrayed the assault, he recognized the dark shrouded figure that was holding an ax to the female figure's head as not only the perpetrator but also himself. Until that time he had not seen himself as a part of the scene. When the couple brought their figures into a conjoint world, he was able to leave the shrouded figure behind and in its place bring in an ordinary male figure who stretched out his hand to the woman.

In future sessions you might ask the couple/family to explore how each member has continued to be affected by the trauma. You may also ask the couple to build a world delving into any of the previously listed aspects of the trauma as well as any other areas that seem relevant. As an alternative to using individual trays in the couple or family context, you might ask the couple or family to begin with a conjoint world showing you how they, as a unit, see the identified trauma. Amplifying sections of individual, couple, or family trays is as important for couple/family work as it is for individual therapy. As therapy progresses, regardless of whether you work with individuals, couples, families, or groups, sand worlds build on sand worlds. Gradually issues are resolved and symptoms of individual and group distress disappear.

Although this section deals mostly with adults, many therapists have asked us how they can use sandplay to help children resolve traumas. To demonstrate how sandplay can effectively be used with traumatized children, we would like to relate a difficult case of an abused child. Although we worked with both Beverly and her mother individually and conjointly using sandplay, we describe only our work with Beverly. Beverly and her mother were referred to us by social services immediately after they had reported that Beverly had been sexually abused by her baby-sitter's husband, Mr. Smythe. Beverly, an only child, was 10 years old at the time of the referral. Mrs. Smythe had been her baby-sitter for three years, and the sexual abuse occurred when Beverly stayed with Mrs. Smythe on weekends. Beverly's mother, who was divorced, worked at a local clothing store. Beverly, according to the mother, felt very close to Mrs. Smythe and regarded her as a second mother. The sexual abuse first came to the mother's attention when she noticed that Beverly had difficulty sitting. When the mother questioned Beverly and examined her, she discovered Beverly's irritated, swollen rectum. Beverly burst into tears and said, "Mr. Smythe did it." The mother, who already felt severely stressed because of lack of finances and a belligerent ex-husband, exploded. She reported the incident to the police immediately. The police sent Beverly to see a doctor and a social worker, who referred her to us.

When Beverly and her mother arrived for their first session, her mother appeared anxious but spoke freely about the situation. She seemed very supportive of Beverly and was willing to be a participant in the therapy process. Beverly, however, was silent throughout the initial session. Until now she had told no one in detail about what had happened to her. In that first session, Beverly's mother spoke about the changes in her daughter's behavior in the previous year. Beverly, normally a friendly, outgoing child, had become more and more withdrawn and at present spent much of her time alone in her room. She would awaken frequently at night screaming. The school was also concerned because her grades had dropped and she no longer spent time with her friends.

Initially, we decided to work with Beverly and her mother separately, because it was clear that the child would not explore her trauma in the presence of her mother. Beverly was immediately drawn to the sand tray and created a spontaneous sand world. Her first sand tray portrayed an idyllic world full of soft fuzzy animals and beautiful flowers and trees near a lake. She did not bring in any human figures. When she told the story of her scene she spoke easily of her love for nature and her pets. As therapy continued, Beverly chose to create sand worlds more and more frequently. Gradually, as she trusted us, she brought in a figure that symbolized her mother, whom, she stated, she loved very much. But Beverly revealed that she felt she needed to protect her mother because of the stress her mother was experiencing. She did not want to disappoint her mother or make her angry. She spoke briefly of her mother's distress about the abuse but was unable to talk about what had happened. A couple of sessions later, Beverly placed an enormous spider, hidden by large rocks and bushes, in her tray. But when she told her story she did not include the spider. Instead, when we mentioned the spider she became very anxious and left the tray. The spider, however, reappeared in each subsequent tray and was less and less hidden. A few weeks passed before she began to talk about the spider. At this time it became evident that the spider represented the man who had abused her.

Eventually, when we felt that she was ready, we asked Beverly to recreate the abuse. She began by having an angry figure of a woman dropping off a small, frightened figure of ET in a girl's dress and hat, at a place she had built out of cardboard pieces. Inside stood a large, plump, smiling figure of a woman, who welcomed her with outstretched arms. Behind a stack of paper that Beverly had torn and placed in a pile hid the spider. As the story progressed, the two women figures left and the spider came out from behind the papers. The frightened ET ran around frantically but was unable to escape from the spider, who jumped on her and "did it to her." She finished the scene with ET pushed half hidden into the sand and the spider sitting on top of the papers. As she told her story she revealed that her babysitter, the plump, friendly woman, would often leave the house shortly after her mother, the angry woman, left in the morning. Her babysitter's husband, Mr. Smythe, the spider, would then take her into a storage shed that was filled with pornographic videos and magazines. He would force her to look at them before he raped her, so (he said) she could learn the finer art of being a good sexual partner.

After she gave voice to the actual abuse, her scenes changed rapidly. Although the spider still remained, it became smaller and smaller. During a family session, Beverly's mother related that Beverly still had periods of intense fear that Mr. Smythe would "come and get her." At Beverly's next individual session, we asked her to create a movie in the tray that would show us how she could make Mr. Smythe less frightening. She recreated the usual scene, but this time she took a normal looking girl figure (as opposed to the ET figure) and had it pounce on the tiny spider and grind it into the sand. Then, at our direction she made a spider out of Play-doh, placed it on the floor, and smashed it with her foot. She ran around the room gleefully yelling, "Mr. Smythe is dead!" Before she left, we devised a way for her to visualize Mr. Smythe as a small bug that she could squash under her foot each time she became afraid of him. For several sessions that followed, she created a "bug" out of Play-doh and stomped on it, yelling and screaming. Her fears and nightmares slowly disappeared.

In this case sandplay therapy was effective because it gave Beverly the opportunity to objectify and work through the trauma both visually and tactilely. It moved her from feeling like a victim to being a master of the experience. In addition, sandplay was particularly powerful because it was the therapy Beverly chose.

. . . .

Redesigning Life Situations

- Ask the client to commit to changing old patterns.
- Have the client recreate in the tray an event that has caused a problem.
- Guide the client through the therapy stage as in a spontaneous tray.
- Instruct the client to select an object in the tray that represents the part of the self creating the problem and place it in the center of the tray.
- Ask the client to find an object that represents a wise entity.
- Place the wise figure in the tray across from the object in the center.
- Ask the client to have the figures dialogue and find a solution.
- Have the client select a third object that represents the capable self.
- Then ask the client to remove objects from the tray while imaging undoing the old pattern.
- Instruct the client to build a new scene representing the changed pattern, using the figure of the capable self in the tray.
- Again guide the client through the therapy stage.
- Have the client take a photograph to reinforce the new behavior pattern.
- In the transition stage ask the client to image the new pattern frequently during the coming week.

. . . .

Ego-Strengthening and Skill-Building

- Prepare the client by establishing a safe environment.
- Provide a follow-up plan in case the client's deep fears are experienced in the session.
- Direct the client to put the "problem" in the tray.
- Proceed through the experiencing and rearranging stage.
- Employ therapeutic strengthening interventions, having the client practice the desired outcome.
- Photograph the scene.
- Discuss the client's experience and how s/he can use what transpired.
- Reinforce her/his sense of security.

. . . .

Negotiating Opposites

- Give the client two opposite figures that symbolize the issue.
- Ask the client to create a scene with these two and any other figures.
- Process the scene as you would a spontaneous sand tray.
- Instruct the client during the transition stage to observe how these opposites manifest in everyday life.
- Repeat the exercise, allowing the client to choose the symbols of opposites in the next session.

. . . .

Subpersonality Integration

- Introduce the client to subpersonality integration sandplay.
- Instruct the client to choose three appealing objects and three aversive objects and place them in the sand tray. With a couple, each chooses six objects and places them on her/his side of the tray.
- Ask the client to describe each object. With a couple, passive partner describes her/his tray first.
- Have the client animate each object, giving it a voice. With a couple, have the partner respectfully listen while the other speaks.
- Encourage the client to consciously identify a part of her/himself with each object. With a couple, have the partner respectfully listen while the other speaks.
- Guide interaction among the objects that can benefit from dialogue, movement, or communication. With a couple, the partners may engage their own objects with each other first, or may engage their objects with their partner's objects.
- Give the client the opportunity to photograph the final scene. With a couple, each partner may take a photograph.
- Facilitate discussion of how the client can apply the experience to her/himself (or to the couple's relationship).
- Thoughtfully dismantle the tray.

Family of Origin

- Introduce the client to family of origin sandplay.
- Instruct the client to choose an object representing grandparents, parents, self, and siblings.
- Have the client describe each object/family member.
- Encourage the client to animate the objects and have them engage in relevant interaction.
- Direct the client to leave the scene as s/he wishes.
- Provide the opportunity for photographs.
- Engage the client in exploring the applicability to her/his current life situation.
- Thoughtfully dismantle the scene.

Amplification

- Allow the client to build a nondirected sand world and process it.
- Introduce the client to the amplification process.
- Choose the area or instruct the client to choose the area in the tray to be amplified.
- Ask the client to select another tray and build a new terrain.
- Direct the client to bring into the new tray those objects s/he wants to amplify.
- Ask the client to complete the scene in any way s/he wishes.
- Process the new world with the client.

Trauma Trays

INDIVIDUAL TRAUMA TRAYS
- Ask the client to recreate the incident as it occurred.
- Direct the client to tell the story as it evolves in the tray.
- Amplify any area in the tray that needs further resolution.

COUPLE/FAMILY TRAUMA TRAYS
- Introduce the couple/family to trauma work in the sand.
- Have each member build a separate tray showing the trauma from her/his perspective.
- Ask each member to tell her/his story to the others.
- Help each member explore her/his world.
- If issues are sufficiently resolved, have the members bring objects from their trays into a conjoint tray.
- Process the conjoint world with the couple/family.

7

DIRECTED SAND TRAYS WITH CHILDREN AND FAMILIES

DIRECTED SAND TRAYS WITH CHILDREN

As with adults, it is often expedient to use directed sandplay rather than spontaneous trays with children and adolescents. Likewise, the same respect, acceptance, and adherence to the clients' needs apply to these directed trays.

Limiting the Number of Objects

Occasionally children dump a huge number of objects into their trays. We usually allow this to occur several times. If the play does not eventually evolve or if we are either unwilling or unable to allow this behavior to continue due to time limitations (inadequate clean-up time between sessions or the number of sessions available), we suggest a directed sand play rather than eliminating sandplay completely. You might also wish to consider using this technique if a child is having difficulty starting sandplay or building a world. Ask the child to find any 12 objects s/he wishes to put into the tray and place them anywhere s/he likes. This structures the play in such a way that children feel safe within the limits you provide. Then proceed through the stages as you would during a spontaneous sandplay session. You might also suggest to the child that s/he find four plants and/or articles made of plants (e.g., nests) and place them into the tray. Then have her/him find and place four animals and/or animal products (e.g., feathers, bones) into the tray. Finally, ask her/him to find four people and place them into the world. Following the introduction of each category of objects, suggest that the child take a little time to be with the sand world as it is. At this pause, give her/him an opportunity to make any changes s/he wishes. This will allow the builder to create a complete, orderly world step by step and experience what it is like to introduce these categories separately. You can then explore this new world as you would when your client has created a spontaneous world.

Games

HIDE AND SEEK

The acts of hiding and finding, burying and exposing, and covering and uncovering often take place without the actual game of hide and seek occurring. If you have a client who seems reluctant to uncover hidden material but is almost ready to do so, the game of hide and seek often facilitates movement. You can recognize this readiness when children repeatedly hide or bury objects in the sand and leave them hidden. We notice that as children move toward greater willingness to work on their issues, they begin to talk about the buried objects but do not uncover them. When you assess that it is timely to intervene and move the process along, suggest the game of hide and seek to the child. Direct her/him to hide as many objects in the sand as s/he wishes. You might say, "You seem to like to hide things in the sand. Wouldn't it be fun to play hide and seek in the tray, kind of like you play hide and seek with your friends?" Once the child has chosen and hidden the objects while you turn away or close your eyes, look for and expose the objects. Notice what objects the child chooses. The nature of the objects that are hidden or buried, as well as the act of disappearing, is significant.

At this point ask the child to tell a story or talk about the objects if s/he wishes. Often, early in this game, children just want to play and not talk. Exchange places—this time you choose the objects. Select items that you believe are therapeutically relevant for the child's situation. Proceed as previously, instructing the child to close her/his eyes, then find the hidden objects. After the child finds the objects, request that s/he tell a story. Some children will say that it is your turn to tell the story. In this case, tell a story. Keep the story nonthreatening but indirectly related to the relevant issues. If the child did not tell a story about the objects s/he buried, you will be modeling storytelling for her/him.

We have Laurie, a 10-year-old client, to thank for introducing the actual game of hide and seek in the sand tray. Laurie was referred to us because she experienced difficulty with her peers, with school performance, and with several irrational fears. In retrospect, her mother suspected that an uncle who had been living with them had sexually abused Laurie from the time she was under 3 years old until she was 7. Laurie either had no memory of the abuse or was in denial. Because of her resistance to allow her imagination and creativity full reign and thus expose painful issues, she suggested we play a game in which she would hide objects and we would find them. She suggested that we turn away while she chose objects and hid them in the sand. She then instructed us to find them. She repeated this activity for several weeks, still reluctant to talk about the tray.

At this point, we decided that it might be therapeutically helpful for Laurie to begin finding hidden objects, because we suspected that she was unconsciously desirous of our finding what was concealed within her. Therefore, we suggested that we take a turn at covering objects, to which she agreed. We chose objects thoughtfully and included those that could have some meaning for Laurie. She enjoyed taking the finding role as much as she had enjoyed taking the hiding role. When we suggested that she make up a story about the objects, she declined. For several sessions we played this game, alternating roles. She spoke increasingly about the objects. Then one day she created an action story about the characters that we had hidden, in which a man on a motorcycle was trying to get away from his girlfriend. They had had a fight and the woman had thrown a hot pot of water in his face. The man's reaction was to hit her hard and push her down. He then ran out of the house. This story revealed the fears of violence and abandonment that she experienced in real life. Following this series of trays, she was less reluctant to disclose these hidden experiences of her past.

MAZES

Life presents many challenges to meet, hurdles to overcome, barriers to eliminate or circumvent, and goals to achieve. Mazes are an appropriate metaphor for clients who struggle with the encumbrances of life. Children approximately 7 years old to adolescence often like to create and successfully traverse a maze. Because sand is so inviting and safe, it is a medium well suited for creating mazes replete with barriers that can be overcome to reach the desired destination. Ask clients to create a maze in the tray. You might say, "I noticed that you like to do mazes and solve puzzles. Today we'll be doing something a little different. I thought it would be fun for you to make a maze in the sand. You can use the sand itself, fences, walls, dangerous areas, or anything you like to hinder and block your journey to the final destination." Have them name what it is they are trying to reach. Then have them make the journey and, at each block they encounter, find a way to get around it or remove it from their path. As they reach their destination they will feel a sense of empowerment; moreover, they will have learned some problem-solving skills along the way. Sometimes children ask you to create the maze for them; sometimes they create a maze for you to traverse; sometimes they ask you to join them in the creation of the maze. These skills are adaptive, and the child can generalize them to her/his life outside the office.

Creating a Story

For children who like interactive play or who have difficulty building sand worlds on their own, creating stories with the therapist as they construct their worlds is valuable. This intervention was adapted to sandplay from a combination of Winnicott's squiggle technique as described in Webb (1991), and other storytelling techniques. In this procedure the child and therapist create a story using sandplay objects that are individually and alternately selected and placed in the tray. If the child requests interactive play, ask the child if s/he would be willing to make a story together with you in the sand. If s/he consents, have the child find any object s/he is drawn to and place it into the tray. Then ask her/him to begin the story with one sentence involving the object s/he has placed in the tray. You might say, "I thought it would be fun to do something a little different today. How would you like it if we make up a story together and act it out in the sand tray? We could take turns and add things to the story. You can begin by choosing any object you want and putting it in the sand tray. Just make up a sentence about the object. Then it will be my turn. You can start the story or, if you wish, I can start." Whoever the child chooses as the initiator of the story will begin.

The story will continue, with each person selecting and placing objects alternately into the tray, until the story and scene are complete. Ask the client to end the story, unless the child or adolescent has difficulty and requests that you end it. We have found that, although some children are reluctant to begin the story, most become immersed in the activity and readily devise an ending. Although we always follow the child's lead or theme, we often select relevant objects or lead the story in a direction that we feel is the most therapeutically helpful. This is particularly pertinent when (a) we want specific information, (b) we feel that it is important for the child to resolve certain issues rapidly (e.g., managed care clients who have a limited number of visits), (c) the child seems on the verge of opening up hidden material but has some trepidation about this movement, or (d) we wish to teach a lesson with the story.

This brings to mind Hope, a bright, creative 10-year-old girl who had been in therapy with us for two months. She had been referred to us because her mother, who was recently divorced, was having difficulty controlling Hope. Hope was very headstrong and frequently engaged in power struggles. Her obstinacy was affecting her interactions with both authority figures (i.e., her mother and teacher) and her peers. Over the two-month period of therapy, Hope had participated in art therapy, storytelling, and other play modalities. She had played in the sand but used no objects. During most of these activities, she had maintained control of the situation and seemed to be disinclined to go beyond a certain point. While the previous therapy had revealed Hope's fear of abandonment and need for control, she managed to sidestep any comments we made that would move her closer to expression of her fears.

Because Hope was so creative and appeared to enjoy storytelling, we decided to combine the creative aspect of storytelling with the objectification of her thoughts and feelings through sandplay. Since she could make changes in the tray, unlike with drawing, we felt that she would feel safer and more in control. Our intuition was correct. As the story evolved, Hope created a scene in which a lost dog was looking for his mother and father. We were careful not to bring resolution to the dog's dilemma with our insertions; instead we added relatively innocuous objects and statements that rounded out the environment. Hope eventually brought in a friend for the dog, and the dog invited the friend to live with him. The friend said he would never go away. This seemed to be a breakthrough for Hope, as she expressed indirectly her need to control the environment because of her fear of being abandoned and alone. The interactive nature of this method of sand-play, which used Hope's active imagination and ability to see and change the scene at will, coupled with our support, facilitated Hope's movement toward healing.

Directed Topic Sand Trays

We have seen time and time again that even the most difficult problem in a child's life can be played out in the sand with less defensiveness than through talk therapy and often even other modes of play (art, storytelling, etc.). As Violet Oaklander wrote, referring to a case example she described, "Such enactments of real situations in a child's life can be done without the use of sand quite effectively. I find, however, that because sand is so appealing to children, it lends itself to freer expression" (1988, p. 168). For child and adolescent clients, recreating a particular situation, relationship, or problem in the sand feels a lot safer than talking about it.

When doing directed trays with children, you may choose to use a full hour session or reduce the amount of time, depending on the client. A colleague told us that she sometimes decreases the time of the session to half an hour for children who tend to use distracting tactics to avoid relevant issues. In such cases she spends the entire half-hour having the client recreate a particular problem in the tray. Our colleague stated that she found this to be a much more expedient path toward progress than a full session. This time limitation gives the child the message that s/he should get down to business.

When time and money are at a premium, a directed, limited session reduces the possibility of waste. You might say to a child who is delinquent in doing his school work, "How about if you create a sand world today about a boy who hates school and doesn't do any of his work?" Or to an adolescent trying to assert his independence, "You have really been having a hard time with your parents treating you like a child. Maybe today it would be a good idea to create a world in the sand tray about someone who wants more freedom to do as he pleases." Alternatively, you might instruct the client to actually recreate her/his own situation. Have her/him create the scene and then process it as you would a spontaneous tray. If you ask the client to create the scene about someone like her/him in the particular situation, have the client use the third person when processing the scene. If you ask the client to recreate her/his own situation in the tray, process it having the client use the first person. In both cases, keep the focus on the tray as much as possible.

The following is an example of a directed topic tray that a young adolescent girl built. It demonstrates the effectiveness of using concrete physical form to help older children and adolescents comprehend their actions. We began seeing a 13-year-old client immediately after her sexual abuse by her father had been reported. She was placed into foster care, and her father, to whom she felt close, was court ordered not to see her without supervision. During the therapy process she secretly continued to meet with her father, and seductive touching and verbal sexual abuse persisted. On a cognitive level she knew that the continued sexual abuse was unacceptable, but that knowledge did not change her behavior. When she finally revealed that she was still seeing her father, we reported this to her social worker, as agreed upon earlier. Even after our discussion she did not seem to understand how her meetings with her father facilitated continued abuse. At this time we suggested sandplay. We asked her to place the situation into the tray. In the tray she created a scene in which a girl figure was standing next to a male figure on one side of a river. The other side was empty. She described the feelings and relationship between the girl figure and the male figure. Suddenly she noticed how close the girl figure and the male figure stood to each other. When she actually saw this scene, the attachment between her and her father became a physical and emotional reality to her.

As the story unfolded it became clear that the girl figure was uncomfortable and frightened but felt drawn to stay. We explored further, and the client divulged that the girl figure was ambivalent. The girl figure was afraid that if she was near the male figure he would hurt her, but if she did not meet with him, either he would come after her and/or she would not get the love she wanted from him. We said, "What would make the girl figure feel less afraid?" She didn't know. We next asked, "What would the girl figure want to say to the male figure?" The client responded, "She's too afraid to talk to him." We then inquired, "What would happen if she moved away from the man?" At first, the client felt incapable of moving the girl figure. After a brief time of quiet, the client very deliberately moved the girl figure to the other side of the river and brought in other objects to support her. This helped the girl figure feel less alone. The client's body relaxed. She revealed that the girl figure actually felt relieved to be away from the male figure. Later, in the transition stage, the client stated that she had not previously realized that being close to her father actually facilitated the abuse or that she had the power to remove herself from an unsafe position. After this session and her talk with the social worker, she did not meet with her father again without supervision.

Individuation Trays for Adolescents

Individuation is a normal developmental process in which adolescents move increasingly toward their own individuality, separate from their parents. For some adolescents, however, this process may be difficult. They may suffer intensely from their pronounced rebellion against authority or their inability to separate and form their own identities. Usually spontaneous sandplay will automatically address these issues. Sometimes, however, it is appropriate to approach the issue in a more direct fashion, for instance, if you see that the adolescent is avoiding the issue or if you have a limited number of sessions. If the client is willing to try a directed individuation tray, you might say, "I'd like you to find an object on the shelves that stands for your mother and place it anywhere in the tray you wish. Then I want you to do the same for your father and then for you. When you have done this, complete the scene in such a way that it represents the relationship between you and your parents right now." After the client has completed the scene, briefly process the tray with her/him. Then ask her/him to pretend that s/he has finished high school and is on her/his own. Instruct the client to create a new world in a clean tray portraying the relationship between the parent figures and the self at this future time. Let the adolescent know that s/he may either use the figures from the first tray or find new ones. Then process this tray. In either this or a subsequent session, you might ask the adolescent to create a tray with a figure representing himself but void of figures representing his parents.

For example, Ryan, 16, requested therapy because he was having difficulty dealing with his parents' divorce. He was living with his mother and stepfather at the time. His father was emotionally close to Ryan but rarely saw him, because the mother and stepfather made sure that Ryan had other commitments during the times scheduled for the father's visits. His father was deeply concerned about his son. Ryan spent part of the summer with his father, who brought him to see us. Ryan stated that he was having difficulty with his stepfather, who expected perfection from him and would withdraw his approval whenever Ryan did not succeed in satisfying his demands. Ryan would then try harder and harder to please. When his stepfather was happy with Ryan, he was a wise, loving, and kind person. At this point Ryan did very little with his peers, because their behavior usually displeased his stepfather. Ryan's mother, who was rarely at home due to job demands, supported the stepfather completely and ended up arguing frequently with Ryan about minor issues.

Because Ryan was able to come to only four sessions while he was staying with his father, we asked him if he would be willing to try a directed tray on his third visit. He selected Cruela from the movie "One Hundred and One Dalmations" as his mother and a bear as his stepfather. He selected a figure of a kneeling, ancient, Chinese warrior as his father. Then he chose a long-eared, sad-looking dog as himself. He placed the bear near and across from the dog in the center of the tray. He then placed Cruela on one side of the tray with her finger pointing at the others. The Chinese warrior was hidden behind some bushes at the other side of the scene; he was looking at the others but doing nothing.

When Ryan constructed the next tray portraying the future relationships with his parents, he smiled and said, "This is wonderful. I can place my parents wherever I want them to be!" First he moved Cruela and placed her behind a large rock. Then he removed the Chinese warrior and stated that he was unsure about where to place him. He took the bear and set him far to one side of the tray, facing away from the center. In the center he built his new life independent from his parents. He included a home, a lake and trees, and a guitar. At last he returned to the warrior and the dog. He selected the warrior and stated, "You know, this warrior is really me. I'm not the dog anymore." He then placed the kneeling warrior at the center of the tray near the house. During the transition stage Ryan stated that he felt different after completing the tray. He knew that it was not very important how his stepfather felt about him anymore, and it was okay for the stepfather to be walking out of his life. He needed to create his own life now. His only concern was that his father might feel hurt because he had physically removed him completely from his new world. Although Ryan was not aware of the process, his identification with his father was clear because of his substitution of the father figure (the Chinese warrior) for himself. In fact, he had actually made manifest the emotional strength he derived from his biological father.

DIRECTED SAND TRAYS WITH FAMILIES

Sandplay with families, as mentioned earlier, is a powerful means of resolving family issues. But as with individuals and couples, situations arise that warrant more directed attention than spontaneous sandplay affords. When families have few funds, have no or limited insurance or are merely interested in brief therapy, and/or when you determine that a more focused approach might be of value, directed family sessions are appropriate. As with individual and couple therapy, have the family create at least one spontaneous tray prior to doing a directed sand tray. As you become more comfortable and confident using sandplay, we encourage you to modify our techniques or develop new ones.

Directed Topic Sand Trays

Directed topic sandplay is especially useful in dealing with a trauma, a dysfunctional family pattern, a strength, or an unsolved problem. You might say, "There is an issue in your family (mention the problem or situation) that we discussed only briefly at the last session. If you are willing, today might be a good time to deal with this in the sand tray. Please show me exactly what happens/happened when this situation occurs/occurred, by making a picture of it." Depending on your assessment, have the family work in one or multiple trays. If you wish to determine how each person perceives the situation or problem individually, have the members use separate trays. If you wish to ascertain how the family sees the issue as a unit, have family members build in one tray, giving them permission to discuss their perceptions with each other as they build. Make sure that each person participates in the construction of the scene.

Resolving Power Struggles

This technique specifically addresses power issues in the family. When you have assessed that family members are in the midst of a power struggle they seem unable to resolve, you might wish to have them work on it in the sand tray. Frequently families with adolescents encounter this problem. Ask each family member to first build an individual sand world portraying the struggle from her/his own perspective and then process the scenes as you would spontaneous individuation trays for families. This allows each person to tell the story as s/he sees it and encourages each person to hear all the others' points of view.

During the next session have the family build a conjoint tray, asking each member to bring in the figure s/he used to represent her/himself in the previous tray. Then let the family know that they may complete the scene in any way they wish, using any objects they choose to depict the power struggle from the view of the family. Briefly process this tray, having each member take you through a brief tour of the conjoint world. Make sure they each claim all the objects. At this point have the family jointly find one object that represents an objective helper or wise one who can see the problem and help the other objects in the tray resolve the issue rationally. You might say, "There is an inner voice in each one of you that knows the answers to these problems. Perhaps you could find one object together that represents this wise voice." Place this figure in the center of the tray. Have each person bring the object that represents her/himself into the middle of the tray, facing the helper. Then ask each member in turn to have the objects in the middle dialogue with each other and the helper, suggesting possible solutions.

If the family members are unable to see the viewpoint of the others, you might suggest that each member give voice to the object that symbolizes her/himself. Then have members take each other's roles (e.g., mother takes the role of the daughter figure and daughter takes the role of the mother figure) and dialogue again. Make sure each family member has an opportunity to give the helper a voice. Keep the play in the tray. If the family members are unable to take the role of the helper, you may offer to do so. Encourage them, however, to come up with their own solutions as much as possible. You might at this point have the family take some time away from the play and do some problem-solving. The decision that the family agrees to implement must include at least partly what those struggling for or needing to maintain power have agreed to or suggested. Without their cooperation the solution will not work. If you have time, ask the family to rearrange the objects in the tray so that they can physically see the solution they have jointly determined. Have the family take a photograph of the solution tray and send it home with them. If you do not have time for the family to rearrange the solution tray, have them create this scene in the next session. By that time they will have attempted to implement the solution and will have discovered other potential answers as well.

Whether the family has had the opportunity to create the solution tray or not, move into the transition stage. Ask family members how each one of them can carry out the solution during the next week. Have the family place the photograph in a location where each one can see it frequently. Ask each of them to assess her/his own (not other family members') progress in changing the family dynamics. In the next session have the family objectively discuss (with your help if needed) how the solution is working and what changes need to be made, keeping the photograph in mind. This will keep the family on track.

A case that demonstrates this procedure follows: Bonnie, a 14-year-old adolescent, was referred to us by the juvenile probation office. Bonnie and a friend had run away from home and had broken into an unoccupied house. After working with Bonnie for a couple of sessions, we were clear that her behavior was closely related to the power struggle between her and her mother. Bonnie stated that her mother was overprotective and would not let her do anything that her friends were allowed to do. At that time we began to see the family for brief therapy. The family appeared fairly functional but needed help through the developmental changes Bonnie was experiencing.

Upon doing a directed sand tray of the power struggle, we noted that each member saw what was happening quite differently. Bonnie's 8-year-old brother portrayed the constant fighting that occurred between the mother and the sister, but placed no blame on either one. He brought in two lions (symbols for his mother and sister) doing battle and a little mouse (a symbol for himself) hiding behind a rock. Bonnie's father, who worked long hours, was only vaguely aware of what was happening and indicated in the tray that he was genuinely puzzled. Although he was confused, he had sided with his wife to keep peace in the relationship. He symbolized himself as an unemotional male figure with a briefcase. The mother created a scene characterizing the conflict between Bonnie and herself, portraying her anxiety about what might happen to Bonnie if she continued on her present path. Her greatest fear was that Bonnie would use drugs, just as some of her friends did. The mother brought into the sand tray a young girl figure for Bonnie, much smaller than the object she had chosen for herself. She did not bring in either the son or the husband. In Bonnie's scene the fighting was completely the fault of the mother figure, and Bonnie stated that there would be no fighting if the mother figure would not be so overprotective of the young woman. She brought in the wicked witch from the story "Snow White" to symbolize the mother, and a normal looking young woman who was as tall as the witch to symbolize herself. She did not bring in either her brother or her father.

During the second session we asked each family member to bring into the conjoint scene the object symbolizing her/himself that s/he had used in the previous sand world. We told the family that they could complete the scene together in any way they wished. After briefly processing this tray, we asked the family to choose a helper. They chose Yoda. We suggested that they have Yoda bring all the members into the center of the tray and ask each member what s/he was willing to do to make things better. We then had the objects dialogue with Yoda, each family member taking all the roles. Because Bonnie and her mother were having difficulty seeing each other's point of view, they were unable to come up with solutions with Yoda that could work. So we had each one take the role of the figure that represented her/himself and we took the role of Yoda. When they were finished talking with Yoda we had Bonnie and her mother switch roles and had the figures again talk with each other and with Yoda. During this process the mother was able to see that the daughter indeed was fully grown and much more responsible and rational than she had thought. Bonnie realized that her mother still loved her and that much of the fighting came out of her mother's fears for her. She also saw that the fears seemed rational, given that some of the friends that she spent a lot of time with were doing drugs. The father saw how distant he had become and realized he needed to take more time with the family and become more active. He was particularly disturbed that none of the others had brought in a figure that symbolized him when they had created their first trays. They all realized how the dynamics in the family were influencing the younger brother.

The family members, at this point aware of their part in the problem, were able to bring out solutions through the voice of Yoda and the figures symbolizing themselves. The father decided that he would come home immediately after work to be with the family. He decided to place himself in charge of organizing an agreed upon weekend family activity. The brother stated that he would stop hiding in his room and become more interactive with the other members. The mother said that she needed to see Bonnie as nearing adulthood and as a trustworthy person and needed to focus more of her energy on herself and her son and husband. She confirmed that she was willing to negotiate more freedoms as Bonnie showed that she was trustworthy. She also was interested in spending more time with each person in the family individually as well as together. Bonnie stated that she would try to become more understanding of her mother's fears and not behave in ways that would trigger them. She agreed to spend more time with the family individually and together. Bonnie felt particularly bad about her brother and decided to play ball with him or read to him when he asked. When they rearranged their tray, they decided to create a scene of an outing they were planning for the next weekend in which they interacted harmoniously. The follow-up sessions helped to actualize and reinforce the family members' good intentions. Real and continuous behavior change tends to be slower than realization of the solution.

. . . .

Limiting the Number of Objects

ANY OBJECTS
- Instruct the child to find any 12 objects and place them in the tray.
- Explore the world as you would a spontaneous tray.

SPECIFIC OBJECTS
- Ask the child to find four plants or plant products and put them in the tray.
- Instruct the child to find four animals and/or animal products and put them in the tray.
- Direct the child to find four people and place them in the tray.
- Have the child find four objects that s/he wishes to use to complete the world.
- Explore the world as you would during a spontaneous sandplay.

. . . .

Games

HIDE AND SEEK
- Have the child hide as many objects as s/he chooses in the sand.
- Find the objects.
- Give the child the opportunity to tell a story using the objects.
- Reverse roles. Hide therapeutically relevant objects.
- Instruct the child to find the objects.
- Suggest that the child tell a story using the objects.

MAZES
- Suggest that the child create a maze in the sand tray, either independently or with your help.
- Have the child name the destination.
- Instruct the child to journey through the maze.
- Help the child apply the experience to her/his everyday life, if appropriate.

Creating a Story

- Ask the child to find one object and place it into the sand tray.
- Instruct the child to make a sentence using the object in the story.
- Find one object that will help guide the story and place the object into the tray.
- Construct an appropriate sentence about the object.
- Select objects alternately and create sentences.
- Have the child complete the scene and finish the story.

Directed Topic Sand Trays with Children

- Instruct the child to create a sand world about someone with a problem similar to the problem the child is experiencing.
- Process the tray in the third person as you would in a spontaneous tray, keeping the focus in the tray.

Alternatively

- Instruct the child to create a sand world depicting her/his problem.
- Process the tray in the first person as you would in a spontaneous tray, keeping the focus in the tray.

Individuation Trays with Adolescents

- Ask the client to find an object that represents her/his mother and put it into the tray.
- Instruct the client to find an object that represents her/his father and put it into the tray.
- Direct the client to find an object that represents her/himself and put it into the tray.
- Have the client complete the scene so that it represents the relationship.

- Process the tray briefly as you would a spontaneous tray.
- Instruct the client to pretend s/he is old enough to be on her/his own.
- Direct the client to build a new world representing the relationship with her/his parents at this future time.
- Process the new scene as you would during a spontaneous sandplay.

. . . .

Directed Topic Sand Trays with Families

- Suggest a topic (trauma, pattern, or situation) for the family to place either in conjoint or individual trays.
- Process as you would a spontaneous world.

. . . .

Resolving Power Struggles in Families

- Have each member build a separate world depicting the power struggle.
- Process the trays as you would an individual spontaneous tray with each member.
- In the next session, direct the family to build a conjoint world bringing in the object that represented them in their previous worlds.
- Ask the family to depict the power struggle by adding other objects if they wish.
- Process the tray as you would a spontaneous world with a couple.
- Have the family conjointly find one "helper" or "wise" object.
- Instruct them to place the helper and the objects representing themselves into the center of the tray.
- Direct each person to take a turn in having the center objects dialogue so that they can come up with a solution to the problem.

- Direct the family to take the play out of the tray and problem solve with your assistance, if needed.
- Have the family build a solution tray.
- Ask the family to take a photo of the tray.
- Send the family home with a practice solution plan.
- Follow up their progress in the next session.

RECORDING THE CREATION
OF A SAND WORLD

Why Record the Creation?

Although most sandplay therapists take a photograph or sketch a diagram of an individual client's or couple's completed sand tray as a document for their files, not all record the process of the creation of the world. Why then, if many therapists do not record process, do we suggest that you chronicle the play during the creating the world stage?

Imagine you could take only one photograph of your entire life. What would you see? You would probably see where you were and who or what mattered to you, and have many memories of how you got there. However, others looking at the picture would see only an image of the finished product, which might or might not evoke an emotional identification for them. They would not see what you see in the photograph nor would they know what you have experienced. They would not recognize the decisions you made, the changes you underwent, or the detours you negotiated. Neither would they see the joys and sorrows, the struggles, the learning and the insights that occurred to bring you to this point in time. You might protest, "But this picture shows so little of what happened and what my life has really been all about!" So it is with sandplay. It is the process that reveals the true movement of the unconscious and conscious course our clients are on. Recording becomes the map of their journey. The photograph of the completed sand tray is but part of the process.

Although in time you will be able to train yourself to remember how a client's world came into being, initially it is difficult to hold in mind all such details with exactness surrounding selection, placement, and sequence. It is important to record in some form so that you can educate your mind to observe exactly what is happening during the building of the world. "This [note-taking] will help you to learn the symbolic interpretive thinking process of the client and permit you to gain insight into the nature and direction of the client's journey" (De Domenico, 1988, p. 65). These notes will also serve you well during the therapy stage. By closely observing the process, you improve the chances that at the end of the creating the world stage you will know what area in the tray needs to be addressed. For example, you might have observed that your client became alarmed when s/he noticed that s/he had brought a lion into the tray and set it next to, and facing, a lamb. S/he might have then moved the lamb across a river, facing it away from the lion; or s/he might have removed the lion from the tray. You would immediately know that your client had issues about these figures that would need further exploration in the therapy stage. Then, during the therapy stage, your notes would serve as a reminder of exactly what transpired as the client moved the lion and the lamb.

There are additional reasons for recording process. Although you may learn to remember long enough to address issues in the therapy stage, it is not likely that you will recall exactly how the world came into being after the session. If you record, you will have a map to refer to later. In case you need to do so, you will be able to recreate the process of the building of the world by retracing the steps mentally or by actually rebuilding the world yourself. You might choose to do this if you are unclear about client issues revealed in the tray, if counter-transference issues arise for you, or if you want to consult with a super-visor. You will also want the information if you conduct a research study, teach sandplay, or are involved in a court case.

When testifying in court, your record of sand worlds can be valuable for you, your client, and the judge or jury. In one of our cases, we were asked to testify for a 5-year-old boy, Johnny, who had been physically abused by his father. Johnny had been removed to a foster home. The judge wanted to ascertain how Johnny felt about his biological father and whether it would be appropriate to return Johnny to his parents' home. The county attorney subpoenaed our records, which included our recordings of Johnny's sandplay sessions, and admitted them as evidence. Although the child had made no negative comments about his father, it was clear to the judge that Johnny was very angry at his father when the judge read the records we had kept of sand worlds the boy had made. Shortly after Johnny began playing in the sand, he brought in a figure that he called the father. Johnny's face became contorted, he started screaming, and then he picked up the father figure and hurled it against the wall. He repeated this play several times in a session and continued to do so session after session, becoming more vehement each time. From our notes, the judge realized that Johnny was not ready to return to his parents' home.

Interestingly, although some therapists object to writing notes during the session because they feel that writing might distract them from being fully present to the client, this is often not the case. Writing can enhance attention to all the details of building and thus facilitate focus for the therapist as well as eliminate unwanted thoughts and analyses. Although some clients prefer not to be recorded, most do not object and some feel that it lends credence and importance to their sandplay process. You will, of course, ask permission to record prior to beginning, just as you would if you want to record during any session. If the client prefers that you not record, keep accurate mental notes that will help you during the therapy stage and, if you choose, document them after the session.

Ways of Recording the Creation

VIDEOTAPING

As we mentioned previously, the most complete way to record a session is to videotape. Although many therapists videotape their regular sessions for review and as a teaching tool to be used with their clients and students, De Domenico first suggested videotaping sandplay (1988). The advantages of this method are apparent. Every detail of the session, including the therapy stage, is recorded. You can rerun the whole tape or sections of it as often as you deem necessary. A videotape can be particularly valuable if you, those you supervise, or your clients have specific questions or thoughts about what happened during the session. Observing yourself on tape can also facilitate your mastery of sandplay as a new modality. For teaching or research purposes and in cases where your client and you appear in court, videos reveal the complete process. When you work with a couple, a family, or a group, videotapes are less cumbersome and more complete than complex notes taken simultaneously on more than one person. Moreover, you can rerun portions of the tape in future sessions to demonstrate issues that arose in the tray.

A couple we saw knew intellectually that their communication patterns (constant put-downs) created problems for them, but they did not truly understand their behaviors or how their actions affected each other. Even after creating worlds in the sand, they were unable to distance themselves sufficiently from the process to comprehend the problem. With their consent, we videotaped a sandplay session and replayed the relevant portions. They were astonished and humbled to see how they related to each other both verbally and nonverbally. The shift in awareness was dramatic.

There are, however, several disadvantages of videotaping. Most therapists find it too costly for their budget. Reviewing the tape of the entire session can be inconvenient and time-consuming for the therapist. In addition, some clients, especially those who have been abused, are fearful that the abuser will somehow obtain access to the tape and use it to hurt the client either physically or emotionally. They prefer to have no permanent record of the things they say or do.

If you decide to videotape, we suggest that you create a consent form for clients to sign prior to the taping. File these signed forms separately from the videotapes in a safe place in case you need to have proof of client permission. Familiarize yourself with your state laws and licensing board regulations on videotaping confidential material. As you request permission from your clients, discuss how the taping will be done, why you are taping (e.g., for their use and/or for educational and training purposes), and where the tapes will be shown (e.g., in the office, workshops, university classrooms). Let the clients know that the tapes will be stored in a locked place for safekeeping. Also let them know that they may view the tapes at a prearranged time. Inform your clients that you will stop the recording at any time they ask. Moreover, advise them that, if they change their minds about having the tapes on file, you will destroy the tapes and will notify your clients if you have already shown the tapes as per your previous agreement.

If the client objects to having someone else in the room taping the session, you can suspend the camera from the ceiling or place it on a tripod in an inconspicuous position and focus the camera on the area where you will be working. If the client objects to being photographed, or if you do not need to record the client's movements or facial expressions, confine the focus of the camera to the tray. In any case, we suggest that the videotaping be as unobtrusive as possible,

because taping may interfere with the sandplay process. If you think
that it may be difficult to identify the objects in the tray when you do
your own videotaping, keep a record of the items as the builder brings
them into the world.

PROCESS PHOTOGRAPHY

If you are unable to videotape a session but would like or need picture
documentation of the process of the play, take a series of photographs
of the construction of the world. Where building is rapid, or where
there is more than one person working in a tray, taking 35mm photographs is often more manageable than recording in detail. Pictures, in
these situations, portray the process more accurately than notes. De
Domenico (1988), who developed the technique of process photography that we describe here, stated that during couple and family sessions
she finds that there are times that still photography combined with
minimal notes is the least cumbersome and most convenient method
of process recording.

Again, make sure to obtain consent from your clients. Most do not
object to picture taking if you are careful not to disrupt their process. Time your photographs in such a way that you record the world
during different phases of its evolution in order to capture major
changes that occur. A zoom lens permits you to include close-ups
of objects or specific areas of the tray. You might take some pictures
during the experiencing and rearranging and therapy stages as well,
if shifts transpire. Take your photographs primarily from your position as observer, so that you do not disturb the builder. If you are
intent on capturing the process precisely, you may well expend an entire roll of film. Additionally, record at least cursory notes and write a
P (the photograph frame #) in front of each note to go with that
particular photograph. If you are working with more than one person,
record in your notes next to the P, which partner is building. Your
pictures will return from the developer already numbered and can be
easily matched to your notes.

Most therapists prefer not to take process photographs because this
form of recording can be expensive, time-consuming, and disruptive to
the client and therapist. Photography can provoke self-consciousness in
clients and may move clients to *shoulds*. In addition, the sound of the
shutter can be disorienting, especially for sound-sensitive people. Even
if clients have given permission for photography, be sure to let them

know that, if at any time they feel uncomfortable or you sense that they are uneasy, you will desist from taking process photographs.

BRIEF NOTE-TAKING

Although we recommend that you record precisely how the world was created, some of you may find that note-taking disturbs your ability to be present to the client. Remember that your presence and availability to the client are of primary concern. It is the blending of your energy with your client's energy that will encourage a transformation to occur. If you find that when you record you are unable to hold the experience for the client or to remain present and/or to provide a safe and protected environment, abandon note-taking. Your ultimate goal is to enter the world with the client both emotionally and spiritually, but still remain the observer. If at all possible, take careful notes of the first two or three worlds the client creates so that you understand the nature and direction of the process.

If you decide not to pursue taking notes, continue to take *mental notes* so that you can recall the sequence in which objects were brought into the world, when and how the sand was moved, the clients' verbal and nonverbal expressions, and any changes that were made. Keep these in mind to address later. If you, like most people, have difficulty remembering the unfolding world, jot down just a word or two to trigger your memory of important observations. During the therapy stage, you can glance at your notes and check with your client as to the relevance of your observations. If possible, leave enough time after the session to review the tray and make any notations or diagrams of the sandplay process that you wish to remember.

IN-DEPTH NOTES AND DIAGRAMS

We have already discussed reasons for itemized recording earlier in this chapter. If you choose not to videotape or take process photographs of the client's tray, but need details of her/his sand tray process, we suggest in-depth note-taking. Make sure to ask permission to take notes, explaining to the client why you are doing so and that the recordings will be a part of your confidential files. You might say, "Is it all right with you if I take some notes while you are building? Note-taking helps me to remember exactly what happened. That way I can refer to them later if I need to. I will keep them with your confidential files." If you are working with a child who is creating a static tray you might say, "I am really interested in what you are making in the sand tray. Is it OK with you if I write it down so that I can remember it?" As we mentioned in chapter 5, children frequently create moving trays, in which you are often an active player. In these cases, and in instances when you work conjointly with several members in a family, recording is unfeasible. You will, however, want to pay close attention to the main themes, progression, and manner of the child's or family's play.

We usually record from the position where the client has asked us to stand or sit during the sandplay. We have found that clients are not disturbed by our recording their process if we remain quiet and inconspicuous. Ryce-Menuhin (1992) sits quietly at a distance and sketches the developing world in his casebook. Katherine Bradway (1990) sits out of view and records the order of placement and the location of objects. How you handle recording is up to you. When you are finished recording, keep the notes beside you or on your lap out of the view of the client, but near enough so that you can refer to them. Occasionally we jot down a few brief notes during the therapy and transition stages if we want to make sure to include them in our records. Allow sufficient time after the session to complete your notes, including significant events that occurred during the therapy and transition stages.

What to Record during the Creating the World Stage

Although you will make many observations and generate ideas of what is occurring during the construction of the world, you will not be able to record all of them. There are specific observations that we suggest you record in the sequence they occur. Often clients place objects into the tray according to their importance or according to the time sequence of the evolution of the sand world. This, however, is not always true. Sometimes clients merely follow the shelves and place objects into the tray as they find them. Check out the meaning of the order later. During the therapy stage you might ask clients to retrace the making of the world in the sequence in which they placed objects into the tray. At that point, the meaning of the sequence should become clear to both you and the client.

As you observe the creation of the world, note the shape of the tray and the grit and color of sand clients choose. Also note how and where the sand is moved and whether clients use water and how much they use (e.g., moisten the sand, flood the tray). If clients choose to use objects, note the objects and their sequence of placement into the tray, the location and direction they are facing, and their spatial placement (on, above, or below the surface of the sand). Note any changes the clients make, the objects they bury, move or remove, or select but do not place into the tray. Note the client's body language and nonverbal as well as verbal expressions, and record them as they occur. Note your own feelings and thoughts. Also record anything that you deem important at the time and would like to recollect at a later stage. Remember that this process is a holistic experience. The succession is not arbitrary and everything the client does and says has significance.

How to Record

Some of you already know shorthand; if you don't, you may want to generate your own to incorporate into the method of recording you develop. We have adopted the recording technique and shorthand developed by De Domenico (1988), and have found it very helpful. Whether you choose to use our system or prefer to develop your own, the following example can serve as a reference.

INDIVIDUAL SANDPLAY RECORDING SHEET

(See sample forms at the end of this chapter.) We find that it is less time-consuming to create recording forms or photocopy them for future use than it is to make new forms during the session. To create the original recording form we used an 8½″ × 14″ sheet of paper. We then turned the page sideways and drew lines dividing the 14″ width into four columns. At the top, we left enough space for the name of the client, the date, what sand (grit and color) and tray (size and shape) the client uses, and whether the sand is wet or dry. Then we labeled each of the four columns as follows. We have a second page that we use when a client includes too many objects to record on one page. If you choose to use this format, you may follow our directions or make an enlarged copy of the form at the end of the chapter. Also at the end of the chapter is an example of a completed form of a client's sand world (see p. 226 and illustration #12, p. 223).

Column 1: Objects/Sand. Number the columns from 1 to 20 so that you will be ready to write down the sequence in which the client brings objects into the tray, moves or removes them, handles them but does not bring them into the tray, moves the sand, adds water, or creates and changes arrangements such as rivers and mountains in the sand. When the world is complete, record the objects that have been selected but not handled or used during the building. Add a check next to the number of the rejected objects and a star or asterisk next to the number of any change you feel is important to remember to address later. If an item is moved, record it again. Leave some space, if possible, following the listed items so that you can later add in parentheses the descriptive terms, names, or attributes given to the objects by the client.

Column 2: Client Nonverbal/Verbal Expressions. Note the body language, the facial expressions, behaviors, as well as the utterances (such as a groan) and verbalizations of the client as s/he creates the world. Remain as objective as possible in your recording. Make sure you record the expression you observe next to the item that was handled at the time.

Column 3: Therapist Reactions. Briefly write your reactions, thoughts, and feelings as the world is being built. Remember not to analyze or interpret the client's world. Focus mainly on the client and hold her/his experiences. The notes in this column will be useful in the therapy stage. They are also valuable when you review the sandplay process after the session. Your observations may give you some ideas about the client's process and, just as importantly, about your process and possible countertransference issues. If you hear yourself in internal dialogue, indicate the conversation in brackets. Again, make sure to write your comments next to the client's objects or expressions so that when you review the process you will understand how the entire picture fits together.

Column 4: Diagram/Map. Draw at least two diagrams of sand trays, one under the other. Sketch four equal quadrants in the diagrams. In order to eliminate or distinguish these lines from recordings you make of the client's process, use a pencil. Like a map of a city, across the top of the diagram write 1, 2, 3, 4, 5, and along the side write A, B, C, D, E. This will help you to accurately show the location of each object or sand formation. As you record the names of the objects or sand formations in column 1, place the number of the item in the tray in its appropriate location. If an object is facing in a specific direction, place an arrow next to the number to indicate the direction. If sand is moved, use arrows to delineate the direction of the action. For rivers and lakes, draw the outline of the body of water. The following sug-gestions help to identify the spatial relationship of objects to the sand. Draw a circle around the number if the object is on the sand or water. If one object is placed on top of or in another object or is on a sky hook, draw a double circle around the number. If an object is buried, do not circle the number. If objects are moved or removed, record the adjustment in column 1 and then place a line through the original number on the diagram. If the object remains in the tray, include the new number and location in the sketch. If clients include many objects or make numerous changes in the tray, you will need to continue re-cording on another diagram.

After the client leaves, turn the sheet over and incorporate the entire process into one drawing. Below the columns and at the bottom of the sheet, leave enough space so that you can briefly record any com-ments you wish to include. If you need more space, finish recording on the back of the sheet. Make a list of the issues addressed during therapy, your assessment, and your plan for future sessions. If the building process is lengthy, rapid or fairly complex, it is likely that you will need more than one recording sheet or will choose to dispense with recording the remainder of the session. In this case, you may wish to complete recording with brief notes. As you can imagine, it is often not possible to include everything we have listed on your recording sheet during the session, so if possible take some time between clients to review the tray, complete your notes, and integrate the session for yourself.

COUPLE'S SANDPLAY RECORDING SHEET

(See sample forms at the end of this chapter.) As we have mentioned earlier, in-depth process recordings of couples may be confusing and overwhelming to the beginning sandplay therapist. We include a method and a form that we have found workable. If this is more than you can record and remain present to the process, take only brief notes of pertinent observations you make during the creating the world stage. Brief notes should include any instances of verbal and nonverbal interaction, as well as constructive and destructive individual and cou-ple dynamics.

If the couple is working conjointly in one tray, proceed as you would if you were creating a form for an individual session, except divide the 8½″ × 14″ sheet of paper into three columns instead of four. Then label the columns as follows:

Column 1:	*Column 2:*	*Column 3:*
Partner #1 _____	Partner #2 _____	Diagram
Objects/Sand	Objects/Sand	
Expressions	Expressions	

For each partner, under the heading "Objects/Sand" record the movement of the sand and the order in which the objects are brought into the tray. Remember to number the items sequentially regardless of which partner places the object. For example, if partner #1 places the first and third object in the tray and partner #2 places the second and fourth object, partner #1's column would include: 1. bird and 3. tree, and partner #2's column would include: 2. house and 4. bridge. Observe significant verbal or nonverbal cues and interactions, and record these under "Expressions." Any thoughts and feelings that you would like to remember are also recorded under "Expressions," with a T (Therapist) in front of them. Under column 3, draw diagrams and record as you would during an individual session. Incorporate both partners' building processes in one sketch. Complete the recording as you would in an individual session, leaving as much time as necessary after the couple leaves to complete your notes.

If the members of the couple are working separately, proceed as before but divide the sheet of paper in half, one-half for each partner, and include a separate diagram for each partner.

Left Half:	*Right Half:*
Partner #1 _____	Partner #2 _____
Objects/Sand	Objects/Sand
Expressions	Expressions
Diagram	Diagram

Comments: After the session, record the therapy issues you addressed, your assessment, and your plan for future sessions.

In your case notes include anything you feel is significant but could not complete during note-taking.

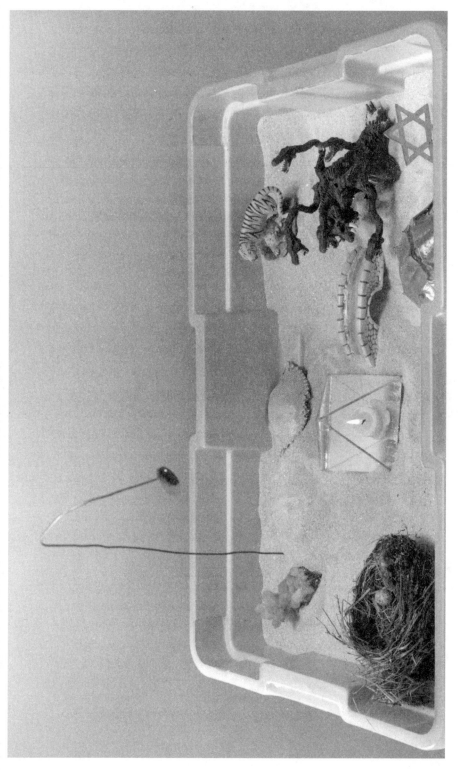

Illustration #12. Sand Tray for Individual Recording Form

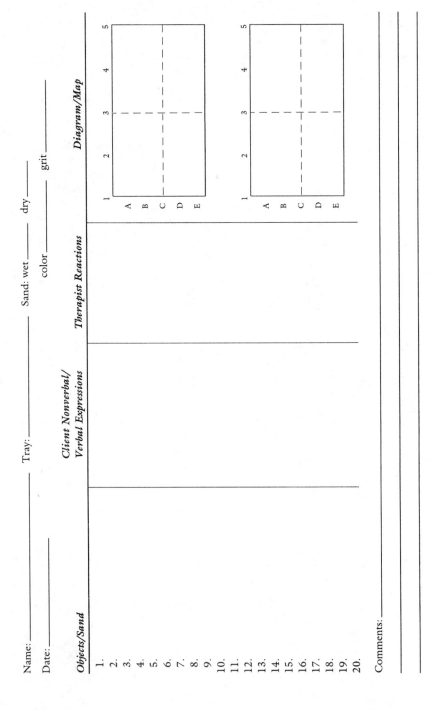

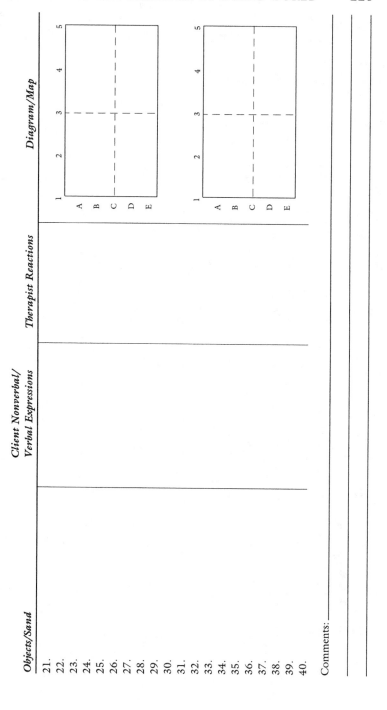

Objects/Sand

Client Nonverbal/Verbal Expressions

Therapist Reactions

Diagram/Map

21.
22.
23.
24.
25.
26.
27.
28.
29.
30.
31.
32.
33.
34.
35.
36.
37.
38.
39.
40.

Comments:

Individual Recording Form: Example (see illustration #12)

Name: Jessica Adams

Date: January 10, 1997

Tray: 20 × 30 rectangular   Sand: wet __x__ dry ____

color ____ white ____ grit __80 mesh__

Objects/Sand	Client Nonverbal/ Verbal Expressions	Therapist Reactions
1. Wet sand thoroughly	Pounded intently	
2. Mound (mountain)		
3. Circle		
4. River		
5. Crab shell (smooth, orange)	Caressed gently	Noticed contrast
6. Crab shell (spiked, brown)	Touching spike, "Ouch"	
7. Bird nest (safety & love)		
8. 2 eggs in nest (rebirth, twin)	"Ahhh," smile	[Client is twin]
9. Crystal (spiritual self)		
10. 5-headed monster (neg. thoughts)	Surprised look	Innger cringe, felt repulsed
11. 6-pointed star (Jewish heritage)	Sat straighter	[Religion facing monster?]
12. Tiger (strength)		
13. Bridge (way to other side)		
14. Pyramid		
15. * Bridge moved	Lifts bridge, hesitates	[Shift occurred?]
16. Candle in the pyramid & lit		
17. Yin Yang on skyhook		Check out hidden vase
18. * Jeweled vase, buried		
19. * Tiger turned to monster		
20. ✔ Feather (handled & rejected)		

Comments: Issues addressed: lack of self-acceptance, negative self-talk, tenuous religious identity

Assessment: movement toward acceptance of shadow aspects and toward integration

Plan: dialogue between non-accepted ego states and balanced self, journalling, observing negative self-talk

Couple's Recording Form: Separate Sand Trays

Couple's Names: _____   Date: _____

Partner #1: _____   Partner #2: _____

Tray: _____   Sand: wet _____ dry _____   Tray: _____   Sand: wet _____ dry _____

color _____ grit _____   color _____ grit _____

Partner #1

Objects/Sand	Expressions	Diagram/Map
1.		
2.		
3.		
4.		
5.		
6.		
7.		
8.		
9.		
10.		
11.		
12.		
13.		
14.		
15.		
16.		
17.		
18.		
19.		
20.		

Partner #2

Objects/Sand	Expressions	Diagram/Map
1.		
2.		
3.		
4.		
5.		
6.		
7.		
8.		
9.		
10.		
11.		
12.		
13.		
14.		
15.		
16.		
17.		
18.		
19.		
20.		

Comments: _____

Couple's Recording Form: Conjoint Sand Tray

Couple's Names: _____ Date _____

Sand Tray: _____ Sand: wet _____ dry _____ color _____ grit _____

Partner #1: _____ Partner #2: _____

Objects/Sand	Expressions	Objects/Sand	Expressions	Diagram/Map

Comments: _____
_____
_____

• •

Recording the Creation

• Why Record?

To train your mind to remember the process. To enhance attention. To guide therapy. To have a map to which to refer later for clarification, research, or evidence. To lend credence to the client's process.

• Ways of Recording:

Videotaping. Process photography. Brief note-taking. In-depth notes and diagrams.

• What to Record:

Tray, grit, and color of sand; wet/dry. Sequence and placement of objects. Direction and spatial relationships of objects. Movement and changes of sand and objects. Buried objects. Objects selected but not used. Client's body language, nonverbal and verbal expressions. Therapist's feelings and thoughts. Other relevant observations and insights.

CONTRAINDICATIONS
FOR SANDPLAY

While we have certainly found sandplay to be a very powerful technique and would like to believe that it could be therapeutic for every client, there are situations and times when sandplay must be delayed, altered, or not used at all. Obviously, as the previous chapters indicate, the most effective sand tray work is achieved by clients who have a desire to heal, are capable of self-reflection, and are willing to play. Most of your clients will probably satisfy these criteria. However, as we and others who have worked in the field have discovered, the client must agree to sandplay for it to be productive. In addition, there are those for whom sandplay therapy would be inappropriate, ineffectual, and even damaging. The client's attitude toward sandplay, her/his developmental stage, current emotional state, personality type, ego strength, and environmental demands have a bearing on your decision to use sandplay.

Some of the clients you will be working with could benefit from sandplay, but it may be some time before they consent to play in the sand. Observe the clients' verbalizations and behaviors as they enter the therapy room; notice their reactions when you mention sandplay as one of the therapeutic interventions you use. You can pick up clues about their attitudes toward the idea of playing in the sand. If clients make negative verbal comments, retreat from the trays, or show tension in their bodies or distaste in their facial expressions when you bring up sandplay, assure them that they do not have to do it. Inform them that if at any time they change their minds, they can let you know. When you are working with a client who is resistant to doing sandplay, do not force the issue. As we have stated earlier, even if you can see how sandplay might be helpful for the client, if s/he feels uncomfortable or shows some resistance to doing sandplay, respect her/his needs by allowing her/him to make the choice.

Often resistance is due to a need not to get *dirty* or a belief that sandplay is just for children, not adolescents or adults. Other resistant clients are highly rational and intellectualizing, although, as we stated in chapter 1, sandplay potentially can be very helpful for these individuals. Some clients are resistant for a combination of these reasons. For example, as Ryce-Menuhin stated, "most of these persons [highly rational] would reject sandplay as 'too infantile' or 'too unscientific'" (1992, p. 34). When a trusting relationship is established, you may suggest sandplay again. We have found that once clients agree to sandplay, their interfering attitudes diminish.

Sometimes resistance is rooted in deep feelings of inadequacy/perfectionism, fear of loss of verbal control and being overwhelmed by unknown material that might be revealed. One client with whom we worked comes to mind. Sally, an artist in her fifties, had been in therapy for about eight months. She came to therapy with several issues: painter's block, relationship dissatisfaction, poor self-esteem, and perfectionism. She seemed hesitant about sandplay when we mentioned it and moved away from the tray. Several months transpired with no sandplay work. We suggested creating a sand world during a session in which we felt that it would be particularly beneficial. She declined but said that she would like to build a sand world the following week. Because it was apparent to us that she had some resistance, we did not suggest sandplay again. At the end of each of the next three consecutive sessions she mentioned that she had not yet played in the sand. At the beginning of the following session Sally reported that she had been thinking about her avoidance of sandplay. She realized that playing put her into a child mode and into a space where she feared her father's judgment. She felt that she could never do anything well enough in his eyes. In that session, however, she decided to build a sand world. She let go of her inhibitions and became playful and creative. When it was time to take a photograph, she did so, then gave us permission to take one. When we asked her from which perspective she wished us to take the picture, she thought for a moment, got under the sand table, and positioned herself as if holding up the world, smiling with a sense of confidence. Had we encouraged her to build the world prior to her willingness, we doubt that she would have been ready to empower her inner child to move toward greater self-acceptance.

There are times when you will be working with clients who enjoy doing sandplay but their play creates problems for you (unless you like to clean up sand, watch your client eat sand or climb into the tray, or feel frantically rushed between sessions!). As mentioned in chapter 2, some clients may be overstimulated by the plethora of objects displayed on your shelves. This is most common for attention deficit/hyperactive children. The client's developmental or maturational stage must be considered. Very young children (under two and a half), developmentally and maturationally immature children and those children subject to overstimulation may not be good candidates for sandplay without special considerations. Their mental capacity and fine motor skills may not be sufficiently developed to keep the sand in the tray, create stories, or manipulate small figures. At times they shove many objects off the shelves, throw or eat the sand, or place the figures in their mouths. Some children may attempt to climb into the tray. These clients appear to need to be literally rather than symbolically in the tray. If a child of any age demonstrates the above mentioned behaviors, you may need to utilize other interventions until the client attains the skills and is ready to adhere to the limits necessary for sandplay.

For those clients who are easily distracted and overstimulated, you might reveal only a small portion of your objects. For some who have the capability of creating a world but need more space or like to throw sand, have them build a world on the floor or on a masonite board larger than the size of the sand tray. If their behavior reveals a need for comfort, you may choose to console and/or hold the child and/or provide a place of safety to hide (e.g., a large box, blankets to make a cave, a space under a table). While sandplay work may not be practicable in the office, if you have access to a large sandbox, you can give the client permission to play as s/he wishes in the box. For those clients who require more gross motor activity and less limitation (e.g., clients who throw sand and/or those who have been confined from activity), substitute a large sandbox, outdoor activity, or indoor active play. An example of the limitations for clients who are not ready for sandplay is a 3-year-old boy in foster care who was very attracted to the sand tray. After a couple of sandplay experiences, we realized that the sand tray was too limiting for him and too labor intensive for us. He was unable to keep the sand within the boundaries of the tray, and we had massive clean-up prior to our next client. We found that having him create worlds on a $40'' \times 40''$ masonite board, play more actively in the office, and play in an outdoor sandbox at a nearby park worked well.

We concur with De Domenico that using sandplay with developmentally disabled children is not effective or appropriate. She stated, "the children made only rudimentary use of the tray, clearly demonstrating their need for a different activity" (1988, p. 17). She went on to say, "Because of their lack of age-appropriate experiences pertaining to the developmental tasks of the first two years of life, they could not yet benefit from the limits of the tray, the nature of the sand, and manipulating and arranging small symbolic objects" (1988, pp. 18–19). In her study she found that after a period of alternative play the children were able to use the sand tray more effectively. Nehama Baum did extensive sandplay therapy with developmentally disabled clients (in Signell & Bradway, 1995, p.18). It is important to make maturational interventions for adults as well as children; we have found that developmentally disabled adults approached the sand tray in a similarly immature manner.

Just as you need to consider the maturational level of the client, you must be aware of her/his emotional state. When a client enters the therapy room in the height of emotion or with an excess of energy that seems important to release (e.g., anger, frustration), s/he may need a more active, less restricted space. If it is suitable and consistent with your philosophy, provide an opportunity for more gross motor acting out. We find bataccas or punching bags, dart boards (not with sharp objects), and clay to be appropriate outlets that both aid the client's resolution and release of the emotion and prevent the scattering of sand outside of the tray. When these materials are not available or appropriate, we utilize Gestalt two-chair work, visualization, art therapy, letter writing, etc., especially for adolescents and adults.

Although we believe that most personality types can benefit from sandplay, there are some clients for whom sandplay is ineffective. We have found that clients with obsessive compulsive personality traits and behaviors may have difficulty using sandplay in a very meaningful way, although there are benefits that may arise from this kind of therapy. As Ryce-Menuhin wrote, "When ritual is compulsive as in the obsessional, sandplay may be tried but will rarely be more than an added 'cul-de-sac' for the pathologically obsessive. It usually becomes another defensive ritual, to be added to the patient's other repertoire of rituals, and although sandplay may reveal some projections from obsessional psyche that escapes words, this happens more often with children (including the autistic) than it does with adult obsessionals" (1992, p. 35). It is often difficult for therapists to do sandplay with autistic children because of the difficulty tolerating persistent protracted, ritualistic, and unproductive play often characteristic of these clients. However, sandplay therapists, Nessie Bayley and Barbara Weller have developed methods to help children with attachment problems such as autism (see Signell & Bradway, 1995, p. 18). If you choose to use sandplay with obsessional clients, you might try a directed sand tray (e.g., subpersonality integration). Your direction may produce a meaningful altered pattern of play and change the usual defensive ritual. Or, if you are working with autistic children, you might wish to contact Bayley or Weller (see Appendix 3, Signell & Bradway, 1995).

For some clients there is a risk in using sandplay, as there is in other forms of therapy that delve deeply into the unconscious (e.g., art therapy, visualization, and hypnosis). We have found that sandplay may be damaging for clients with poor ego strength, such as psychotic, schizophrenic, borderline, and severely dissociated individuals, unless they are in a controlled environment (e.g., an inpatient setting) where they can be safe with regression or psychotic ideation. Exclude from sandplay clients who tend to severely dissociate when interventions provoke regression, particularly if they are suicidal or self-mutilating, become incapable of taking care of themselves, or do not have a support system in place. Borderline clients or those in a prepsychotic state "may be so vulnerable to 'flooding' by the unconscious that they feel immediately threatened by any limitation of ego control" (Weinrib, 1983, pp. 72–73). Ryce-Menuhin stated that the borderline psychotic client "will discover a toy spider or an anaconda snake and 'flip' at once into the psychosis with very definite clinical, phobic features in a way that is not helpful to therapeutic process" (1992, p. 34). As an alternative intervention, you may wish to use a more verbal, conscious, reality-based approach, because "the unconscious, due to its autonomy, is responsive, but . . . the ego . . . is unable to integrate the experience" (Weinrib, 1983, p. 73). Ryce-Menuhin also suggested that "the control of words chosen by an analyst enables verbal treatment to be more clinically helpful over time to psychotics than sandplay" (1992, p. 34). If you choose to use sandplay, it is imperative to work very slowly and carefully. You may wish to take a more interactive role than usual to slow the process.

A client came to us after she had attended a personal growth workshop in which art therapy and imagery were used. Although she was a highly functional adult at the time of participation in the workshop, she had historically experienced psychotic episodes. According to the client, the art therapy and imaging exercises evoked sufficient unconscious images to flood her to the point of losing touch with reality. When we saw her we realized that sandplay would probably exacerbate the psychosis. Instead we referred her to a psychiatrist for medication, and in our sessions we employed talk therapy and suggested grounding activities such as knitting, gardening, and focusing on her daily chores. This helped to keep her in the here and now.

There are times and situations in clients' lives when we believe that it is essential for clients not to regress. You must use your discretion to determine if reducing the client's defenses would place her/him at risk in some way. This will be a difficult judgment call, because the client's needs change as circumstances alter. As we all know, work at the unconscious level breaks down ego control and defenses, and clients may become more open and regressed. When a client lives in a dangerous neighborhood or home, attends an unsafe school, or works in a precarious work setting, it is inadvisable to thwart her/his level of alertness to the potential dangers around her/him. Returning to an abusive setting necessitates that the client's defense structure be intact. While working with inner-city adolescents, we found that it was essential to know their home, school, and neighborhood conditions. A case that clearly portrays the need for caution is a 14-year-old client who returned to a very dangerous school following our sessions. His peers taunted him with knives and verbal abuse. Had he used sandplay, he might not have been sufficiently defended to protect himself. We focused therapy on ego-strengthening and problem-solving techniques instead. You must also consider the circumstances of a client who must operate at a high level of performance when s/he leaves the session. Although you prepare clients to reenter the world outside the therapy room in the transition stage, this is often not adequate when a level of excellence is required (e.g., an examination, a presentation, a physically hazardous job). In such cases, you may wish to schedule the client either after the task is completed or at the end of her/his workday.

The above examples are guidelines to remind you that sandplay is neither effective nor safe with all clients. Although most clients can benefit from sandplay, you must use your judgment on a case-by-case basis.

* *

Contraindications for Sandplay

- Strong resistance to sandplay
- Insufficiently developed maturational level
- Excessive emotional energy
- Poor ego strength, as in psychotic, severely dissociated, or border-line clients
- Obsessive-compulsive ritualistic behavior and thinking
- Need to remain alert to dangers outside the therapy office
- Need for high level of performance following the session

·· 10 ··

PERSONAL SAND TRAYS FOR THE THERAPIST

The benefits of sandplay apply not only to clients but also to you, the therapist, if you decide to build sand worlds for your own personal growth and healing. As you are aware, it is vital that you take time for your own work. Unless you know who you are and what is going on inside of you, it will be difficult to be effective as a therapist and as a human being. Not only will you be much clearer if you remove the debris of unresolved issues, but you will find that you will naturally grow in understanding and become a more integrated, mature person emotionally and spiritually. In addition, self-exploration helps you release blocks to creativity. It opens a space in you that invites innovative ideas as well as peaceful and centered feelings. This inner stability increases your ability to deal with life changes and stressors and allows you to work more effectively with clients. It makes it less likely that you will place your judgments or project your shadow aspects onto them. Instead, you will be a steady person in their lives whom they can trust and use as a support, especially when they are in crisis. Whether you like it or not, you are a model for your clients.

Personal Growth

Although there are many ways to accomplish personal growth, sandplay is a particularly effective tool if you are drawn to approaches that allow you to express the unconscious through physical means. For many years we pursued our own growth through self-hypnosis, dream

analysis, Gestalt therapy, group therapy, and supervision using talk
therapies. However, we did not see sandplay as a technique for personal healing and understanding until we experienced the creation of
our own worlds. Although we had both done our own trays, we had
not used sandplay consistently until after Anna's training with De Domenico, who suggested that all sandplay therapists routinely create personal trays for their continued growth. As with therapy in general, it
is important for therapists to have experienced their own therapy, particularly the type of therapy they will be practicing. This is frequently
not done in play therapy. We shared Barbara's first personal experience
with sandplay in the preface. Now we would like to share the experience that convinced Anna to use sandplay regularly for her own
growth.

It was not until I studied extensively with Dr. Gisela De Domenico
in Oakland, California, that I truly understood just how powerful and
unique sandplay could be in my own healing and growth process.
Shortly before I participated in one of Gisela's trainings, I received
news that my mother was dying of a stroke. I rushed to Canada to be
with her and, as I sat beside her holding her hand, I realized how
privileged I was to be with her in her time of leaving. Within 24 hours
she was gone. I mourned briefly and spent some time processing the
event. I felt that I had resolved my mother's death. Then in the course
of the sandplay training, I built my own sand world. When I began
selecting objects, I felt I had little to explore. As I worked, my hands
moved without thought to objects that seemed insignificant to me. I
created frantically, and when my world was complete, I was surprised
to see a little child frightened and lost, looking from afar into her
mother's grave. I wept silently for my mother and the young child that
I had ignored in the grieving process. She had lost the one person in
her life who had given her unconditional love as a child. With the
weeping came the healing of the past and the present. Although I had
previously processed my mother's death from the adult perspective, I
had not reached into the depth of the heart-pain the child in me felt.
During the week of the workshop, I completed a series of trays culmi-
nating in a powerful memorial service. The entire class stood reverently
by and witnessed as the child knelt in the center of the tray beside her
mother's body, laid to rest in a glass pyramid. I lit a ring of candles
that circled the pyramid as the child sent her mother on her last journey home. The pictures of these trays remain precious to me to this

Illustration #13. Anna's Personal Growth Initial Tray

day (see illustrations #13 & 14). It was after this experience that I began using sandplay regularly for myself.

Before we discuss how you can build your own scenes in the sand and process your own work, we would like to briefly mention our philosophy of personal growth. Each person, no doubt, has her/his own belief about the human being. From our perspective, we see people as a union of the body, mind, emotion, and spirit. Why are we here? For each person the answer may well be unique. However, what we observe in general is that life is a process, experience linked to experience, and on this path life's lessons are learned. It appears that the psyche

Illustration #14. Anna's Personal Growth Culmination Tray

naturally moves toward healing, growth, and integration. Regardless of the choices people make, they are constantly propelled toward a higher level of understanding. As people experience and reexperience events, inner reality as well as outer behaviors change.

Ruth Ammann, a Jungian analyst, defined inner growth as the process of transformation of the personal world view of a fundamentally healthy and stable ego confronting the shadows of the self. She believed that the psyche is continuously changing. There are times when an individual's ideas and values fluctuate. S/he then regains stability and order "until such time that from the depth of the soul the archetype of the Soul once again constellates a change and introduces a new process of transformation" (1993, p. 8).

Whether you choose to build worlds, or how often you do so, we leave to your discretion. We find that we create sand worlds approximately once a week. This allows us to resolve issues, answer questions we have, discover new insights, and, in general, check in with the psyche, especially when we are engrossed in hectic daily activities. These worlds are usually created in the presence of another therapist or supervisor who is familiar with sandplay, or with a person we know and trust who is a good listener and is nonjudgmental. If you decide to create your own worlds, remember, it is not as important that the person holding the space has the *right* questions and answers or knows therapy techniques, as it is that s/he can create a safe, protected environment for you to explore your unfolding world cognitively, emotionally, physically, and spiritually. Although the observer often says very little, it is important for you to feel psychologically held and heard. It is also easier to explore the scene if you can actually talk to someone. Often this process results in *hearing* yourself.

It is not, however, always feasible to have an observer present when you wish to create a sand world. In situations where you are alone, you can build, experience, and process the world on your own. This, of course, will probably not be as effective as if you were with someone else. If you create worlds by yourself or with someone who is not a therapist familiar with sandplay, follow the protocol you would use with your clients. Remember, it is important to trust your own inner wisdom to release the answers you need.

First, empty your mind as much as possible. You might want to close your eyes and take some deep breathes to help you relax. Once you are relaxed, imagine all your thoughts floating away as you breathe out, until your mind is blank. Then take some quiet time to give yourself unconditional regard, letting the inner child know that it is safe to come out and play. Tell the child there is no right or wrong way to play and that regardless of what comes up you will be there to support her/him without judgment. If you have an issue to resolve or need an answer to a problem, give your unconscious mind permission to release the solution to you.

With your mind empty of judgment and analyses, select a tray (wet or dry, the color and grit of sand you want). If you choose to create a scene in the sand, it is now time to build a terrain, go to the shelves to choose objects, and compose a world. For those of you who tend to slip into therapist mode, it may be important to work fairly quickly and with little thought as to what you are doing. Then take time to experience the world fully. Take a little time at the end of the experiencing stage to rearrange the scene if you wish, and then center yourself. Note any emotions or thoughts you had while building and experiencing, and make them conscious. Give yourself permission to feel the emotions for as long as you wish.

During the therapy stage, take yourself or the observer on a tour of the world. This is best done out loud, whether you are with someone or alone. Speaking aloud allows you to hear what you are saying and often leads to increased insight. If you are alone you may wish to use a tape recorder so that you not only have an audience but can also replay the tape and listen to what you have said. During the touring the world phase, ask yourself similar questions as you would ask your clients and answer the questions without much thought, so that the unconscious can release answers to you as it would in a dream. If you are puzzled by the answers you give, but realize that the object has significance because of a physical or emotional reaction you are experiencing, continue to explore and speak about whatever enters your mind, even though what you say may seem unimportant or irrelevant. Note any memories that are evoked as you speak. You might also create a story about the object or section of the tray. If the connotation of the object remains unclear, continue the tour and see how it relates to the rest of the scene. Sometimes the meaning is only significant as it pertains to the whole.

Throughout the tour, note your body sensations and emotions. Allow yourself to have them and deal with them as they arise. You can also come back to them later. When the tour is complete, take some time to reflect on the process. At this point you will usually know what areas in the tray call for resolution. Dualities and conflicts become clear. In some instances, your tray may be an altar to your strengths and inner peace and joy. If this is the case, experience the feelings fully and carry them with you into your daily life. Take a picture if you wish, and if possible leave the scene untouched until you create a new one. That way you can come back to it at any time.

In most situations, however, you will be facing an unresolved issue in the tray. If this occurs, use some of the therapy techniques you usually use with clients, such as reworking memories, dialoguing with objects, imaging, and psychodrama. Move and remove objects or bring in new ones as you wish. Try not to analyze the tray or place negative judgments on what unfolds. If something frightening occurs, stay with the fear and explore the unconscious message.

We'd like to share one of our personal experiences. While processing one of my own sand worlds, I felt a strange twinge in my gut as I talked about an old man in the tray. At first I thought that the fear dealt with the impending death of my father, but my anxiety remained even after I had dealt with this fear. My first impulse was to move on to the next object without further exploration. But as I stayed with the feeling of dread and asked my unconscious mind to present an image that I could work with, the face of my husband appeared in my mind. At first I could not see the relevance of the image, because my husband was not an old man, but then it became clear to me that I was dealing with the fear of my husband aging and dying and of my being alone. Although I would have preferred not to deal with these feelings, I felt much calmer and stronger after my tears. I knew that my husband would always be "present" in some form even after physical death, and I would be able to continue on without him.

After the experience, when you feel you are finished processing the world, take a photograph of the scene, and then take some time to journal and/or create a picture, such as a mandala, to help you integrate the experience. Ask yourself if there is anything that you can take with you into your daily life. A sand world comes to mind that we created some time ago. We wanted to understand the difficulty we were experiencing with a colleague. When we processed the scene, we noticed that we had placed a medical filter mask between us and the figure that represented this person. After dialoguing with the mask, we realized that the mask prevented a connection with our colleague. We deliberately removed the mask and the energy shifted. We took the image of the mask with us and imagined removing it from our relationship whenever we interacted with our colleague. The distance between us gradually disappeared.

Make sure you are not rushed when creating sand worlds. Take a photograph of your sand world so that you can refer to it later. If you wish, you can dismantle the world immediately after your experience or you can choose to leave it intact until you are ready to disassemble it.

Countertransference

Regardless of how much inner work each of us does, "countertransference happens." As therapists and human beings we have times when we react, at least internally, to a client's appearance and mannerisms and/or to what a client says and does. These internal reactions can be positive as well as negative. The thoughts and feelings we experience often reflect past situations and relationships in our lives and are not necessarily closely connected to our present interaction with our clients. We tend to carry these past memories and reactions into present relationships, just as couples do. In fact, as soon as we build a relationship with a person, as we inevitably do with the client, we have formed a partnership. Even though we may be fairly clear emotionally, it is impossible and probably ill-advised to remove ourselves completely, because the energy we bring to the relationship is important for the client's growth. We will, however, become part of the client's system and will influence the client and be influenced by her/him.

There is nothing wrong with the reactions we as therapists have as long as we are aware of what those reactions are about and where they are coming from, so that we do not take our unresolved baggage into the relationship. Once we have worked out our own issues, we are usually clear enough to help our clients work out theirs. As we resolve countertransference issues with our clients, we grow not only professionally but also personally.

Irrespective of the method of therapy you use with clients (e.g., talk, art, Gestalt, hypnosis, or sandplay), we suggest that, to resolve your own issues in the relationship, you become cognizant of your inner reactions and feelings as you work with the client. Whenever you feel an inner response to what s/he does and says, note it mentally and remember what you were talking about or what you were doing at the time. After the session or when you have sufficient time, process your reactions. Countertransference issues can be resolved in many ways.

Self-examination through meditation, journaling, or sandplay, as well as working with a therapist or supervisor, is effective. For those of you who like a more tactile and visual approach, building your own sand world is particularly useful. Usually your issues stare back at you from the tray and are hard to disregard.

Your use of the sand tray to resolve countertransference issues can be accomplished whether or not your client has constructed a sand world. If you decide to use sandplay to work through these issues when your client has not created a sand world, prepare yourself as you would for a personal growth tray and ask your unconscious mind to release to you the issue within yourself that stimulated the response. You might also ask to be shown the dynamics that occur between you and your client. Immerse yourself in the feelings with no judgment or censoring. Experience them fully and note any associations and memories that develop at this time. Then build a spontaneous scene and process it, preferably with another therapist or a supervisor who is familiar with sandplay. If this is not possible, process the world on your own, using the techniques discussed in the preceding section on personal growth. If the issue eludes you or you are unable to resolve it on your own, rebuild the world later when you find a therapist you trust to help you.

An example of how countertransference and its resolution through sandplay can affect the client and the therapist follows. A therapist we supervised, Nell, identified the person she was working with, Jim, as very similar to Nell's brother, whom she loved deeply. The therapist had a strong positive reaction to the client. What Nell did not realize, however, was that as she worked with Jim she placed expectations on him similar to those she had placed on her brother for many years. Jim was trying to decide whether to return to college to complete his doctorate. Nell subtly pressured Jim to return to school, just as she had pressured her brother when he had suddenly dropped out of college. Nell had always blamed her brother's difficulties in life on his decision to leave college and had felt that if she had been able to persuade him to remain in school he would have succeeded. Nell felt guilty about her inability to help her brother secure a better life for himself. The expectation that it was best for Jim to return to college, however, impeded the therapy process, blocking Jim from resolving the issue in the way that was best for him.

In a supervision session Nell built a countertransference world in the sand. She realized that the figure of an angry woman that she had placed in the sand world was actually her, and the figure of a man in the tray was not her client, but her brother. After she had the figures dialogue with each other she was able to let go of her expectations and to support Jim fully in making his own choice. She was also able to process the interaction with Jim and apologize for her confusion. The resolution of Nell's issue obviously profited Jim, but it also benefited Nell in her professional work as well as her personal life. She was finally able to let go of her anger at her brother and her guilt about not being able to help him. This awareness also helped Nell let go of her need to save her clients.

Countertransference issues are somewhat easier to recognize and explore in the sand when your client has created a sand world in the therapy session. The following exercises are adapted from ones taught by De Domenico, the originator of the idea of using sandplay for countertransference issues. As with other interventions, notice your inner feelings as the client builds and processes the scene. Although your primary concern is your client, be aware of your reactions when s/he brings objects into the tray, buries, moves, or removes them. Also observe your responses to the client's verbal and nonverbal expressions. If you are videotaping or recording the process in depth, refer to the details after the session. Sometimes your reactions may be strongest before an explanation of the world has been given and then dissipate when you know the actual meaning. But do not disregard your reaction. Note the occurrence and, at a later time, work with it. There are, after all, times when you may react without full cognizance. The initial reaction you had to your client's tray gives you an opportunity to get in touch with your unknown material.

A specific session comes to mind that illustrates this type of situation. Just before our client completed her scene, she tore a sheet of paper into many little pieces and dropped them into her world. Our reaction was one of dismay. To us the world appeared messy and chaotic after the paper fell on the scene. When our client began to talk about her tray, her eyes filled with wonder as she spoke of the magic (the shreds of paper) that had showered the world. Although we immediately released our image of mess and chaos, we decided to take time to process the client's world after the session. As we processed the scene, we slowly and deliberately removed every piece of paper until the scene appeared ordered and peaceful to us. We realized that because our life was very chaotic at that particular time, we needed order and stability. This understanding helped us to not project our issues onto our client.

Before dismantling the scene after your client leaves, take some time with the world and focus on the object or area where your reaction occurred. If you do not have time between sessions and need the sand tray for your next client, clear the tray and reconstruct the client's world from your photograph or diagram and notes at a later time. We suggest you rebuild the world at the end of your work day so that if the personal issues you are facing are unsettling, you will have adequate time to deal with them. Again, if possible, process the world with a therapist or supervisor you trust. Take time to experience the world as if it were your own. Then take yourself (if you are alone) or the witnessing therapist on a tour of the world as you see it, focusing more thoroughly on the troublesome objects or areas. Usually, by verbally designating your meaning to the object, area in the tray, or client's expressions, you will become aware of how your client's world reflects your own issues. After the tour, proceed with the therapy as you would during personal growth sessions. Remember, you are dealing with your own tray at this point, not your client's tray. The issues you discover are yours, not necessarily your client's. Finish by rearranging the tray (moving, removing, and bringing in new objects) in the way you would like to leave it. Take a little time to process the new scene and ask yourself what has changed after you moved the objects or sand. Then record your insights in your journal.

Another approach to resolving countertransference using sandplay is to go through the processes already delineated but, instead of rearranging the tray, amplify the area in the tray where your reactions occurred. Take the objects in this area out of the tray and use them to build a new world, bringing in any other objects you wish. In one situation, a therapist we were supervising rebuilt a client's world according to her records to determine what it was about the scene that bothered her. She finally realized that she felt anxious about the empty pyramid in the middle of the tray. She removed the pyramid and placed it in the center of a new tray. Then she built the scene as she wanted it to be. As soon as she began processing the world, she realized she had filled the pyramid with people, and she recognized her discomfort with emptiness. Emptiness symbolized loneliness to her. To the client it had represented a place where unknown but new possibilities could arise. The therapist realized how lonely she had been feeling since her recent move. Her first impulse was to fill the space with people rather than face her feelings.

Another way to resolve countertransference issues is to create a completely new world of your own, not necessarily using any of your client's objects. Ask your unconscious mind to create a reply to the client's world or to the area of the world that troubles you. If you would like to deal directly with transference as well as countertransference issues with a particular client, you might choose to have a client create a sand tray about your therapeutic relationship. Process this tray with the client, and when s/he is gone, use her/his completed world to delve into your own feelings about your relationship with the client. Then create an answer world to your client's world. By associating her/his world with your issues and past experiences, and then dealing with them, you can minimize countertransference. In fact, your heightened understanding may well enhance your relationship with your client and others in your life.

In some cases the issues you discover may not be resolved easily, and it becomes impossible to continue working with the client. This is probably one of the most painful situations that you will have to deal with as a therapist, but it is important for your growth and the client's growth that you admit your limitations and deal with the problem. If you determine that you cannot or would prefer not to work with the client, discuss your feelings with her/him and refer her/him to another therapist. Because the client is probably aware that something is amiss, addressing the issue will validate her/his perception.

This process may also be very painful for the client because s/he may feel that there is something wrong with her/him and may think that you are rejecting her/him. It is best, therefore, to have already worked out your own feelings prior to addressing them with the client so that you do not place blame on her/him. Be careful of what you tell the client about your own thoughts and feelings so that you do not reinforce existing dysfunctional patterns and low self-esteem (e.g., her/his perception of doing something wrong and then being abandoned). Let the client know that these are your issues and may have little to do with her/him. You might say, "You may have noticed that I seem to be somewhat distant lately. I have recently felt that I have not been very helpful to you because of my own limitations. How are you feeling about what is going on in these sessions?" Process the feelings with the client. The processing may well lead to termination of therapy and referral. If there is resolution during this interaction, therapy will often proceed with the client at a deeper level.

We have found that doing our own sand trays is invaluable. When issues arise for us, whether professional or personal, one of the first places we turn to find clarification is the sand tray. For us, the immediacy and objectification catapult us into a deeper level of awareness. We can see, touch, and manipulate the objects. With the issue before us in the tray, we find it hard to deny that from which our defenses may have otherwise protected us. We cannot stress enough how important it is for both you and your client that you deal with your own unconscious material.

Personal Growth

- Empty your mind of extraneous thoughts.
- Give your inner child unconditional regard.
- Ask your unconscious mind to release answers to any questions you have.
- Build a spontaneous world.
- Experience the world fully.
- Take yourself or an observer on a tour of the world. Ask yourself similar questions you would ask clients and answer aloud.
- Rework memories, dialogue with objects, and/or use appropriate therapy techniques.
- Take a photograph, if you wish.
- Take time to reflect on the process.
- Journal important insights and feelings.
- Dismantle the world when you are ready.

Countertransference Options

Creating a tray when sandplay was not used with a client:

- Notice your thoughts and feelings as you work with the client.
- When you have time, prepare yourself as you would for a personal growth tray.
- Ask your unconscious mind to release the issue that stimulated your response to the client.
- Immerse yourself in the feelings and memories.
- Build a spontaneous world and process it, preferably with another therapist.

Creating a tray when sandplay was used with a client:

- Note your inner feelings and reactions as the client builds and processes the scene.
- When you have time, focus on the area in the client's tray that disturbed you. If you dismantled the tray, recreate it.
- Experience the client's world as if it were your own.

- Take yourself or a guiding therapist on a tour.
- Rework memories, dialogue, etc., as you would in your personal growth tray.
- Rearrange the scene in the way you would like to leave it.
- Briefly process the new scene.
- Take a picture and record your insights in your journal.

Amplify the troubling area of your client's world.

Create an answer world to your client's world.

CONCLUSION

We close this book as we began it, with a story. Many years ago, in Russia, shortly after the revolution ended, there lived a young woman of aristocratic descent. Antonia had lost all her wealth and property when the soldiers had taken everything of value she owned. Although she now lived in poverty like the other villagers, she still possessed a beautiful fan given to her by her mother just before her death. When Antonia felt particularly depressed about her present situation, she carried the fan with her. Whenever she carried the fan, she remembered her mother and the olden days and felt radiant and confident again. From time to time she found snippets of ribbon or shiny objects that she added to the fan to make her feel it was truly hers.

One day, on her way to the marketplace, she came upon a band of Gypsies dancing in the town square. As she watched the group, she noticed a girl of about 14 who danced self-consciously with eyes turned to the ground. When the music stopped, the girl looked up at Antonia. The girl's face lit up when she saw the fan that Antonia carried. As Antonia was leaving the square, the girl's eyes followed the fan with longing. Antonia's heart went out to the girl. She remembered what it was like to not believe in herself. She turned around and walked over to the Gypsies' wagon. "Here, this is for you. I don't need it anymore. I carry it in my heart," she said as she held out the fan to the girl. The young girl smiled and curtsied as she graciously accepted the gift.

A few weeks later, when Antonia returned to the marketplace, she saw the Gypsy girl, face glowing, dancing and twirling confidently in the square. In her left hand she held the fan high as she waved and swished it around her body. Antonia noticed that the girl had collected wildflowers of various colors and tied them to the handle of the fan. Antonia visited the square many times and saw that the Gypsy girl had developed more intricate ways to use the fan in her dances.

Then one day when Antonia returned to the marketplace she saw the Gypsy girl dance with pride and confidence, but the fan was gone. Tears welled up in Antonia's eyes, because she feared that the fan had been lost. But as she looked around, she saw a crippled child of about 8 sitting at the edge of the square. The child wore clothes that were tattered and torn. In her hand she clutched the beautiful yet well worn fan. With her other hand, she stroked the fan gently and spoke to it. Antonia approached the child and sat down next to her. She said, "How did you get that beautiful fan?" The little girl replied, "Oh, the dancing Gypsy girl over there gave it to me. She said that it was no ordinary fan, but that it was magical. She told me that she had gotten it from a pretty lady. Then she said that she didn't need it anymore because she held it in her heart. She told me that I could change it any way I wanted to, so I added my most favorite trinkets right here. When I carry this fan, it makes me feel special. I almost feel as if I can run and play like the other children." Antonia smiled at the child and gently touched her shoulder. She knew that the treasure was in good hands.

Sandplay, with its wonderland of symbols and images, is a little like this fan. We would again like to thank those who passed sandplay on to us. We have added our personal touches to this gift, as the children in the story did to the fan, and we have used it with respect and care. And so we pass our knowledge, ideas, and experiences on to you for you to use and change in ways that are most compatible with your own needs and visions. Then, when you are ready, you can pass on your knowledge and ideas to someone else. We hope that you will use sandplay wisely, but remember, just like the fan, this technique is merely a tool that can help you and your clients think and feel differently and aid you and them on the journey to wholeness.

Our wish is that those of you who venture on this journey will learn to trust your own and your clients' inner wisdom to guide you. We hope that the incorporation of sandplay into your life and into the lives of your clients will be an enriching, provocative, and enlightening experience.

TROUBLESHOOTING

Below are some common questions from our workshops and supervision.

What do I do if a client seems to be staying on a very superficial level?
This is sometimes frustrating for us as therapists, because we want to feel that the sandplay work is having some meaningful impact. Although movement may not be evident, it is important to trust that work is occurring on an unconscious level. Allow the client to create several sand worlds. Sometimes the client needs to experience sandplay over time to learn to trust the therapist and the process. As a number of our examples in the text have shown, this then permits the client to go into the unconscious and potentially painful material. But if it appears that the client continues to remain on a shallow level, explore verbally what s/he is experiencing. Often what is revealed by the client's outward appearance belies what is occurring internally for her/him. However, some clients remain too defended to let go (e.g., they talk incessantly, intellectualize, or race through the process). Others make the sandplay activity ritualistic, thus maintaining distance and control. If you assess that a client is not able to utilize sandplay as a tool to move beyond the surface level, find an alternative approach.

What can I do when clients persist in using "I" through the therapy stage or in taking the action out of the tray and personalizing it?
Because using the third person helps to create some distance from the action in the tray and thus is less threatening to the client, we recom-

mend that you continue to refer to the objects in the tray in the third person (i.e., "that woman" as opposed to "you," or "that man" as opposed to "your husband"). Do not correct the client's language; instead model the use of the third person. If the client persists in personalizing the objects, and it seems appropriate and safe for her/him, follow her/his lead in naming the objects what the client is naming them. However, continue to keep the activity in the tray as opposed to turning the process into talk therapy. As a man we worked with commented at the end of the sandplay session, "It was really helpful when you had me have the man and the boy talk with each other. It seemed to evoke answers to emerge from my unconscious that I hadn't thought about before."

Should I allow children to light matches in the sandplay session?
This decision must be made on a case-by-case basis. Children's safety (as well as your own and that of the building you are in) is the primary concern. However, there are also other factors to consider. If the child is very young, developmentally immature or emotionally disturbed, or inclined to be destructive or impulsive, we would not recommend allowing her/him to light matches. We generally ask parents and caretakers what their preferences are regarding the lighting of fire. Even if we deem it appropriate but they don't, we honor their requests. If the client has a history of starting fires, we recommend that you assess what would be most helpful for the child. We have found that the child who is merely curious, wants control, or is destructive but has not developed an obsessive pattern, may actually benefit from the permission to light matches in a controlled environment. The child can learn the limits and internalize them so that s/he can use matches in a safe and appropriate way. However, if the pattern of fire-setting is ingrained and compulsive, we do not permit the use of matches/lighters in the office. If you have clients in this category, you may wish to either remove the matches from your display or refrain from having matches on your shelf. Let those who ask to light candles, incense, sage, or paper as a symbolic gesture know that you have matches available.

How can I use what the client does in the tray to determine where s/he is in her/his growth process?
There are several theories that can indicate a client's progress in her/his growth process. See the "Developmental Stages in Sandplay" in

chapter 5 for Charles Stewart's paradigm. Bradway and McCoard (1997) reported that Kalff's three sequential stages are often portrayed in children's first sand trays at the stage-related ages, e.g., if a child is 5 years old, her/his first tray will reflect the developmental stage of a 5-year-old.

Lowenfeld observed that the first tray could reveal how the client felt about therapy, her/his relationship to the unconscious, her/his personal problems, and a possible solution (Mitchell & Friedman, 1994). Bradway wrote that the sandplay therapy process passes through loose stages to come to completion. These stages may or may not occur, but when they do she knows something is happening. She stated that she finds that the first tray often depicts a problematic situation and a possible solution. She noticed that after the first tray there is usually a gradual or sudden "going down" or regression into the collective unconscious. Bradway found that at this time clients tend to use more water, as well as water plants and animals, and fewer land animals and humans. Eventually more land animals, people and buildings return to the scenes. This period appears to be a time of greater creativity. The process of "going down" and returning may occur several times.

Another stage that Bradway observed is what she identified as the period of mother-child unity. The unity seems to appear first with animals and then with people. She also observed a time of differentiation between masculine and feminine, which is then followed by an integration of the two. Eventually the play in the sand leads to what she called a "Self" tray. The client creates what is to her/him a profound cosmic scene where there is peace within the self. Often a deep, enlightening experience occurs, and there may be a feeling of having contacted the spiritual. This world usually releases energy and is often followed by a strengthening of the ego. Bradway (1997) stated that, although the life process is not finished until death, the therapist will recognize when some form of resolution has occurred and the particular stage that the client and therapist are working on is complete.

The remaining questions address interpretation and meaning-making. Although we are not Jungian analysts or experts in Jungian symbology and we emphasize client interpretation as opposed to therapist interpretation, many therapists who use sandplay have extensive Jungian training and this group currently dominates the sandplay field. Because of the potential readership of this book, which may include those who are familiar with Jung, and because we agree with many of Jung's concepts, we include some questions and answers on interpretation. Although familiarity with Jungian archetypes and symbology can be helpful, we do not think that it is essential.

Is it important for me to know and to interpret the symbology of the tray?

While we have focused in the text on allowing the client to determine the meaning of objects, there are varying opinions about whether therapists should or can interpret the meaning of a client's sand world. Jungian therapists believe in the collective unconscious and archetypal symbols. They emphasize that the therapist's understanding of these symbols is vital in order to lead the client to a deeper level of awareness and integration. Kalff (1980) believed, as did Jung, that it is important that the symbols that allow clients to move toward wholeness be correctly understood by the therapist. Jungians believe that there are appropriate times to interject their interpretations.

We believe, as Lowenfeld did, that the interpretation of the world is best left to the client. Although we may have ideas of what the world means on a deeper level than the client is indicating, it is important to trust the client's wise inner self to reveal to her/himself as much as s/he can tolerate and in the appropriate time frame. As Lowenfeld suggested, the client will move towards individuation and amelioration of the presenting symptoms regardless of our efforts (Ryce-Menuhin, 1992). We also, as Clare Thompson (1990) mentioned, encourage the client (and ourselves) to focus on the experience rather than the analysis. Being overly committed to particular interpretations could at times actually impede your clients' progress. "The current trend seems to be moving away from a rigid reliance on specific rules, which are confining and limiting" (Mitchell & Friedman, 1994, p. 84). We encourage you to choose whether to make interpretations according to your professional orientation.

When do I share interpretations with the client, if I assess that it is appropriate?

If you decide to interpret your client's sand tray, we concur with Jungian analysts that initially you do so only *internally*. We caution you not to relate your assumptions to the client before s/he is ready. Weinrib (1983), a Jungian analyst, wrote that after the scene is complete and the therapist has asked the client pertinent questions or evoked client comments, the therapist evaluates the scene according to Jungian symbology and any archetypal meanings that seem appropriate. The therapist does not tell the client of these interpretations, but can use any ideas s/he has derived in an indirect way. The client's response will or will not validate the therapist's deductions. Bradway and McCoard stated that after the sandplay series has been concluded, a joint viewing with the client of the pictures of her/his trays allows the therapist to exchange observations on what s/he has seen. They believed that "at this time cognition can beneficially join the feeling experience" (1997, p. 115).

Where can I go to learn more about cultural and archetypal meanings?

Although we ordinarily do not recommend attributing meaning to the client's sand tray, there are times when it may be valuable for you to be aware of culturally and archetypally determined meanings. If you and/or the client are still confused about the meaning of a sand tray and how the scene relates to a client's issues or the process of therapy, and you have already asked the questions we discussed in chapters 3, 4, and 5, you and/or your client may refer to a symbol or mythology dictionary. You may also want to refer to our suggested reading list and Jung's works themselves. We both have gleaned valuable information from those more knowledgeable in cultural and Jungian interpretation, and at times this has led to deeper understanding of a client's tray. The following were valuable resources for us:

- Martin Kalff, a Jungian analyst and a founding member of the International Society for Sandplay Therapy, has an informative article, "Twenty Points to be Considered in the Interpretation of a Sandplay" in the *Journal of Sandplay Therapy*, II (2), 1993. He wrote, as Jung did, that interpretation must include not only the thinking process, but also the therapist's intuition, feelings, and sensations.
- Rie Rogers Mitchell and Harriet S. Friedman, in *Sandplay Past, Present and Future*, described sandplay as a multilevel process. As with dreams, the client's comments and work in the tray can be understood "at three levels: the personal level (what does this story represent in the client's life?); the archetypal level (what are the underlining motifs?); and the cultural level (what cultural issues are seen as motivating factors in the story?)" (1994, p. 116).
- Ruth Ammann, in her book *Healing and Transformation in Sandplay* (1993), elaborated on her ideology. Among her tenets regard-

ing meaning in the tray are her interpretations of spatial phenomena. She attributed distinct meanings to each of the quadrants in the tray.

- Dora Kalff, throughout her book *Sandplay* (1981), ascribed Jungian interpretation to many symbols her clients used.

GLOSSARY

There are varying ways of defining the following words and concepts. Our brief definitions below connote how we are using these concepts in this book.

Active imagination: A method of deliberately and actively fantasizing. The process of focusing on dream images or on fantasy figures in an effort to elaborate and embellish them purposefully. This enables a person to capitalize knowingly on unconscious content and self-knowledge that would otherwise remain untapped.

Aha experience: A type of experience in which there is sudden insight into or solution of a problem, at which time the features of the problem suddenly fit together in a unified pattern.

Amplification: Elaboration and clarification of symbols derived from the unconscious in the sand world (also from dreams and the imagination), often understood by moving an object or group of objects into another sand tray and creating a new scene.

Archetype: Inborn patterns of experiencing. The archetypes are preexistent forms inherited in the psychic structure. Only the form is inherited; the content is filled in by the life of the individual. Just as the instincts seem to account for recurrent behavior patterns in people, so the archetypes seem to account for recurrent patterns in the psyche.

Child within/inner child: The child part of the self who, when there is unresolved emotional content, often propels the adult to act from that maturational level. When psychological work is done to address the past needs and irresolution, healing occurs and the client is able to act out of a more mature stance.

Collective unconscious: The part of our unconscious side that cannot be traced as the product of individual subjective experience; the archetypes are the content of the collective unconscious.

Complex: Split-off ideas, images, etc., that are related to each other and cluster around a central core. This entity interferes with ego functioning and disturbs conscious performance.

Confront: The act of addressing the client in such a fashion as to move her/him in her/his process. To reflect back that which the client has put forth.

Conscious/consciousness: That part of mental life of which the individual is aware at any given time.

Constellate: The stirring and clustering of related unconscious content so that a new entity or gestalt is formed and its effects are perceived or felt to some degree in the conscious.

Countertransference: A part of the sandplay process in which the therapist's unconscious perception and understanding of her/his client's productions come about, typically by means of partial and short-lived identifications with the client or a projection of the therapist onto the client. By recognizing and addressing her/his own issues that are evoked, the therapist can separate her/his own material from the client's and gain insight and understanding of the client's previously incomprehensible and confusing productions.

Ego: The center of consciousness; the carrier of consciousness within which the faculty of willpower and decision-making reside.

Gestalt techniques: Techniques used that incorporate a philosophy that takes into account the whole individual and her/his inner and outer environment. The interventions involve the total person in a creative and active manner.

Growing edge: That place for a client where s/he is challenged to move beyond her/his current status and toward her/his fullest potential.

Individuation: The process of moving toward one's own totality, potential, and consciousness of oneself; the process of becoming a psychologically whole and separate individual.

Intra/inter: intra—situated, originating, or taking place within the unit, as in intrapersonal, intrapsychic, intra-integration; **inter**—between or among, as opposed to within, units.

Introjection: When one incorporates into her/his ego system the picture or attitudes of an object or person as s/he conceives the object or person to be. The replacement of a relation to an external object by a relation to an internal object.

Mandala: Jung's term for the circle that symbolizes total unity of the Self, of order and integration. Is often symbolically created in the sand tray when the client is approaching integration.

Persona: The mask; the personality we wear for the world; the bridge from the ego to the outer world.

Projection: The process by which a person perceives an unconscious quality belonging to her/himself as belonging to another outer object or person.

Psyche: All of the human being that is not physical; the dynamic process, conscious and unconscious, that makes up the human personality.

Regress: To return to an earlier time or developmental stage, often to a place that needs healing or can provide insight into the etiology of an issue.

Self: The central archetype expressing wholeness; the center of the psyche, embracing both the conscious and the unconscious. Jung refers to it as both the center and the circumference of the psyche; it is the most complete expression of one's individuality.

Shadow: A composite of personal characteristics and potentialities which have been denied expression in life and of which the individual is unaware. The ego denies these characteristics because of their incompatibility with the person's chosen conscious attitude.

Symbol: An image or form giving the best expression to a content whose meaning is still largely unknown; the language in which the unconscious speaks via dreams, fantasy, sandplay, etc.

Transference: Projection of feelings, thoughts, and wishes onto the therapist who has come to represent an object/person from the client's life. In sandplay, the projection can be onto the objects in the tray.

Transitional object: An object in the outer world that represents an attachment or security figure (originally something that acts as a maternal substitute) and serves to facilitate separation and independence from the attachment figure. An object that acts symbolically to provide a person with comfort and a sense of security.

Two-chair intervention: A Gestalt technique in which a client dialogues with another person or aspect of her/himself, imagined to be present in the room. In the sand tray world, the client gives voice to symbolic objects, which dialogue with each other.

Unconscious: The unknown in the inner world; everything inside which is not known, i.e., not related to the ego.

SELECTED READINGS AND RESOURCES

SELECTED READINGS

Allen, D. M. (1988). *Unifying individual and family therapies.* San Francisco: Jossey-Bass.

A presentation of Allen's suggested approach to integrating individual therapy with family systems theory.

Ammann, R. (1993). *Healing and transformation in sandplay: Creative processes become visible* (2nd printing; W. P. Rainer, trans.). La-Salle, IL: Open Court Publishing.

An excellent book describing the role and workings of sandplay therapy from a Jungian perspective, including Ammann's views on the process of sandplay, the symbolic interpretation of spatial phenomena, and case histories.

Ammann, R. (1994). The sandtray as a garden of the soul. *Journal of Sandplay Therapy, IV* (1), 46–65.

An articulate metaphorical look at sandplay as tending a garden.

Baker, C. (1993). Navaho sand painting and sandplay. *Journal of Sandplay Therapy, II* (1).

An elaboration on Navaho sand painting and its parallel to sandplay.

Berne, E. (1964). *Games people play.* New York: Grove Press.

An introduction to Transactional Analysis.

Bradway, K. (1990). Developmental stages in children's sand worlds. In K. Bradway et al., *Sandplay studies: Origins, theory and practice* (2nd ed.; pp. 93–100). Boston: Sigo Press.

Description of children's sand worlds as related to Kalff's stages of ego development.

Bradway, K., & McCoard, B. (1997). *Sandplay—Silent workshop of the psyche*. London, New York: Routledge.

Both an introduction to sandplay and in-depth case studies of sandplay processes of a wide variety of clients, including the authors' detailed explanation of interpretations of sandplay and use of symbols.

Bradway, K., Signell, K., Spare, G., Stewart, C., Stewart, L., & Thompson, C. (1990). *Sandplay studies: Origins, theory and practice* (2nd ed.). Boston: Sigo Press.

A collection of articles covering the use of sandplay with children, men, and women; foreword by Dora Kalff.

Cirlot, J. E. (1971). *A dictionary of symbols*. New York: Philosophical Library.

A dictionary of symbols and their meanings.

Cooper, J. (1987). *An illustrated encyclopedia of traditional symbols*. London: Thames & Hudson.

A dictionary of symbols and their meanings.

Cunningham, L. (1997). The therapist's use of self in sandplay: Participation mystique and projective identification. *Journal of Sandplay Therapy, VI* (2), 121–135.

A clear discussion of projective identification, participation mystique, and empathy as they apply to sandplay.

De Domenico, G. S. (1986a). *Applications of the Lowenfeld world technique: A comparative illustration of the analysis of the final world and the analysis of the sand tray play process in clinical practice*. Vision Quest Into Reality, 1946 Clemens Rd., Oakland, CA 94602.

A paper describing how the observation of the world-building process reveals much more about the unconscious workings of the builder than just viewing the final tray.

De Domenico, G. S. (1986b). *A child's sandtray play mirrors the world of her father*. Vision Quest Into Reality, 1946 Clemens Rd., Oakland, CA 94602.

A paper focusing on the process of creating a sand world, expanding the focus to include the play process as opposed to only the final product.

De Domenico, G. S. (1988). *Sand tray world play: A comprehensive guide to the use of sand tray play in therapeutic transformational settings*. Vision Quest Into Reality, 1946 Clemens Rd., Oakland, CA 94602.

A self-published training manual describing many aspects of how to do sand tray world play, what to look for, stages to go through, etc.

De Domenico, G. S. (1989). *Experiential training level 1: Workbook.* Vision Quest Into Reality, 1946 Clemens Rd., Oakland, CA 94602.

A workbook used in sand tray world play training.

De Domenico, G. S. (1991). *Sandtray worldplay with couples: Applications and techniques.* Vision Quest Into Reality, 1946 Clemens Rd., Oakland, CA 94602.

A paper describing the rationale and various methods of using sand tray world play therapy with couples.

Dundas, E. T. (1990). *Symbols come alive in the sand* (2nd ed.). Boston: Coventure, Ltd.

A description of the sandplay therapeutic technique and the theory behind it, including detailed descriptions of several cases.

The Educational Center. (1995). *Centerpoint I* (2nd ed.). St. Louis: Author.

A course on Jungian studies.

Gil, E. (1994). *Play in family therapy.* New York: Guilford.

A discussion of the need for play in family therapy, including a comprehensive collection of play techniques.

Hall, C. M. (1991). *The Bowen family theory and its uses.* Northvale, NJ: Aronson.

A thorough description of Murray Bowen's family systems theory and its many applications.

Hegeman, G. (1992). The sandplay collection. *Journal of Sandplay Therapy, I* (2), 101–106.

A description of collecting sandplay items.

Jung, C. G. (1960). The transcendent function. In *The structure and the dynamics of the psyche, Collected Works* (Vol. 8, 67-91). (R. F. C. Hull, Trans.). New York: Pantheon Books.

Jung, C. G. (1963). *Memories, dreams, and reflections* (3rd ed.). (Richard and Clara Winston, Trans.). New York: Pantheon Books.

An excellent account of Jung's life and experiences as recorded by Aniela Jaffe.

Jung, C. G. (1971). *Psychological types, Collected Works* (Vol. 6). London: Routledge.

Kalff, D. M. (1980). *Sandplay: A psychotherapeutic approach to the psyche.* Boston: Sigo Press.

Written by one of the early developers and proponents of sandplay: a description of this Jungian analyst's use of sandplay, including theory and case presentations.

Kalff, M. (1993). Twenty points to be considered in the interpretation of a sandplay. *Journal of Sandplay Therapy*, II (2), 17–35.

Keirsey, D. & Bates, M. (1984). *Please understand me*. Del Mar, CA: Prometheus Nemesis Book Company (distributor).
Describes the four temperaments, derived from Jungian typology, and discusses how awareness of personality types can enhance understanding of oneself and one's relationships.

Lowenfeld, M. (1935/1967). *Play in childhood*. New York: Wiley.
Written by the founder of worldplay, covers all aspects of play.

Lowenfeld, M. (1979). *The world technique*. London: George Allen & Unwin.
A posthumous bringing together of Lowenfeld's works through 1960.

Maier, Henry W. (1978). *Three theories of child development* (3rd ed.). New York: Harper & Row.
A comprehensive view of the child from cognitive (Jean Piaget), affective (Erik H. Erikson), and behavioral (Robert R. Sears) perspectives.

Mitchell, R. R., & Friedman, H. S. (1994). *Sandplay past, present and future*. New York, London: Routledge.
Examines the history, current trends, and future of sandplay.

Oaklander, V. (1988). *Windows to our children*. New York: The Gestalt Journal Press.
The author's vast experiences in working with children therapeutically, including her interactions using a multitude of therapeutic interventions.

Piaget, J. (1951). *Play, dreams and imitation in childhood*. London: Routledge.
Discusses the individuation process and source of development.

Ryce-Menuhin, J. (1992). *Jungian sandplay: The wonderful therapy*. London: Routledge.
An analytical presentation of clients' work in the sand tray.

Signell, K., & Bradway, K. (1995). Some answers to Skamania questions. *Journal of Sandplay Therapy*, V (1), 16–35.
An article which provides answers to commonly asked questions.

Spare, G. H. (1990). Are there any rules? (Musings of a peripatetic sandplayer). In K. Bradway et al., *Sandplay studies: Origins, theory and practice* (2nd ed., pp. 195–208). Boston: Sigo Press.
An article addressing possible fears or questions of non-Jungian therapists.

Steiner, C. M. (1974). *Scripts people live.* New York: Grove Press.

Based on the Transactional Analysis paradigm, an exploration of the patterns in people's lives that originated from early decisions in life.

Stewart, C. T. (1990). Developmental psychology of sandplay. In K. Bradway et al., *Sandplay studies: Origins, theory and practice* (2nd ed., pp. 39–92). Boston: Sigo Press.

An article addressing the culmination of Stewart's research, in which he synthesized Neumann's, Erikson's, and Piaget's developmental stages and play that occurs at those stages for the analysis of sandplay.

Stewart, L. (1982). On sandplay and Jungian analysis. In M. Stein (Ed.), *Jungian analysis* (pp. 204–218). LaSalle, IL: Open Court Publishing.

A discussion of sandplay, including its adaptation from Lowenfeld's World Technique to Jungian analysis.

Thompson, C. (1990). Variations on a theme by Lowenfeld: Sandplay in focus. In K. Bradway et al., *Sandplay studies: Origins, theory and practice* (2nd ed., pp. 5–20). Boston: Sigo Press.

An overview of sandplay, including history, methodology, and benefits.

Walker, B. (1983). *The woman's encyclopedia of myths and secrets.* San Francisco: Harper & Row.

A dictionary of symbols and myths from a feminist perspective.

Webb, N. B. (1991). Play therapy crisis intervention with children. In N. B. Boyd (Ed.), *Play therapy with children in crisis* (pp. 26–42). New York: Guilford Press.

A collection of in-depth writings on cases demonstrating a multitude of techniques applied to working with children in crisis.

Weinrib, E. L. (1983). *Images of the self.* Boston: Sigo Press.

An excellent book describing the theory and practice of sandplay from a Jungian perspective.

Wells, H. G. (1975). *Floor games.* New York: Arno Press.

A reproduction of the 1912 Boston edition of his book elaborating on the games that served as a catalyst for the development of sandplay.

RESOURCES FOR SELECTED MATERIALS

Catalogs of sandplay materials are available from the following sources:

Bijou Archetypes Miniatures &
  Ethnic Artifacts
P. O. Box 4525
Walnut Creek, CA 94597
(925) 939–3111
Fax: (925) 939-3430

Bell Pine Art Farm
82535 Weiss Road
Creswell, OR 97426
(800) 439–6556
(Handmade stoneware sculptures)

Archie McPhee & Co.
2428 Northwest Market
Seattle, WA 98107
(206) 297–0240

Phyllis Kirson
39 Belmont Avenue
Fairfax, CA 94930
(415) 454-8775
(Goddess sculptures)

Dharma Crafts
405 Walthon Street
Lexington, MA 02173
(800) 794-9862
www.DharmaCrafts.com
(Buddha's Delight)

Pryor-Giggey Co.
12393 E. Slauson Avenue
Whittier, CA 90606
(562) 945–3781
(sand)

Playrooms
P. O. Box 2660
Petaluma, CA 94953
(707) 763–2448

Myoshi Gift Shop
18942 Brookhurst Street
Fountain Valley, CA 92708
(714) 968-9100
(Japanese artifacts)

Way of Life, Inc.
P.O. Box 3087
Fayville, MA 01745-0087
(508) 865-7462
(12 Steppers)

Thera-a-Play
P.O. Box 2030
Lodi, CA 95241
(800) 308–6749

There are many stores that carry unique objects for sandplay. If you
are interested in wooden sand trays or objects that you cannot find
(e.g., sky hooks, coffins, open glass pyramids), please contact us at
Center for Creative Endeavors (see appendix 4 for address).

WORKSHOPS AND VIDEOS

WORKSHOPS

The following workshops are 15-hour experiential trainings for psychotherapists, social workers, counselors, and graduate students in mental health fields. Our workshops have been approved in the past for continuing education credit by the state licensing board for counselors and social workers, the national certification board for counselors, and the Office of Public Instruction for school counselors, psychologists, and educators. Psychologists have completed our workshops and earned continuing education credit. Workshops are conducted in Bozeman, MT, in the beautiful Rocky Mountains, 90 miles north of Yellowstone Park. Arrangements can be negotiated for workshops in locations other than Bozeman upon group request.

Sandplay Therapy—Level I: A Workshop for Using Spontaneous Sand Trays with Individual Adults. This workshop is comprised of didactic presentations on theory, history, and benefits of sandplay. The roles of the therapist, the stages of a session, and how to set up a sandplay space are included. A demonstration and video portray actual sandplay work. The majority of the workshop is experiential. Maximum enrollment in Bozeman is ten participants.

Sandplay Therapy—Level II: A Workshop for Using Directed Sand Trays with Individual Adults. This workshop is comprised of brief didactic presentations of the theory behind a variety of directed interventions that we teach. The majority of the workshop is experiential. A demonstration and video of directed sandplay work are included. Maximum enrollment in Bozeman is ten participants. Level I is a prerequisite.

Sandplay Therapy—Level II: A Workshop for Using Spontaneous and Directed Sand Trays with Couples and **Sandplay Therapy— Level I: A Workshop for Using Spontaneous and Directed Sand Trays with Children** are in progress and will be available upon request. We prefer that therapists register as a group of at least eight. Level I is a prerequisite for the couples workshop. Also, if you wish to register for the couples workshop, we suggest that you do so with a colleague you know, because you will be coupling with a partner as you experience each exercise.

VIDEOS

Teaching videos portraying sandplay sessions are available. They consist of both the actual experience of sand tray work and explanations of the stages as they occur. In addition, a discussion about the clients, the construction of each world, and the dynamics are addressed. Topics include spontaneous and directed sandplay work with adults, children, and couples.

To order videos or obtain further information about the workshops, contact us at

Center for Creative Endeavors
321 E. Main, Suite 402
Bozeman, MT 59715

Telephone: (406) 586–7515
Fax: (406) 522–7154
E-mail: BLBoik@aol.com

INDEX